Tips and Traps for Writing an Effective Business Plan

Tips and Traps for Writing an Effective Business Plan

Greg Balanko-Dickson

McGraw-Hill

New York   Chicago   San Francisco   Lisbon   London
Madrid   Mexico City   Milan   New Delhi   San Juan
Seoul   Singapore   Sydney   Toronto

The **McGraw·Hill** Companies

1 2 3 4 5 6 7 8 9 0   DOC/DOC   0 9 8 7 6

ISBN-13: 978-0-07-146751-3
ISBN-10: 0-07-146751-3

This publication is designed to provide accurate and authoritative information in regard to the subject matter covered. It is sold with the understanding that neither the author nor the publisher is not engaged in rendering legal, accounting, or other professional service. If legal advice or other expert assistance is required, the services of a competent professional person should be sought.

> —*From a declaration of principles jointly adopted by a committee of the American Bar Association and a committee of publishers*

McGraw-Hill books are available at special quantity discounts to use as premiums and sales promotions, or for use in corporate training programs. For more information, please write to the Director of Special Sales, McGraw-Hill Professional, Two Penn Plaza, New York, NY 10121-2298. Or contact your local bookstore.

*Dedicated to the memory of my father,
Donald Marquis Dickson, who always encouraged,
believed in, and taught me to be open
to lifelong learning opportunities.*

Contents

PART 2 THE 10 SECTIONS OF A BUSINESS PLAN

3. Industry Analysis 23

4. Market Analysis 39

5. Products and Services 59

PART 3 WRITING A BUSINESS PLAN IN 30 DAYS

13. Writing a Business Plan in 30 Days 199

14. Common Mistakes in Writing a Business Plan 209

15. Working with Professional Advisers 221

PART 4 SPECIAL CONSIDERATIONS FOR SPECIFIC BUSINESSES

16. Business Planning for Inventors 229

Tips and Traps for Writing an Effective Business Plan

PART 1

Introduction

1

What Is a Business Plan?
Why Do I Need
a Business Plan?

Does Every Business Need a Plan?

Absolutely. Every business needs a plan.

Developing a detailed business plan will provide you with an opportunity to shape a powerful business development strategy, whether your goal is to:

1. Get financing to start a business.
2. Get financing to expand your business.
3. Be more organized and increase your odds of success.
4. Identify the value of your business and prepare a plan for selling your business.
5. Create a plan to buy a business.
6. Create a management succession plan to facilitate your retirement.
7. Revitalize your business and identify new markets and business opportunities.
8. Reorganize to allow you more free time away from the business.
9. Build a financial plan to improve profitability.

10. Decrease your margin for error and increase profitability through rigorous management of staff and resources, as well as leveraging market conditions.

11. Clarify goals, objectives, and strategies in a partnership or corporation with multiple directors.

12. Improve effectiveness and management of operations.

I promise that if you follow the process in this book you will be excited by what you learn about yourself and your business. You will find yourself systematically reviewing every area of the business. Your business background, skills, and writing ability don't matter. If you are curious and willing to learn, I will guide you each step of the way toward creating an effective business plan.

TIP

If this is your first time writing a business plan, relax. I am only an e-mail away. If you have a question that you feel is not answered here, visit my Web site (www.sbishere.com), and I will do my best to help you. Even if you consider yourself an old pro at business planning, I'll still read and answer your e-mail!

Ten Sections of a Business Plan

I have devoted a complete chapter of this book to each of the 10 business plan sections listed below. These chapters will provide you with the information you need to understand, research, and write each section. The 10 sections (in the order you write the plan) are:

1. *Industry analysis:* describes the trends, demand outlook, barriers to entry and growth, impact of innovation and technology, impact of the economy, role of government, and the financial health of the industry.

2. *Market analysis:* identifies market trends, market size, competition analysis, and projected market share as well as how you will make decisions on the products and services you will offer.

3. *Products and services:* defines the outputs, sales mix, costs and profits, expansion of services, product positioning, and product/service life cycle.

4. *Business description:* describes the company, including your brand, identity, vision, mission, ethics, goals, and legal structure.

5. *Marketing strategy:* explains how you will utilize location, distribution channels, sales, pricing, and market positioning. This section will also

include a sample or description of the sales and marketing tools (Web site, telemarketing, brochures, sales systems, etc.) that you will use to acquire market share.

6. *Operations and management:* provides details on how you plan to manage the business, including organizational structure, responsibilities, and professional services.

7. *Financial plan:* includes copies of past financial statements (if any) and pro forma financial projections including start-up costs, the balance sheet, the income statement, cash flow, and sensitivity analysis.

8. *Implementation plan:* this is where you explain how you will use staff, systems, communication, bookkeeping, equipment, software, office, furniture, fixtures, land and buildings, as well as research and development.

9. *Contingency plan:* identifies all potential risks (liability, contract termination, etc.) and your plan to reduce or eliminate the risks or threats identified: for example, how you will deal with emergencies, major accidents, or disasters.

10. *Executive summary:* the executive summary is always written last but it appears as the first page in the plan.

TIP

If you are starting a business from scratch or expanding a business into a new market area, start with Chapter 3, "Industry Analysis," and then move on to Chapter 4, "Market Analysis." The third step before writing a complete business plan is to write your sales forecast. Discussion of this can be found in Chapter 7. There is no sense in putting work into writing a business plan if the industry and market cannot support a viable business.

When your plan is complete, organize it in the following order.

1. Executive summary.
2. Business description.
3. Products and services.
4. Industry analysis.
5. Market analysis.
6. Marketing strategy.
7. Operations and management.

8. Implementation plan.

9. Financial plan.

10. Contingency plan.

Business Plans as a Communication Tool

A business plan is used to communicate how your strategy will increase your chance for success in a new venture or improve the performance of an existing business. Plus, it can be used to facilitate a discussion among business partners who need to agree upon and document their plans. It can also be used to communicate with government officials who may need to approve aspects of the plan, and, of course, with potential investors, banks, or private individuals who may decide to fund the business or its expansion.

TRAP

If you are writing your business plan for a business with partners or other shareholders, do not give them the entire business plan—give it to them one part at a time. This will allow you to flesh out changes and have a quality discussion before you meet with your banker. Plus, it makes them feel like they are part of the process, which is always a good thing.

What Is a Business Plan?

A *business plan* is an instrument used to document the intent and plans of the owner regarding every aspect of the business. The document itself can be used to communicate plans, strategies, and tactics to your managers, partners, and investors. It is also used when you're applying for business credit.

The business plan contains both strategic and tactical objectives, and it can be either informal or formal. A plan can be on a napkin or in your head, or it can be a simple to-do list. If you asked average business owners or entrepreneurs if they have a "plan," they would say, "Of course." Ask them to explain their plan, and you will most likely end up with an overview of their major goals.

Goals + Research + Strategy = Business Plan

A list of goals might be a plan of what you want to achieve, but that does not make it a business plan.

A goal only reveals your intent or where you expect to end up. A formal business plan details the exact formula you feel you need to put together to attain your primary goals. My definition of a business plan is *a formal document written to capture and communicate the planned direction and maneuvers required for the business to accomplish its most important goal—profitability.*

Profit is no accident, and by writing and following a business plan, you increase the odds of achieving profitability. A business plan incorporates the same methods good managers use to guarantee the ongoing viability of the business. It is much more than notes on a napkin or a to-do list. A business plan is a roadmap to guide the business, its owner(s), and its employees on the journey to success.

TIP

Your completed business plan can be used to compare actual results achieved to the goals you originally set in your business plan. The review process will help keep your business on track, make sure you are taking appropriate actions, and ensure that they are in alignment with the strategic direction spelled out in the business plan.

Planning Stops Problems before They Start

You are most likely reading this book because you want to improve the effectiveness of a business, whether your own or one you are thinking of buying. Like I say to my coaching clients, without a formal plan, it is easy to become distracted, fall back on past schemes, or, even worse, end up reacting to crisis after crisis. The side effect of a poor planning is increased costs, confusion, and a drop in profits.

Without a clear purpose, managers and employees are left to "figure it out" on their own. The business is like a car that needs an alignment: It takes you places, but it is hard to handle because something is out of balance, causing excessive wear and tear. The same holds true when your business is out of balance: it does not perform to your expectations.

TRAP

It is always amazing to me when business owners try to justify not making an investment in planning. If you fall into this trap while writing your plan, nip it in the bud and get right back at it. Otherwise you will have wasted all the time you've already invested. Remember, help is just an e-mail away at gregbd@sbishere.com

TIP

Writing a business plan is like giving the organization a "tune-up." It's important to do this periodically, because some components will need to be rebuilt to get the business back to optimal performance.

Planning Is Part of Our DNA

Believe it or not, you are a natural born planner. Planning happens constantly throughout your day. From the time you get up in the morning, drive to work, and check your to-do list, you're making and executing plans. Some people are better at planning than others, but that is because they have worked at it. Just like an athlete trains to build muscles, you have to work at writing a business plan to enjoy the benefits.

TRAP

Beware of feelings of frustration, confusion, and negative self-talk. Do not buy into the reasons you feel inadequate. Be "un" reasonable; writing a business plan is an endurance race, not a sprint. When confused, you are simply missing information. Go back and reread the appropriate chapter. Ask yourself, "What information do I need to finish this part of the business plan?"

It's Worth the Effort

Business planning can become as natural as breathing, but you have to pay the price first. Spend time reading this entire book, then start researching, writing, and finish with editing. You can do it! Know that, when you finish your business plan, it will make a significant contribution to your organization's success. Look closely at any successful organization and you will find that business planning is routine, an exercise in due diligence that protects shareholders, creditors, directors, and customers.

Good Management

A manager's role is to provide leadership, maintain focus on core objectives, and prevent distractions from diluting the company's strength or slowing momentum.

Planning allows you to think about the details of your operation and how they all need to work together to form a viable, ongoing, and healthy entity.

Business planning mirrors the practices that good managers use as an ongoing evaluation process. They gather information, identify the resources needed, set business goals, and create a blueprint for accomplishing those goals.

Impress Your Bankers and Investors

A business plan is especially crucial for entrepreneurs seeking financing because a plan that is well prepared is a reflection of the entrepreneur's ability to manage the business. Bankers, investors, and financiers might appear cynical, but remember that it is their job to separate the viable businesses from those that may close owing them money.

Financiers want to verify that you have a working knowledge of the major functions of the business, including marketing, finance, sales, human resources, and production. They expect to see a true picture of the business's financial position or of the expected financial needs of a new enterprise.

You can bet that financiers will be looking to confirm your competence while reading your plan. Presenting a meticulously prepared and well-thought-out business plan is unmistakable evidence of your ability to plan and manage your business operation.

The process of writing a business plan helps to crystallize your thoughts. As you commit them to paper, you demonstrate an intimate knowledge of the business. After all, the last thing your financier wants to hear is that you need to consult someone else in order to answer questions. Being able to answer lenders' questions will go a long way to assuring them that the money they provide is in the hands of a knowledgeable and competent manager. Trust the business planning process. As you write, you prepare yourself to answer questions posed by your financier.

Business Plans as a Management Tool

In reviewing U.S. and Canadian studies of business failures, I found that bankrupt and successful firms had similar business plans and financial plans. According to the U.S. Department of Commerce in their publication *Failing Concerns: Business Bankruptcy in Canada, Characteristics of Business Owners 1992,* the major difference between success and failure was that 81 percent of successful firms periodically took stock of where they stood with respect to their goals, and they followed up by making adjustments to their practices and expectations. The sad news is that less than 33 percent of bankrupt firms with financial forecasts in their business plans actually compared their results with their forecasts, and only 40 percent of those took any remedial action when their forecasts differed from their goals.

This strikes me as just plain silly. If you do not know what is going on in your business (what's working, what isn't), you will never know what you need to do to make sure you reach your goals.

TRAP

Not making adjustments after reviewing your business plan seals your fate and substantially increases your chances of failure.

2

Understanding the Process and Getting Prepared

The benefits of writing a business plan are often misunderstood. Yes, a business plan will help you get the money you need when you're starting a business. But it will also help you make an existing business more effective.

Trust the Process, and You Will Gain New Insights

Most important is to remember that a business plan is made up of at least 10 major sections and many subsections. If you follow the process outlined in this book and do the work, you will gain a unique understanding that will help you to grow, evolve, and innovate.

These insights are gained only if you either take the time to write a business plan or have psychic abilities. Even if you have operated your business for decades, you will not have the same insights that come from critically evaluating every aspect of your business.

TRAP

Avoid procrastination. If you have a strong aversion to writing of any kind, never mind a business plan—change your mind and think of it as a very long set of notes to yourself. These are notes about what you want to do with the business.

What's Your Learning Style?

Everyone has a preferred learning style. Depending on your learning style, you can adjust your approach to organizing yourself in order to make the writing of your business plan less stressful than it might otherwise be.

Writing a business plan is as much about learning as it is about writing. In fact, if you are unable to articulate your thoughts and get them down on paper, it is most likely because you have not taken the time to articulate and express your knowledge of your business in an organized fashion.

> We do what we are. We are what we think. What we think is determined by what we learn. What we learn is determined by what we experience and what we experience is determined by what we expose ourselves to and what we do with that experience.
>
> MIKE VANCE, founder and dean
> of Walt Disney University

The actions we take are predicated on our behaviors, and our behaviors are determined by what we learn. Writing a business plan should be a learning experience.

TIP

Think about your business plan as an opportunity to gain a fresh perspective on what is driving or inhibiting your business progress.

A big part of the way you learn is based upon the way you "take in" and process information. In coaching hundreds of business owners, I have discovered the reason that some of them never start or finish writing a business plan. It is based partially on a bias toward action and partially on the way they have learned to operate their business. They feel a sense of guilt because they know they should have a written business plan but often have misconceptions about the value of a business plan and write one only when a banker or investor asks for one. I can see their eyes rolling and head tilting back when they first hear someone ask for a business plan.

No one has ever told them that the guilt is inappropriate or explained that what they are experiencing is simply the fear of having to learn something new. The good news is that, by identifying your learning style, I can help you overcome the roadblocks that prevent you from writing a business plan.

Learning Styles—Everyone Has One

Our learning style is based upon the way that we prefer to "take in" information. This is called VAKOG (visual, auditory, kinesthetic, olfactory, and gustatory). Everybody has visual, auditory, kinesthetic, and analytical capabilities. It is just that we each have a "preferred" learning style, and by gaining a greater understanding of your preference, you empower yourself and even prevent common obstacles and roadblocks to the planning process.

Visual

Visual entrepreneurs tend to overlook details and give short shrift to the business planning process. Why? Because they already have a good grasp of what they need and what they will need to do to achieve their goals. The problem for them is getting their ideas down on paper. If you are a visual entrepreneur, I recommend that you learn how to create a mind map to capture your ideas and then make notes following your mind map.

A mind map is a diagram used to link words and ideas to a central concept. A popular brainstorming technique, you can create a mind map with just a piece of paper and a pencil or purchase computer software. In Figure 12.1 you can view an example of a simple mind map I created on my computer to illustrate the process of writing an Executive Summary.

Auditory

If your primary learning style is through what you hear (auditory), you will speed your business plan development by finding someone with whom you can discuss your ideas. The discussion will help to solidify your ideas and organize your thoughts. If you do not get this type of support, you may find that you get stuck and are not sure why you are stalled. The process of "thinking out loud" is how you clear your mind, organize your thoughts, and make sense of your business plan. Another option is to use a digital/dictation recorder to capture your thoughts and then have someone else transcribe them into the business plan format.

Kinesthetic

As a kinesthetic learner, you take in information best when you experience a physical sensation or "feel" something. So using a computer and business planning software to write your business plan are important to you because you will get the tactile feedback you need. Plus, making a connection with someone else who will support you throughout the process will make the writing of your business plan go smoothly.

Olfactory and Gustatory

Unless you are starting a restaurant, winery, or a food product, the olfactory and gustatory senses will not impact your planning process.

People who are olfactory learners rely on their sense of smell. You will hear someone say, "That deal just stinks."

Gustatory learners take in the world through their sense of taste. They can be heard to say something like, "I could just taste victory."

If you are in the food services industry, make sure to include photographs of your product and provide samples or a taste test when presenting your business plan. When writing your business plan I recommend that you get someone to help you put your ideas down on paper, use business plan software, or use a digital/audio recorder to capture your thoughts. Make sure to allocate a portion of your marketing budget to samples and taste testing.

TIP

You can also use these learning styles when training your staff and for other major projects. For example, when training using the kinesthetic style, you want to focus your training by doing it with your staff.

Your Personality

Just as your learning style influences the way you learn, your personality affects the way you communicate, perceive information, and interact with others. The following are personality types that I have observed while working with business owners who were writing a business plan.

The Analyzer

You are a person who loves details, and you will love the process of writing a business plan. If at any point you get confused, go back and review your previous work and the appropriate chapter of this book. Do not try to write anything when you feel confused. Once you identify what it was that you found confusing then dig for the information you need, and you will be ready to continue writing.

The Socializer

As the name implies, socializers are people who are most concerned with and motivated by relationships. If forced to make a choice, socializers will preserve a relationship even at their own expense. They love to connect with people, and sitting down at a computer to write a business plan is a chore because it does not involve a relationship. If you are a socializer, to overcome the problem of writing in isolation, picture the person whom you will be meeting with to review the business plan. This will help keep you motivated and focused. Another option is to work on the business plan with a buddy.

The Promoter

Promoters make ideal salespeople. They can be highly intuitive, and they like to talk. They are quite good at influencing people. Despite this, they lack confidence, and they know it. This lack of confidence will be either an excellent motivator (they have a goal they really want) or a completely demotivating factor. If you are a promoter, the good news is that you will do a good job of selling and promoting your plan. But first you need to actually write the plan. I highly recommend that you plan your day and make an appointment with yourself to write the business plan. Make sure that you choose a time when you won't be interrupted and distractions will be minimal.

The Controller

Controllers are driven. They do not lack confidence. They are often considered aggressive, but, when you want to get something done, the controller is the right person for the job. If you're a controller, you have clear goals and do not like to waste time. Your weakness is in the details. Depending on your schedule, you might be prone to outsource or delegate the preparation of your business plan. Resist the urge to do this and get organized. Make the most of your time by either getting someone who is more detail-oriented than you (i.e., an analyzer) to help you put your plan together.

TRAP

Do not let the computer or software write your business plan. Think for yourself. I strongly recommend that you use templates as a guide—after you have read this book. As you read each chapter, make notes and highlight the parts that you want to pay special attention to.

The Process of Writing a Business Plan

I remember the first time I wrote a business plan for my own business. It was an intimidating task. But the process taught me so much that I wrote the

Business Plan Coach as a guide to help me keep on track while writing the business plan.

I realized I had something because, when I used it and just followed the process step by step, it was much easier.

TIP

My system for writing a business plan is read, think, journalize, do. Sure you can buy software or use templates to speed the writing process, but it is your knowledge, passion, and expertise that will sell the plan to your banker or investors.

The bottom line is that you do not need someone to write your plan for you; you just need a system to draw out your passion and a process to help you put it down on paper. That is what this book does. That is exactly what makes it so valuable—that, and what you learn about your business in the process.

One Bite at a Time

I have heard many people say that they cannot write. If you can think and speak, you can write. All you need to do is break the process down into small, manageable parts.

I highly recommend that, before you write one word for your business plan, you first take the time to read this book, think about each section, make notes, and journalize your thoughts—then and only then should you move on to the next step.

TIP

As you read, make notes in the margins, earmark pages, and highlight at will. Then, when you have notes for each section of your business plan, sit down at your computer and begin transferring your notes.

TIP

Stop at the end of each chapter of this book and think. Ask yourself questions, and then make notes for yourself on separate pieces of paper with the chapter number at the top of each page. Then, when you have finished reading the entire book and made all your notes, sit down in front of your computer and begin to transcribe your notes. Then organize them in order of priority.

Financial Projections for Your Business Plan

The one area in which you will likely need help is your financial projections. If you have some familiarity with financial statements I highly recommend using Business Plan Pro for this. It includes 400 templates plus a wizard to help you create your financial projections.

If you do not know a financial statement from a bank statement, you will need to get some help creating your financial projections. Here are your options:

1. Use a spreadsheet program. If you are an Excel wizard and understand financial statements and accounting, then certainly a spreadsheet application like Excel or Lotus is all you will need. However, I do not recommend this for anyone except accountants, bookkeepers, and those that have a working knowledge of financial statements.

2. Your accountant can create pro forma financial statements for you. Most accountants typically charge by the hour, and my clients have spent a few thousand dollars to as much as $10,000 for their accountant to prepare pro forma financial statements.

3. Purchase Business Plan Pro software ($99.95 at the time of this writing, available from Palo Alto Software, https://secure.paloalto.com). It has a great tool to help you put the financial portion of your business plan together.

Remember, there is nothing magic in the computer or software; it is the planning process plus your knowledge that makes a business plan come alive.

TRAP

A business plan without pro forma financial projections is like running a marathon without any training or preparation. You might get off to a reasonable start, but you will not have the endurance (money) to finish the race.

Ignore the Order in Which Sections Appear in the Final Document

The order in which the sections of your business plan appear in the final document is not the order in which you should write them. In fact, you will jump around from section to section because each is dependent on others. Jumping from section to section is a normal part of the process of writing a business plan.

It would be quite abnormal for someone to sit down and actually write one complete section and then move on to the next without considering the impact that one section has on the others. For example, the assumptions made in your marketing plan will affect the financial plan. It is like a large jigsaw puzzle: you start with what you know and keep trying new pieces and ideas until you get the result you want.

TIP

For your business plan, start with what you know and work the puzzle by following the background, tips, and instructions included in each section of this book.

To help you in assembling your business plan, Part 2 of this book, "The 10 Sections of a Business Plan," is organized based on the order in which you should begin writing the sections, not the order in which they should appear in the finished document. When all your sections are written, the finished document should be organized in the following order:

1. Executive summary
2. Business description
3. Products and services
4. Industry analysis
5. Market analysis
6. Marketing strategy
7. Management, operations, and organization
8. Implementation plan
9. Contingency plan
10. Financial plan

Sample Business Plans Are Too General

Just like a generic legal agreement that lacks specifics, using a business plan template or sample plan without checking its details cannot adequately identify risks and liabilities, and it runs the risk of getting the business and directors in trouble.

TRAP

Sample plans can increase your risk unless you use them only as writing tools and not as planning tools. You are always much safer with more detail than less. With more detail you are less likely to miss an important assumption, and after all, the whole point of planning is to reduce risk.

The problem arises because, unless something is spelled out, disclosed, or excluded, it will be considered to have been included because of the general and broad terms of the business plan. For example, a general statement in a business plan that does not disclose a tendency of the business to seasonal revenue fluctuations could be considered an oversight or even fraud if the sample plan projected steady growth in sales. This kind of discrepancy could become an issue, especially if you planned to finance your business using private investors. If the business were to get into trouble and go out of business and you failed to disclose (for whatever reason) the cyclical or seasonal nature of sales, you could find yourself being sued.

TRAP

Beware the sample business plan. Making changes to the names and numbers in a sample plan is always a bad idea. On my site, I do provide links to my friends at Palo Alto software who provide sample business plans, but remember that using these samples can get you into trouble.

Director's Liability

If you are incorporated or plan to incorporate, you will want to learn about your director's liabilities. Typically the president and treasurer are considered the directors of a company. A vice president also can be a director if this is specified in your corporate bylaws.

Directors have a fiduciary responsibility to act in the corporation's best interest. This obligation is as important as that between a trustee and a beneficiary. For example, it is illegal for a fiduciary to misappropriate money for personal gain or to take a paycheck before paying suppliers or the IRS.

TRAP

A director's position is a very serious matter. Keep this in mind when writing your business plan. I knew of a businessman in Canada who went to jail because the court found that he had not exercised his fiduciary duties. Even though his manager was the one who embezzled money and disappeared, the court held that this businessman and his partner, as directors of the company, were responsible for ensuring that the manager was managing the affairs of the company correctly. Their defense was that they trusted the manager and dealt in good faith, but this did not hold up—they spent 18 months in jail.

PART 2

The 10 Sections of a Business Plan

3

Industry Analysis

The industry analysis and market analysis (this chapter and chapter 4) both seek to identify the factors that will influence the external environment in which the business operates, whereas all the other sections of your business plan focus on the internal environment over which you have control. While the industry and market analyses look at the external environment, they view through different lenses.

TIP

In the industry analysis, you identify strategic opportunities you can use to your advantage. In the market analysis you scrutinize your local market to identify a profitable niche.

When you're writing your industry analysis, you provide answers to many questions including: Is the industry in decline or experiencing a fundamental restructuring? What is the size of the industry? Who holds the lion's share in the market? What percentage of market share do you need to acquire in order to achieve your business goals? What is the short-term and long-term outlook for your industry?

Industry Analysis = External Focus

The industry analysis shows the big picture—external factors that are beyond your control. Local market conditions are not part of the industry analysis (these are covered in Chapter 4, Market Analysis).

Identifying the external factors that could affect your business while you're writing your business plan allows you time to form a response or make adjustments to your plan. External factors include industry trends, the makeup of your market, the competitive environment, the economic climate, demographic trends, and the role of technology. The last areas you need to examine are the social, legal, and political aspects that could interfere with business activity.

TRAP

If you have direct experience in the industry, you will tend to feel quite confident in your industry knowledge. Do not assume that your context and understanding of the industry are comprehensive. Make an extra effort to acquire third-party clarification of your assumptions. You can conduct research and obtain information from libraries, the Internet, and trade organizations and associations. Expect to do a lot of reading and note taking. Your goal is to gain additional insight into how your industry is performing on a local, national, and international level.

Competitive Environment, Industry Trends, and Market Environment

The world and business climate are constantly evolving. What was hot a few years ago may be an anchor today. Identifying trends, competitive components, and market factors will allow you to create a strategy and respond proactively to customer needs.

Emerging Industry

While an emerging industry is ripe with opportunity, it may also present a significant risk. Factors indicating success and growth may be difficult to identify. Identifying your skill sets and a plan to quickly shift and evolve your business will be the "critical success factor," and you will want to make sure that your business plan clearly illustrates how you plan to respond to industry growth.

Mature Industry

Mature industries pose a different risk. It is much easier to identify factors that contribute to success. However, major players tend to dominate mature industries. Identifying the size of the market and the amount of market share you require are checkpoints to determine the viability of your business idea/plan.

Industry in Decline

An industry in decline or in a period of economic downturn presents a different set of issues. Opportunities may develop that would not normally be available. Determining and confirming realistic assumptions for economic growth will help support the assumptions made in your business plan. For example, what will it mean to your business plan assumptions if the economic indicators show an extended slump? On the other hand, if there are indicators that the industry is coming out of the slump and you anticipate real economic growth, the timing of your venture, start-up or expansion would be a critical factor in determining success.

Industry Restructuring

An industry undergoing restructuring or a process of reorganization generally shrinks in market size. For example, since the early 1990s the oil and gas industry in Canada experienced substantial reorganization and restructuring. Beginning in 1992 the industry saw marginal recovery in product demand and significantly improved profitability as a result of severe cost cutting, plant closures, and downsizing. While your expertise, financial resources, and anticipation of opportunities may indicate great potential, investors and bankers may not agree. You must prove that your assumptions and indicators are both accurate and attainable.

TIP

What are the factors driven by industry that contribute to growth or decline? Research, read, and describe the primary competitive factors affecting the industry in obtaining new customers. Is it price, delivery, change, evolution in products or services? Or is the reputation and image of the industry having an impact?

Economic Climate

A healthy economy can make a substantial difference in demand for your products, services, and business momentum.

Industry Financial Health

Both the IRS and Revenue Canada produce an industry balance sheet. This is an aggregated balance sheet that is compiled from corporate tax returns. It is an excellent tool to use for assessing the financial health of the industry as well as to compare your own financial projections with those of the industry and analyze your business assumptions.

For example, I conducted a comparison for one of my clients. We took his balance sheet and compared it to the industry balance sheet. We discovered that his staff costs were almost 50 percent higher than industry averages. We also discovered that his profit margins were double that of industry averages. This tool can be a valuable and unbiased way to test your business plan assumptions. Do your best to answer these questions:

- What is the financial status of the industry?
- How many new companies are opening?
- What is the split in size (i.e., number of small vs. large companies and sales volumes)?
- Which markets are being served well, and which are underserved? Which show the most potential for growth?
- How aggressive are the advertising and promotions strategies?
- What value-added factors are being used successfully?
- How many substitute products or services are available?
- Who holds the bargaining power? Customers? Suppliers?

TIP

The whole purpose of looking at the financial health of your industry is to make comparisons to see how you are doing. I guarantee that you will learn something important and spot areas of your business that may need attention.

Scale of Economy

How important is it to decrease the unit costs of a product or service? How much more money can you make per unit by increasing the number of units per production run?

What are industry experts saying? What do you hear people saying about your industry? What is the status and reputation of the industry?

Customer Loyalties and Differentiation

What is the loyalty factor in your industry? If the industry and competition are strong, how realistic is it that you can get customers to change their buying patterns? Is being a first mover in an industry a help or hindrance?

TIP

If you are in a highly competitive industry segment, maintaining customer loyalty can be challenging; but when successful, it will make you nothing but money.

Cash Flow Demands

A growing business can be in just as much of a crisis as a shrinking business. For example, there may be cash shortfalls for paying suppliers and staff. The need to purchase large amounts of inventory delays the return on investment. If your industry demands carrying large amounts of accounts receivable, this may negatively affect your ability to pay suppliers and staff. Identify the factors that can negatively affect your cash flow.

Staff and Delegation

What role do skilled workers play in your business? If your business relies heavily on skilled workers, how will your business attract the right people? Are there adequate systems and information controls developed to allow an effective balance between delegation and control? As an entrepreneur, are you reluctant to delegate and trust staff?

Idea and Business Development

Use this part of your business plan to describe how you will experiment with and test new business ideas. How will you balance your schedule to allow time to work on business developmental issues? After all, business moves at an accelerated pace today, and no business idea lasts forever.

TRAP

Back in the 1960s, companies could count on a product life cycle of five to nine years. Today, many have only a nine-month advantage. Do your customers have access to offshore competitors? What is the risk that someone can easily copy your product and flood the market with a low-cost knock off? A patent provides some protection and documentation of who did it first. However, protecting a patent can be expensive and difficult to enforce overseas. Document your plans to develop and protect ideas.

Diversification, Growth, and Expansion

Changes in your marketplace and customer demographics may require the owner to let go of long-held cherished beliefs. There is always going to be a certain amount of imbalance between marketplace needs and business strategy. The key is being able to identify changes that need to be made and then make an objective decision.

TRAP

Every business has a limited capacity to absorb change. Startups tend to focus on survival when they need to be diversifying, and established business owners try to cope with business growth by working harder. Without a solid plan to adapt to a market growth, diversification, or expansion, a business can quickly become insolvent.

Identify what tools, strategies, and changes, if any, you plan to implement.

The Role of Technology

For an example of how technology can disrupt normal business activity, look at the changes in the music industry and how Apple Computer came along to dominate the online music market. The business model for selling music was fueled by the more than 200 million computers that have installed Apple's iTunes software.

When you combine the widespread adoption of Apple's iTunes with the deep market penetration of the iPod, you get massive market disruption. This has forced brick-and-mortar stores (the traditional business model of selling music) to adapt by discounting CDs. Now Yahoo!, Napster, and AOL among others are all competing for a share of the online market.

TIP

When you're writing your business plan, make sure to identify how you will leverage the use of technology to compete or gain a technological advantage.

Exit Strategy

The strategies used by investors and owners to liquidate or cash out their investments are called *exit strategies*. These can range from selling the business, liquidating assets to repay debts, or selling a portion of the business to an investor.

TIP

An Employee Stock Ownership Plan (ESOP) is great way to exit your business, cash out, and save a bundle on taxes if it is set up properly with an attorney that specializes in this area of tax and legal planning.

Coping with Management and Emotional Factors

During times of economic change or crisis, it may be difficult for the entrepreneur or manager to decide to shut down a part of the business or the whole business. This decision can be made even more difficult because of the manager's emotional attachment to employees or the business.

TIP

To avoid making bad decisions based on emotion instead of reason, it is important to identify the types of situations (events, acceptable losses, and market changes) that would trigger your exit strategy.

Impact on Relationships

Are your investors family and/or friends? Shutting down the business may affect relationships with investors, friends, suppliers, or other business units. Concern over maintaining image and identity may encroach on your ability to make a quality decision to close the business.

TIP

The closer the relationship, the more difficult it can be to close a business. Every business that has more than one owner, investor, or shareholder should enter into a legally binding agreement that spells out the events, conditions, or circumstances that trigger an exit strategy.

Specific Assets

Lease financial commitments for equipment and facilities often survive the closure of the business. In a manufacturing organization the need to maintain a parts supply is often a legal if not moral requirement. Other issues include agreements with labor unions, customers, and suppliers.

TRAP

The more specialized your equipment and facilities are, the more difficult it may be to expand or liquidate quickly. Carefully consider the restrictions or impediments there could there be to expanding or closing the business.

Government Regulations

Are there any existing or anticipated government regulations that could affect your ability to start, expand or exit the business?

TIP

Make a list of government regulations that affect your business or the area in which your business is located. If you are not aware of any, call the local chamber of commerce for suggestions and access to government agencies. Research the issues and then develop a plan for dealing with these issues.

In some industries and locales professional accreditation or certification is required for getting a business license. Engineers, architects, and automotive mechanics are a few examples of businesses that require a degree or certification to be able to operate.

Demographic Trends

Gathering demographic data will allow you to select the area with the best mix of demographic characteristics to support your business.

Baby Boomers

Baby Boomers are the single largest demographic segment of the population, and by the sheer size of their buying power have disrupted entire industries and created business opportunities as they have aged.

From the huge increase in demand for housing, furniture, and appliances in the 1950s and 1960s to the heavy demand for retirement and financial planning services in the 1990s, and the growth of recreational vehicle sales, the effect of the baby boom is massive.

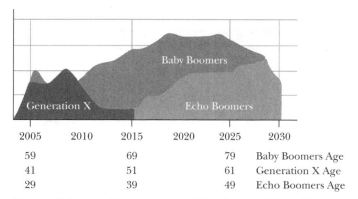

2005	2010	2015	2020	2025	2030	
59		69		79		Baby Boomers Age
41		51		61		Generation X Age
29		39		49		Echo Boomers Age

Figure 3.1 Age Progression and Distribution of Baby Boomers

Baby Boomers' influence on North America will extend several decades into the twenty-first century as they continue to age. The decline in the proportion of elderly in the population is expected to reverse as the Baby Boomers (born from 1946 to 1964) reach age 65, starting in 2011. (See Fig. 3.1.)

Many Baby Boomer business owners' greatest problem is to figure out a way to retire and extract the equity that has built up in their businesses. For many Baby Boomers, that will mean selling their businesses and converting their equity into cash or retirement income.

TIP

Look at your customer profile. How many of your customers are in the Baby Boomer business owner demographic? How many should be? Is this a market you have been missing? Consider how you could include marketing and positioning for Baby Boomers in your business plan.

Generation X

While the exact definition of Generation X is still hotly debated, I will be referring to their primary characteristic of being sandwiched between the Baby Boomers and the Echo Boomers (Baby Boomers' children), because they were born between 1966 and 1979. They are Web savvy, mobile, and have the entrepreneurial bug just like the Echo Boomers. Compared with the size of the baby boom, this segment is relatively small.

Members of Generation X seek out authentic and genuine products and services. They dislike being pushed to make a buying decision, they like a variety of choices and options when making a purchasing decision, and their brand loyalty is lower than Baby Boomers' and Echo Boomers'.

Often referred to as "latchkey kids," they were widely credited with a growth spurt of entrepreneurship and the resulting dot-com boom. They tend to have fewer kids and are oriented toward entrepreneurship, perhaps as the result of being self-reliant while growing up.

TIP

Generation X is somewhat controversial in that demographers do not all agree on the definition or the term itself. What is important to remember is that they are the group that was born at the end of the baby boom.

Echo Boomers Seeking Self-Employment

Children of Baby Boomers are known as Generation Y, the Echo Boomers, or the Millennials, and were born between 1977 and 2002. They are increasingly becoming known as the Entrepreneurial or "E" Generation.

Jeff Cornwall, director of Belmont University, using information from the Small Business Administration, has this to say about the Echo Boomers, or as he calls them, "The Entrepreneurial Generation":

Over the past decade or so, the emergence of a new entrepreneurial economy in America has begun. There has been significant growth in entrepreneurial start-ups and small businesses now are the engine of this economy. The number of small businesses has grown steadily: 4.5 million small businesses in 1955, to 18 million by the late 1980s, to 23 million today. New business formation has grown from about 200,000 per year in mid 1900s to over 3.5 million per year in the early twenty-first century.

Cornwall goes on to point to some interesting statistics about today's small businesses (from the Small Business Administration), including:

Business survival rates are now over 50 percent; with education and training this increases to 80 to 90 percent. Small businesses contribute 50 percent to the GDP (gross domestic product), and 5 million to 6 million small businesses have employees. Of the total number of employers in the United States, 99 percent of employers are small businesses. Over 50 percent of the workforce now is employed in small businesses with 45 percent of total payroll in the United States coming from small businesses.

Cornwall goes onto to state that "These businesses have become the engines of job creation for the United States. In fact, entrepreneurs and small business owners are responsible for 77 percent of new jobs created in past twenty years."

TIP

How can you utilize this information about the Echo Boom Generation in your business plan? You should consider what services or products you could offer and what you could do to customize specific products or services for them.

Industry Analysis Questions

Answering the questions in the following list will help you gather information to write and critique your own Industry Analysis.

- What influences customers to buy your product or service? How does the industry meet customer needs?

- What are the key performance indicators of this industry? Is it sales, profit, or the number of active businesses operating?

- What do industry experts say about the performance of this industry for the past five years? What is anticipated for the next five years?

- Who are the primary suppliers, distributors, and key players in the industry?

- What is the distribution model in this industry?

- What new services or products have been introduced in the last few years?

- How is technology affecting industry growth?

- What is the SIC code for this industry? The U.S. Department of Commerce uses the Standard Industrial Classification System to categorize industry and business types (see http://www.osha.gov/pls/imis/sicsearch.html). However, the U.S. Census Bureau uses the North American Industry Classification System (NAICS: http://www.census.gov/epcd/www/naics.html) to replace the U.S. Standard Industrial Classification (SIC) system. Unfortunately, the system is still under development and provides definitions for service businesses at the time of writing. You will most likely need both the SIC code and NAICS code to locate for information about your industry.

- What other industries, products, or services compete with this industry?

- Which are the major companies that you expect to compete with when starting or operating your business?

- What is the economic outlook for sales and profits in this industry over the next decade? Include at least a three- to five-year period of the economic forecast.

- What is the strategic opportunity for businesses in this sector? How can you create a new opportunity?
  - Improve the service levels?
  - Develop a new or untapped market?
  - Create a new product or an innovative service?
  - Use technology to develop ways to lower costs?
  - Meet an unfilled need or fulfill a new market demand?
- What are the major threats to this industry?
- What impact are the Baby Boomer, Generation X, or Echo Boomer generations having on the industry?

Sample Industry Analysis

Following is the industry analysis section of the business plan. The complete business plan can be found in Appendix A.

Industry Analysis

Government Regulations   The trucking industry is a highly regulated industry. Some of the areas of regulation include:

- *Motor Vehicle Safety Act:* http://www.tc.gc.ca/actsregs/mvsa/tocmvs.htm.
- *Uniform Cargo JOE'SmentStandard:* For highway transport vehicles, http://www.ab.org/ccmta/ccmta.html.
- *Federal Register online via GPO access:* The *Federal Register* is the official daily publication for rules, proposed rules and notices of federal agencies and organizations, http://www.access.gpo.gov/su_docs/aces/aces140.html.
- *Running authorities:* Individual extra regulations per province.
- *National Safety Code:* Covers hours of service regulations, commercial driver's license explanations, pre- and posttrip inspections, brake problems to look for and CVSA inspections, weights and dimensions, tires, differences between Canadian and U.S. regulations, etc.
- *U.S. Department of Transport (DOT) Compliance:* JOE'S is compliant with all aspects of U.S. DOT.

- *Transportation of Dangerous Goods (TDG):* Covers the transportation of dangerous goods. It covers TDG training requirements; classification and identification of dangerous goods; shipper, carrier, and consignee responsibilities; incident reporting; emergency response planning; and other crucial topics.

The Trucking Industry Two main segments characterize the Canadian trucking industry:

- For-hire companies, which transport the freight of others for compensation. For-hire fleets are three times more likely to use owner-operators than are private fleets.

- Private firms transport their own products. In dollar terms, private trucking accounts for nearly one-half the industry. These companies are typically involved in private trucking as they have a need to control service. Private firms tend to use smaller units and trailers. Private trucking dominates the urban goods movement, accounting for approximately 85 percent of truck movements in this market.

At distances of 300 miles, private trucking accounts for approximately 25 percent of trucking movements. In 1998 Canadian-based, long-distance for-hire carriers experienced an increase of almost 5 percent from 1997.[1]

Transborder traffic has grown by 9 percent per annum over the past five years.[2]

On distances above approximately 300 to 600 miles, for-hire trucking accounts for approximately 90 percent of all trips. For-hire trucking accounts for 78 percent of interprovincial trips, and 59 percent of longer distance intraprovincial trips.[3]

The for-hire trucking industry in Canada had $13 billion in revenues in 1993 (for-hire carriers and couriers). The industry is a $37 billion (including the value of private fleets) a year industry (1995)—an increase of $6 billion over 1993 estimates. Private trucking accounts for $19 billion of the total. 90 percent of private fleets consist of 10 vehicles or fewer, with most of these fleets consisting of 1 or 2 vehicles. However, there are many private fleets with up to several hundred vehicles. The same data indicate that overall private fleets outnumber for-hire fleets by a factor of 2 or 3 to 1.

Economic Impact of the For Hire Canadian Trucking Industry
Trucks handle over half of all Canada's trade as measured by the value

(*Continued*)

(Continued)

of the commodities. In 1994 two-thirds or $218 billion of all truck shipments were carried across the Canada–United States border. No wonder there are close to 10 million truck trips a year back and forth across the border.

The trucking industry (for-hire carriers and couriers) accounts for one out of every three dollars spent on commercial, for-hire transportation in Canada (this includes both freight and passenger transportation).

Another estimate, considering private trucking as well as for-hire trucking, suggests that trucking accounts for 47 percent of all commercial passenger and freight transportation in the country.

For-hire trucks account for 29 percent of the transport component of Canada's gross domestic product.

A 2001 estimate puts the total level of taxation of the trucking industry at 13.5 percent of revenues. A rough extrapolation from this indicates that highway tractors generate between $30,000 and $40,000 in taxes every year, and this does not take into account the taxes paid by the people driving those trucks.

Every job created in the for-hire trucking industry creates 0.7 jobs somewhere else; every dollar of output adds $0.69 in sales to some other industry; and every dollar of Gross Domestic Product (GDP) produced by the trucking industry creates an additional $0.73 in GDP for other industries.

Over the last three decades (1970–2000), the total economy has grown at an average annual rate of 3.8 percent. For-hire trucking has grown at an average annual rate of 4.2 percent; faster than airlines, shipping companies, railways, bus operations, and urban transit.

Barriers to Entry and Growth   The three primary barriers to entry and growth in this industry are:

- *Capital cost:* Obviously the high capital cost of trucks and trailers makes entry and growth a challenge.

- *Human resources:* The demand and growth for trucking services has outstripped the ability of the industry to attract new people to enter the field. The driver population is at least two years older than the age of the average worker. The under-25 age group is attracted to the trades, secondary education and technology jobs.

- *Customer perception:* To be a credible trucking company that can consistently meet the needs of the average industrial customer, you need to have approximately six or more trucks. That is the number needed to be able to cope with the dynamic nature of the trucking industry and changing customer needs.

Impact of Innovation and Technology Probably one of the most important technology issues for the trucking industry is the impact of the Internet. In the last two to three years a number of companies have launched load-matching services online. These services take one of four forms:

1. *Software:* This approach requires the purchase and installation of special software designed for the trucking industry.
2. *Online load matching:* For a small monthly fee you can search for and find a load or post truck availability.
3. *Complete solution:* This service looks after all billing, credit approval, and collection.
4. *Auctions:* Online auctions provide an opportunity to list equipment and shipments available and allow shippers and trucking companies to bid competitively for loads. These services are relatively new. Shippers place loads they need moved and trucking companies use the auction to bid for the load. Because the load is placed in a competitive auction, the practice tends to drive down the rates and sometimes the load descriptions can be misleading and the trucking company ends up having to take the load regardless.

Using the Internet to match equipment with loads is here to stay. The Internet will reduce costs by helping to eliminate empty miles.

Another trend is trucking companies that have special sections in their Web sites that are password-protected and allow customers to log in and request a quote, track a shipment, and even get an invoice.

Notes

1. Statistics Canada—The Daily, June 10, 1999.

2. Profile of Private Trucking in Canada, 1998, a joint report of Industry Canada and the Private Motor Truck Council of Canada. http://strategis.ic.gc.ca/epic/internet/ints-sdc.nsf/en/fd01101e.html.

3. Profile of Private Trucking in Canada, 1998, a joint report of Industry Canada and the Private Motor Truck Council of Canada. http://strategis.ic.gc.ca/epic/internet/ints-sdc.nsf/en/fd01101e.html.

4
Market Analysis

One of the easiest mistakes to make in your business plan is to assume that there is a market for your business. Just because you think you have a great idea does not mean that a market exists or is accessible without spending a lot of money.

Benefits of the Market Analysis

The market analysis, marketing strategy, and financial plan are three of the most important parts of your business plan. The market analysis will provide you with insight into the structure and size of the market as well as information concerning the environment that influences the market. It should answer the following questions:

- What do customers want to buy? How do they want to buy it? When do they want to buy it? What are their preferences, purchasing behavior, and perceptions?

- Where is the market located?

- What is the size of the market or the total number of potential buyers for your services or products?

- What are the external factors influencing business activity in this market? Your analysis should include social, economic, and environmental factors such as the legal, government, and competitive environment controlling the market.

- What are the pressures that shape business activity in this market? How sensitive is the market to changes by large employers that downsize, being dominated by one industry that suffers a downturn, an increase in unemployment, and changing demographics?

- What is the average income in your market area? Is the price of your products or services in alignment with the income, lifestyle, and demographics of your market segment?

- What is the primary market niche(s) that you plan to serve with your company? What are the current trends influencing this niche?

- Are any of the trends identified in the industry analysis having an impact on your local market? If so, how will you address these concerns in your business plan?

- How does the local market compare to the industry as a whole?

- What trends could alter the market over the time period covered by the business plan?

- What is the anticipated growth rate for sales and profits for your market?

- What do you know about your customers and the marketplace?

- What competitive products or services have the potential to gain market share?

- What strategies do your competitors use to compete in this market? How do service, price, positioning, quality, or exclusive products factor into the buyers decision?

- Where is there an opportunity to innovate and compete on a new level?

TIP

Now is the time to show your knowledge of the local market. As a result of working on this section, you should have identified a segment of the market that describes your "ideal customer." If you have not clearly identified your ideal customer, keep digging.

Identify Your Competition

The goal of marketing is to communicate clearly your primary competitive advantage to your target audience. To identify the clear advantage you have over your competitors, you will need to compare your business to that of your direct and indirect competitors. Competitors come in all shapes, sizes, and flavors. For example, let's look at a professional sports team. In today's marketplace the competition for entertainment dollars is fierce.

- *Direct competitors:* Direct competitors would include other professional sports teams and concerts or other events that take place on the same day your team is playing.

- *Indirect competitors:* Indirect competitors are substitute products or services, for example, businesses like video stores, movie theaters, restaurants, exhibitions and fairs, the local symphony orchestra, and the opera. Can you think of any other indirect competitors?

Make a list of direct and indirect competitors. Who else in your market is competing for the same portion of the customer's budget?

TRAP

Your market has only a certain amount of disposable income for the particular type of expenditure made for your business. When doing your competition analysis, remember that your goal is to come to a better understanding of your competitors and what motivates their customers to do business with them. Then you can use that information to improve your marketing strategy.

With this information you can strategize and position your products or services to ensure that you have a fighting chance to win market share. What you learn here will be very valuable and helpful in writing your marketing strategy.

Competition Analysis

Once you have described your direct, indirect, substitute, or potential competitors and have identified them by name, it's time to perform a thorough competition analysis. Gather the following information about your competitors:

- *Strengths:* What do they do well? What do they say is (in their advertising, Web site, etc.) their primary competitive advantage? Identify their market share, volume and profitability. Are they bigger or smaller than you?
- *Weaknesses:* Where are they weak? What could they improve upon? What is lacking?
- *How they compete:* Describe their characteristics, strategies and operational methods. For example:
    - How is their business model different?
    - How are they positioned with respect to price?
    - How would you describe the quality of what they sell?
    - How do credit terms factor into a purchasing decision?
    - What do they do to service their customers?
    - What is their approach to sales and distribution?
    - How would you describe their reputation?
    - What is the background and expertise of their management?

How to Gather Information about Your Competitors

The following are 10 sources and strategies you can use to get information about your competition.

1. *Suppliers:* You might be surprised how much information suppliers might give you if they trust you and want your business.

2. *Annual reports:* If one of your competitors is a public company, its annual report may reveal important information.

3. *Phone the competition:* Call your competitors. Introduce yourself and get to know them. Some industries are ultra competitive and information will be tough to obtain, and others are quite cooperative. If you can gain their trust, they may begin to share their expertise and knowledge out of sheer ego. Remember, the business is their baby, and they are proud of it.

4. *Talk to their customers:* Most of them will be willing to speak with you because you represent another source of services or products.

5. *Check periodicals and trade journals:* See if any articles have been written about them. Often these articles reveal an amazing amount of information.

6. Review the company's Web site.

7. *Talk to some of their employees:* Be careful what you disclose. But a little give and take might yield surprising results.

8. *Visit your competitors at a local industry trade show:* It will give you a good idea of how they present themselves to the public, and you might be surprised at how much information you will get before they start asking you questions.

9. *Review reports and profiles of the local industry:* Local trade associations and larger community groups often have these. If not, take the executive director out for lunch or coffee. He or she will see you as a potential member and will be quite open to your questions.

10. *Look at your competitors' advertising:* Check the local telephone directory, newspapers, magazines, and trade publications.

TIP

Create a comparison chart or spreadsheet to help organize the information you've gathered on your competitors. Include a brief overview and analysis of the competition in the following areas: financial strength and health, reputation and image, business model, price, range of product(s) or service(s) offered, quality of services and/or product offered, reputation and quality of their human resources, location and appearance of their facility as compared to yours, and marketing and advertising.

Identify Sales and Profits by Market Segment

Now you need to identify and describe how many products or services you will sell—and when and to whom you will sell them. This will help you create a sales forecast, which you will need to complete your financial plan. Conducting this type of market research can have three results:

1. It will confirm your assumptions. Having confirmed key assumptions, you will feel secure and confident knowing that you are on the right track.

2. It will prove which of your assumptions are wrong. It is always better to find out that your assumptions are incorrect sooner rather than later. It will save you money and time.

3. You will learn something new. Everyone brings knowledge, skills, and expertise to a business. While conducting research, watch for information or ideas you had not previously considered. When you identify an opportunity or idea, write it down, and then see how you can modify your business plan to implement the idea.

Any one of these three results will make the effort worthwhile. In my experience, most research and survey efforts provide insights on all three levels.

Your sales and profit estimates will be made up of information from two sources: new data you gather from your research and information from local governments, institutions, or associations.

TIP

Create a spreadsheet and list your products or services on the left side. Across the top, from left to right, estimate by percentage of sales how much each market segment will represent to overall revenue.

Other Sources of Information

Digging for and locating information about your market will provide a fresh perspective on your customers' needs, preferences, and motivations, which will aide in the development of your business plan.

- *Industry analysis:* Take some time to compare your market research with the information you obtained while writing the industry analysis. What are the differences? Are they major? If so, what will the impact be on the business plan? How can you compensate for, explain, or justify your findings?

- *Competition analysis:* Once you conduct your competition analysis, you need to determine whether the information you collect would change or alter your assumptions for market share, marketing strategy, and promotion.

- *Customer profile and preferences:* The next chapter covers customer profile and preferences. Once you have completed those sections, be sure to go back and compare that information with what you have learned about the market. Are your assumptions still valid? If not, what will you need to change to make the business plan work?

You can also buy market reports from www.bizminer.com for U.S., state, and metropolitan-area markets. These include count of firms, small businesses and start-ups, three-year industry volume and average sales, three-year sales per employee and employment, failure rates, industry vitality measures, and three-year industry concentration rates. The reports are affordable and provide a foundation that you can build upon by add your own research and findings.

TIP

Some economic development authorities and certified development authorities maintain a library of local market trends, statistics, and other information that you can access for free.

In-Depth Marketing Research

You can conduct marketing research in a variety of ways:

- *Focus groups:* A focus group is formed when a group of potential customers come together to provide feedback and suggestions on a company's products, services, or marketing strategy. The information gathered using this method is very valuable. It will help you qualify your ideas and confirm customer preferences, emotions, and attitudes toward your company and its products or services. Focus groups always provide a new and fresh perspective of your customers.

- *Test marketing:* Test, test, test because we never stop testing and learning about how to build a business. This will involve going to a small part of the marketplace to test selling your services and products. You can test your marketing ideas and verify customer attitudes and preferences. You can then use this information to revise and evolve your product and service offerings. If you cannot afford to do a focus group, this is an excellent alternative.

- *Survey:* You can create a survey and then ask the questions and record the responses. Usually surveys are conducted face to face, but they can also be successful over the telephone. I would avoid mail surveys since our purpose is to obtain data on their buying motivations, feedback on marketing concepts, and the emotional connection they have to your products or services.

- *Observation:* Watching people in real life situations, in a store or on video, will provide insights into shopping patterns, behaviors, and perceptions.

- *Experimentation:* You can interview people in a real-life situations, observe them from afar, or any combination of the above strategies.

TRAP

In-depth marketing research is expensive. If you decide to have an independent third party do the research for you, make sure you are clear about what you want to uncover and that the contract clearly reflects your desired outcomes (information). This means you need to have a good basic understanding of the market before investing in market research, otherwise you could end up paying a lot of money for information that is not that useful or insightful.

Market Segments and Innovation

You can create a market segment by identifying specific variables and then establishing a market niche based on those criteria. For example, some of the variables could be geographic location, demographics, psychographics, buying habits, consumer behavior, consumer inclinations, and socioeconomic patterns. You can use these criteria to segment your market as well as reveal key performance indicators (see Chapter 9).

Do not be intimidated by this task. There is so much that can be learned by studying your industry and market. In fact you will never stop learning about your industry. The twenty-first century is all about innovation and creativity. Innovation almost always builds on something that already exists.

TIP

The next great innovation could be right under your nose. Educating yourself about the industry and market will provide you with a unique perspective that will help you see things in a new light.

Calculate Market Size and Market Share

It can be a challenge to quantify the size of your market and calculate your market share, but it is an important viability test. Let me explain. Let's say that your financial projections show that in order to be profitable you need a 20 percent market share. If your business is in a mature industry and you are just starting up, gaining a 20 percent market share would require taking business from your competitors. This would likely be unrealistic and unattainable; it's just not good economic sense. On the other hand, if you only require a 0.5 percent market share, the business plan could work.

TRAP

Do not get caught in the trap of making this overcomplicated, but do not skip estimating the size of your market and market share because it will help you understand the financial realities of your business.

How to Determine the Size of Your Market

There are a number of sources you can use to calculate the size of your market. For example:

1. *Government data:* Many local, state, and federal governments offer public access to market information. In the United States, seek out your local small business development center (SBDC) which may be able to help you connect to information sources. You can also check with local authorities including the chamber of commerce and economic development organizations; some counties also have general statistics available.

   In Canada you can use the Industry Canada Web site (http://sme.ic.gc.ca/) which, in conjunction with Revenue Canada, compiles an "industry balance" sheet. This will show you income and expense averages, gross profit, assets, and accounting ratios. Many civic governments and economic development departments have a lot of data available that may assist you.

2. *Sales trends:* Are sales volumes going up or down or are they level? Use articles from trade magazines, newspapers associations, and industry studies to support your assumptions.

3. *Alternate industry comparison:* If you are really stuck, you could compare your business to another in a similar industry whose financial performance data is easier to obtain.

4. *Extrapolate from industry data:* If you are able to find out the sales volume for your industry in your area, then a simple calculation may be just the ticket. Divide reported sales by the total number of businesses competing in your market. A source for estimated data is the Survey of Buying Power, which breaks down the information for every state, Core-Based Statistical Areas (CBSA), county, major city, and Designated Market Area (DMA) in the United States. The report includes population, effective buying income, retail sales, and buying power. It is likely available at your local library or can be purchased online at www.salesandmarketing.com.

TIP

If you visit your local library and it does not have these surveys, ask the local librarian to order them for you. Libraries are always looking to improve their selection of books, and, if you can spare the time, this is an excellent way of getting almost any business book without spending any money.

Determining the size of your market could be as simple as counting the total number of competitors in your area (from Yellow Pages listings) and estimating sales for each one to come up with the total market size. If you choose this method, be sure to show your calculations so the reader will know how you arrived at your statistics.

TRAP

If purchasing your product is unbudgeted and/or unplanned, your marketing and sales strategies will need to help your customers to come up with the money (create the budget), which adds friction and time to the sales and marketing cycle. The best market to go after is the one that has a lot of money and already has a budget for purchasing your product or service.

Market Area

Choose your battles carefully, because no business can sell to the whole world. Only the largest of corporations can do that. Even an online business is going to sell its products and services to people within a specific market area.

TIP

What geographic area will you serve? Customers in the closest proximity to you are going to be the most cost-effective to sell to and service. You will also be able to better penetrate the markets that are closest to you.

External Factors

Identify specific factors, trends, or issues that are going to affect sales performance. Look into these factors and comment about them in your business plan. External factors include:

- *Sales cycle:* Every business endures sales fluctuations. What are the times of year that things tend to get quiet or busy? Create a chart that shows the estimated peaks and valleys in your sales cycle.

    Using data gathered from your market research, compare your sales forecast to the market trends. Do the sales trends (peaks and valleys) differ greatly? If so, is your forecast realistic? If needed, compare your forecast to a similar business or ask an industry expert.

- *Interviews:* Seek input from other business owners who are no longer operating, former employees, or suppliers. Suppliers can be an excellent source of information because they see the purchasing patterns of all their customers. In test marketing campaigns you may be able to pre sell or book advance orders. If your test marketing was successful, a number of your assumptions will be confirmed, which will support your business plan.

- *Survey and research results:* You should have gained insight from the work you did in these two areas. If your survey was well designed and asked about buying patterns, preferences, and volumes, you should have some sort of an indicator of sales potential.

TRAP

At first glance you might think that writing about the external factors that could influence your local market and what you plan to do to offset negative events is overkill. In reality, anything that can impact your sales cycle, buying behavior, and purchasing patterns should be taken seriously, because these factors also have the potential to affect your cash flow and your ability to pay your bills.

Sample Market Analysis

Following is the market analysis section of a business plan. The complete business plan can be found in Appendix A.

Market Analysis

The nature of the trucking industry is to serve local businesses that need to move products and manufactured goods. Typically, the majority of a trucking company's loads are generated by a local business. Therefore, the economic outlook for Edmonton and the surrounding area is an important success indicator for JOE'S.

Positive Economic Trends   According to the Conference Board of Canada, Edmonton has the most diverse economy of any area in Canada. Major projects in northern Alberta are now valued at $43 billion. Statistics that support economic growth include:

- In 1996, exports of manufactured products reached more than $12 billion—39.6 percent of Alberta's total exports.[1]

- Manufacturing shipments in the Edmonton region—Alberta's leading manufacturing area—are valued at more than $14 billion a year.[2]

- $8.3 billion of manufactured commodities were imported by the United States. Exports to the United States were $1.0 billion higher in 1998 than in 1997.[3]

- Alberta's manufacturing industry grew in 1998 by 12.8 percent, while Canadian overall industry grew by 6.5 percent.[4]

- Valued at $38.7 billion in 1998, manufacturing in Alberta now outpaces revenues from the agriculture, construction, and business services sectors.[5]

- Exports of manufactured goods more than doubled between 1993 and 1998.[6]

- In 1998, Alberta surpassed British Columbia for the first time in industrial manufacturing shipments. Manufacturing accounts for about 10 percent of Alberta's economy.[7]

- There were 2,190 manufacturing companies registered in the Edmonton region in June 1999, a 6 percent increase from June 1998. Much of the manufacturing activity in the Edmonton capital

(Continued)

(*Continued*)

region is concentrated in the areas of agrifood products, chemicals, metal fabrication, oil refining, and machinery.[8]

- Manufactured products are the fastest growing category of export in Alberta. In 1996, exports of manufactured products reached more than \$12 billion—39.6 percent of Alberta's total exports.[9]

- Manufactured products represented 75 percent of Alberta's total exports in 2002. Currently, two-thirds of all manufacturing shipments are value-added resource-based (food-processing, refined petroleum, and forest) products.[10]

For-Hire Trucking (Commodity Origin and Destination)—Second Half of 1999   Canada-based, long-distance, for-hire carriers carried more than 269 million tons of freight in 1999, an increase of 15 percent over 1998.(See Fig. 4.1.)

Regional Transborder Market Splits   On a regional basis, private trucking accounts for 9 to 16 percent of long-distance transborder

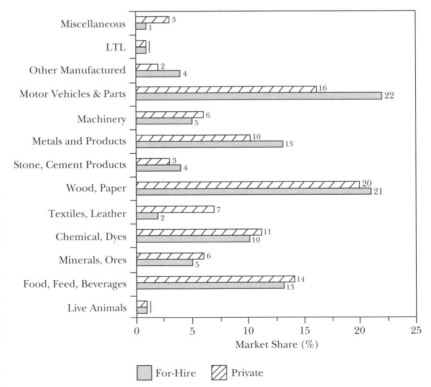

Figure 4.1   Transborder Commodity Types

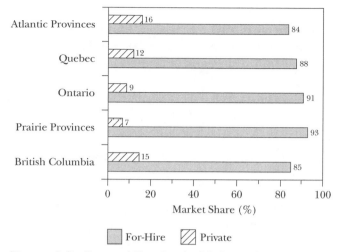

Figure 4.2 Regional Transborder Market Splits

trips. Use of private trucking is greatest in the Atlantic Provinces and British Columbia. (See Fig. 4.2.)

Commodity Types Commodities hauled by private trucks are similar to those hauled by the for-hire sector. (See Fig. 4.3.)

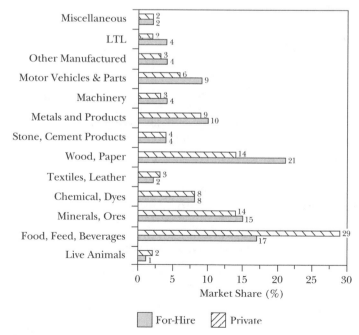

Figure 4.3 Intraprovincial Commodities

(*Continued*)

(*Continued*)

Figure 4.3 shows the type of commodities that JOE'S hauls include LTL, machinery, other manufactured goods, metals and products, wood and wood products, and food.

Northern Alberta Major Projects, 2000[11]

Industry	Value ($millions)
Oil, gas, and oilsands	26,220.0
Pipelines	5,233.9
Chemicals and petrochemicals	2,806.0
Infrastructure	2,452.4
Power	1,640.0
Forestry and related	1,420.0
Commercial/retail	940.4
Agriculture and related	626.2
Institutional	578.2
Tourism/recreation	380.4
Other industrial	322.0
Residential	283.9
Mining	257.5
Manufacturing	84.5
Total projects	43,245.4

Note: Major projects are defined as projects valued at $2 million or greater that are currently under construction or are proposed to start construction within two years.

Individual Projects in Edmonton Service Area Worth $1 Billion or More[12]

Company	Value ($billions)	Location	Project Description
Syncrude Canada Ltd.	$3.0	Muskeg River	Oilsands Mining/ Extraction plant
Alliance Pipeline Ltd. Partnership	$2.4	Muskeg River	Natural gas pipeline to Shell Co-gen Facility

Syncrude Canada Ltd.	$2.3	Cold Lake	Heavy oil pilot plant
Suncor Energy Inc.	$2.2	Cold Lake	Heavy oil commercial facility
Albian Sands . Energy Inc	$1.8	near Elk Point	New facility
Mobil Oil Canada Ltd.	$1.7	Cold Lake and Beartrap, Charlotte and Pelican Lakes	In situ bitumen production
Shell Canada/ Western Oil Sands/ Chevron Canada Resources	$1.7	Primrose/ Wolf Lake	In situ bitumen production
Syncrude Canada Ltd.	$1.5	Empress to Fort Saskatchewan	Straddle plant and pipeline
Mobil Oil Canada Ltd.	$1.4	Surmont	SAGD bitumen commercial project, phase 1
Koch Exploration/ UTSEnergy	$1.3	Surmont	SAGD bitumen commercial project, phase 2
Petrovera Resources Ltd.	$1.2	Lloydminster	Upgrader expansion/ debottleneck
NOVA Chemicals/ UnionCarbide Canada	$1.1	Joffre	Polyethylene plant (PE2)
Alberta Infrastructure	$1.0	Cold Lake area	Highway 28 upgrading
Syncrude Canada Ltd.	$1.0	Cold Lake	Heavy oil plant expansion
Nova Gas Transmission Ltd.	$1.0	Fort McMurray toHardisty	Wild Rose pipeline, phase 2

Trucking Market Trends in Canada

Growth of the Canadian trucking industry in Canada tends to follow increases in manufacturing, resource, and economic cycles. Long-distance

(Continued)

(*Continued*)

highway trucking has continued to grow from year to year despite regional economic realities.

1999	Tonnage	Shipments	Revenue Share[13]
Transborder	26%	22%	46%
Domestic	74%	78%	54%

1998	Tonnage	Shipments	Revenue Share[14]
Transborder	24%	20%	42%
Domestic	76%	80%	56%

Market Share   There are $2.7 billion in transportation services by Canadian-based for-hire carriers and couriers across the Canada-U.S. border. Revenues earned on this cross-border traffic have been growing at an annual rate of 12.6 percent since 1980—much faster than revenues for domestic business.

To meet its revenue and profit objectives in the first year of operation, JOE'S requires a market share of 0.000618 percent. This is a small and attainable projection. This does not include growth in JOE'S's western Canadian marketplace, where four new contracts totaling over $800,000 are in place. Further growth in the western Canadian market is anticipated because of these contracts, and the $43 billion in major projects in northern Alberta over the next two years. (see Table 4.1 for details).

Table 4.1   Market Share Analysis

No. of Units: 7

Annual average dollar amount per unit	$192,000.00
Annual volume	$1,671,000.00
Transborder volume, in dollars	$2,700,000,000.00
Market share	0.000618
Canadian industry average per unit	260,000

JOE'S Major Accounts

Customer	$ YTD	Next 12 months
Right Here Products	$39,321.06	Increase
Next Door Logistics	$147,208.46	Varies
Hard Steel	$19,689.28	Increase

We Know the Way Transportation Ltd	$17,151.90	Varies
No One Knows Metals	$44,481.42	Varies
Black White & Gray	$20,534.96	Increase
Canadian Imitation Products Co.	$53,921.95	Increase
Edmonton Growers	$63,484.54	Varies
Oilfield Tubes	$63,464.17	Increase
Big Tanks & Equip Ltd.	$28,833.72	Increase
ABCD	$125,786.90	Increase
To and Fro Transportation (TO AND FRO)	$34,500.00	Varies
Big Guy Industries	$40,006.17	Increase
Metal Buildings Inc.	$37,154.50	Increase
Heavy Equip. Sales	$17,840.00	Increase
Big Bird Transportation Inc. (Sunpine)	$85,980.34	Varies
Both Sides Intl. Transport Inc.	$11,520.00	Varies
Transportation Company	$9,100.00	Varies
Always On Time Logistics Ltd.	$43,928.00	Varies
Three Small Men Holdings Ltd.	$88,991.99	Increase
The Weather Is Bad Here	$46,675.00	Increase
Oilfield Welding & Overhead Cranes	$105,843.21	Increase
Total business YTD	**$1,145,417.00**	

For-Hire Motor Carriers of Freight, All Carriers—Third and Fourth Quarter 1999 In the second half of 1999, there were approximately 2,500 for-hire trucking companies based in Canada with annual revenues of $1 million or more compared with an estimated 2,350 carriers during the same period in 1998.

Second half of 1999 operating revenues climbed to $9.0 billion ($4.4 billion in the third quarter and $4.6 billion in the fourth quarter). Operating expenses reached $8.3 billion ($4.1 billion in the third quarter and $4.3 billion in the fourth quarter).

Average operating expenses increased by 11 percent over the second half of 1998 to $3.35 million. In particular, for-hire trucking companies reported a 19 percent increase in average owner-operator expenses and spent substantially more on fuel (+12%) compared with the last six months of 1998. The operating ratio (operating expenses divided

(*Continued*)

(*Continued*)

by operating revenues) was 0.93, unchanged from the same period in 1997. Any ratio under 1.00 represents an operating profit.[15]

For-Hire Motor Carriers of Freight (Top Carriers)—First Quarter 2000   The top 82 for-hire motor carriers of freight (Canada-based trucking companies earning $25 million or more annually) generated operating revenues of $1.65 billion during the first three months of 2000. Although there were two fewer top carriers in the first quarter compared with the first quarter of 1999, average revenue per carrier increased by 14 percent. Average operating expenses for top carriers also increased by 14 percent over the first quarter of 1999 to $19.1 million. After higher fuel expenditures in the third and fourth quarters of 1999, top carriers in the first quarter paid 34 percent more for fuel than in the first quarter of 1999.

The operating ratio (operating expenses divided by operating revenues) for all top for-hire carriers and the largest subgroup, general freight carriers, was unchanged from the first quarter of 1999 at 0.95 (a ratio of greater than 1.00 represents an operating loss). However, revenues outpaced expenses among carriers hauling bulk liquids, dry bulk materials, forest products, and other specialized freight, resulting in an improvement of 2 points in the specialized freight carrier operating ratio (0.94) over the first quarter of 1999.[16]

Notes

1. Alberta Economic Development.

2. Alberta Economic Development.

3. Alberta International Trade Review 1998; Alberta Economic Development.

4. Alberta Economic Development.

5. Alberta Economic Development.

6. Alberta Economic Development.

7. Alberta Economic Development.

8. Conference Board of Canada (Metropolitan Outlook, Autumn 1999), Canadian Business Register, Alliance of Manufacturers & Exporters Canada.

9. Alliance of Manufacturers & Exporters Canada (Manufacturing in Alberta—1999), Alberta Economic Development.

10. Alliance of Manufacturers & Exporters Canada (Manufacturing in Alberta—1999), Alberta Economic Development.

11. Alberta Economic Development. Prepared by Economic Development Edmonton, February 2000.

12. Alberta Economic Development. Prepared by: Economic Development Edmonton, February 2000.

13. The Daily, May17, 2000.

14. The Daily, June 10, 1999.

15. Statistics Canada—The Daily, June 7, 2000.

16. Statistics Canada—The Daily, June 19, 2000.

5
Products and Services

The next step in creating your business plan is writing the description of what your business sells. Do not gloss over this section. Just because you are familiar with the products or services you sell does not mean that the banker or investor reading your plan is.

TIP

Remember that the person reading your plan does not have your experience, knowledge, or desire. As a result of reading your plan you want to gain their confidence and trust. Demonstrate that you know how to run your business and achieve your goals and objectives. Whenever possible customize your plan for each person that will be reading it. Modify and edit the appropriate sections of the plan with an eye to details that the reader will be looking for by customizing the Executive Summary plus any sections you know they have a special interest in. For example, a banker will be interested in financial projections, while a seasoned businessperson might be more concerned about your commitment and skills and the business concept and viability.

To get started, simply write a brief description of what you sell. Then read this chapter and come back to rewrite your description applying what you have learned.

Background Information

Start with a clear and simple statement of what your product(s) is or what service(s) your business will provide.

TRAP

Avoid the temptation to compare your offering to similar services or products. Reserve that for the competitive and marketing analysis section of your business plan. Instead, focus on what makes your offering unique and preferable to customers. Explain what it does, how it works, how long it lasts, what options are available, and any proprietary rights that give you an advantage.

Of particular importance is whether you are selling a stand-alone product or service or one that must be used with others (e.g., computer software or peripheral devices). Be sure to describe the requirements for any associated products or services.

Do you hope to sell items as a one-time purchase, on an infrequent basis, or as repeat sales? A retail store, bakery, or restaurant will be counting on repeat customers returning on a regular basis, whereas a consultant helping a client implement a new order processing system may not get much repeat business.

How long will the product or service last? Do you intend to upgrade or supersede the product or service at some point in the future?

TRAP

Do not get sidetracked explaining the life cycle of your products or services. This will be dealt with later in this section.

Define the Line of Products or Services

What do you plan to sell, how are they used, and what are the main product or service characteristics? (Note: Do not describe customer preferences, a topic that is discussed later in this chapter.)

- *Products/services mix:* What is the collection of the various products or services offered by your business?

- *Breadth:* Explain the number of products or services you provide, and describe all services including the different features offered within a single service.
- *Depth:* Describe the assortment of services offered. How many possible variations are there within a particular service? Remember, 80 percent of your revenues will come from 20 percent of your services. The better able you are to identify that 20 percent, the greater your chance of success will be.

Write a paragraph or two about the services or products you plan to sell. Then create a table that illustrates the mix, depth, and breadth of your offerings. See Table 5.1 for a sample.

TRAP

Do not make the mistake of thinking that you know what your customers want. Take the time to talk to them. Ask open-ended, probing questions that they cannot answer with a simple yes or no. Keep asking and probing until you uncover an unmet need—something that you can do better than your competition.

Be cautious and try not to be everything to everyone. There is a fine line between diversity and distraction. If your product or service selection is too wide and varied, it will be difficult to find a strong marketing position and create a winning marketing strategy. Less is more. Focus on the 20 percent of your services or products that create 80 percent of your revenue.

To analyze your product or service offering, analyze how much profit or sales will come from which each line. Make a spreadsheet that shows how each product or service contributes to your overall sales and profits. Then review your product line and eliminate those low-margin and high-maintenance items that are not in alignment with your positioning strategy. Invest in services or products that are more complementary and in alignment with your positioning strategy.

Table 5.1 Sample Product Mix Table

Revenue		Gross Profit (GP)	
Auto parts	$45,000	Auto parts	$11,250
Accessories	$15,000	Accessories	$6,750
Oil, fluids	$20,000	Oil, fluids	$3,000
Total Revenue	$80,000	Total GP	$21,000

Service and Product Positioning

"Positioning is identifying what you can deliver better than anyone else that meets an unmet need in the marketplace," says Jennifer Rice of Mantra Brand Consulting. *Positioning* is making a statement about what your business is going to stand for.

Positioning strategies come in all shapes and sizes. A strategy could be as simple as increasing the quality of your customer service or adding a complementary product or service; and it could also mean taking up a cause and becoming its champion.

For example, near where I live there is a little company called the Running Room that has grown nationally. It sponsors fun runs and marathons, conducts running classes, and sells running shoes and gear. It has made a name for itself. When I think of the Running Room, I think "fitness," because whenever there is a running event, the company is there supporting the community with infrastructure (timing devices, runner registration, etc.).

Writing about your positioning strategy will require that you formulate your position and align three areas: product selection, marketing strategy, and selling strategy. (See Fig. 5.1.)

Positioning your business depends upon balancing all three of these areas. As you read through this book, you will learn more about these areas. For now, just write about how your product or service selection will meet an unmet need in the marketplace.

Start-Up and Expansion Costs

In a service business the start-up costs can be minimal. However, as the business grows, requirements change. New staff members are hired, and new facilities, equipment, and tools are required.

Figure 5.1 Positioning Strategy

TIP

If you have a service business, document your start-up costs for now. What do you need to purchase? Will you maintain an office? If so, what are the costs to set it up or renovate, buy fixtures and furniture, move, and pay monthly maintenance?

For every other kind of business, your start-up costs could be substantial, especially if you are setting up a repair shop, manufacturing facility, or retail location.

Make a complete list of everything you will need to purchase or invest in to start your business and open the doors. Make sure to include insurance premiums and other prepaid expenses.

Document Revenue, Costs, and Profits

In a spreadsheet, document the revenues, costs, and profits of each individual item. You will use this information to help you build your income and expense projections when it comes time to assemble your pro forma financial statements.

TIP

If you are new to spreadsheets or just want to save yourself some time, visit my Web site, http://www.sbishere.com/, where you can download spreadsheet templates to help get you started.

Service

Record revenue, costs, and profits on your services and products by category or item if necessary. Identify the time required to prepare, manage, and create the service yourself.

TIP

Multiply your time by what you would have to pay to have the service performed by someone with your level of experience, education, and reputation. Remember to add the cost of materials used directly in the project (if any).

Products

Create a spreadsheet of all the products you plan to sell including revenues, costs, and profits.

Growth, Expansion, and Redesign

Your business will grow and change over time. It is important to show the reader of your plan the growth path (evolution, growth milestones, stages) of how you expect to grow over the next three to five years.

TIP

In service businesses, the time available and reputation of the service provider can limit the initial scope and capacity of the business. Then, as your revenue grows, you can afford to hire new staff. Record the path or evolution you anticipate and include the milestones, costs, and benefits of expansion.

Identify products or services that can be added or expanded to grow revenues. Timing is an issue. Be realistic about the time it will take to develop and evolve the business and systems. Timing issues are also reflected in your financial projections and affect the marketing strategy. Remember to record all associated costs in the income and expense budgets.

Change in Costs and Profits

A lot of the writing of a business plan entails what I call "blue-sky" scenarios. In most planning we always look for positive results. Rarely are the results all positive in the real world because things happen that are out of your control.

Therefore, to make your plan more practical and realistic, you need to anticipate and plan for changes in costs and how those will affect your profits. For example, in the last decade I have seen energy costs increase substantially. Substantial increases in fuel costs affect every business from airlines to trucking companies to retailers. Manufacturers can be especially hard-hit because they often consume large amounts of electricity or natural gas.

Regardless of the type of business you have, you will feel the pressure of increased costs, and in some cases (like trucking companies) your entire profit margin could be consumed by increases in energy costs. How will you deal with this issue? Will customers pay a fuel surcharge, or are you locked into a long-term, fixed-price contract? If so, that needs to be identified as a risk and worked into a contingency plan (see Chapter 11).

In sectors like the insulation or HVAC industry, higher energy costs simply increase the demand for energy-efficient solutions and insulation products as consumers and businesses scramble to rein in their energy expenses. Even in those businesses, trying to meet the demand can be a formidable problem while the business owner tries to find enough workers to deliver or install the product.

What changes in your costs and profits do you anticipate? What are the factors that will influence costs and profits? Will you be able to achieve any economies of scale or an increase in market share? Following the start-up phase, what are the ways you will reduce costs, improve productivity or handle simultaneous projects?

What about business momentum? As the company's reputation grows with an aggressive marketing, sales, and promotional campaign, the business should be able to attract more customers. If the business has little or no competition, the business may attract competition thereby reducing market share in the second and third years. How will inflation or price increases in staff or raw materials affect your prices?

Service Life Cycle

Every product or service has a natural life cycle. Is your service a fad, trend, or choice? Is your product or service a new and emerging trend, or is it relatively mature? Some trends have been around for years and may become obsolete or simply lose market share over time. Write a brief overview of the history of your products or services.

TIP

Document the changes you have witnessed and what you anticipate might happen over the next few years.

Every product or service goes through a series of phases: introduction, growth, maturity, and decline. The length of time for each phase varies. Fads go through all phases in less than two years. Following are approximate time lines:

1. *Fad:* less than 2 years.
2. *Trend:* 2 to 10 years.
3. *Lifestyle/choice:* 10 years plus. (Products or services in this category become absorbed into the culture or community.)

Other products may be pushed ahead by technology and innovation. Take the changes in the online music industry and the growth of the MP3 player (iPod, for example). The technology of digital rights management (software that prevents unauthorized duplication of music files) when combined with the popularity of personal music players has fundamentally changed the music industry.

Another example is podcasting. In mid 2005 Apple modified its popular iTunes music player (over 200 million installations to date) to include the automatic downloading of podcasts. In one strategic move Apple accelerated the growth of the recording equipment industry. There is now a whole new market segment seeking quality, low-cost recording equipment to do a podcast.

Write a paragraph or two on how you see technology affecting the life cycle of your product or service.

Customer Profile

Knowing exactly what your market really wants as a result of doing business with you is so fundamentally important that when you get this wrong, the problems created trickle down to every other area of your business.

TRAP

 Include information in your business plan about customer needs should not be an exercise of your sitting down and making a list of needs and wants based upon what you think. You need to get away from the computer and talk to the customer.

Be prepared with a set of open-ended questions that make customers reveal what they think about your products or services and what goes into their making a decision to buy. Record their answers on a notepad, and gather enough of a sample so that you feel you have learned something. You will use this information throughout your business plan.

Customer Analysis

After gathering a fair sampling of answers to your questions, it is time to sort customers' answers into identifiable segments. Combine your own market sense with the answers from your survey. Sort your information into geographic, demographic, socioeconomic, and psychographic segments. Include behavior, consumption, and consumer perceptions or predispositions.

By taking the time to identify each target market group and its distinguishing geographic, demographic, psychographic, and behavior variables and characteristics, you are segmenting your market.

Look for common characteristics and trends across all segments. If there are no common trends or characteristics, you need to narrow your business focus to a smaller, more identifiable group or you need to rewrite your survey questions and start over.

In a business-to-business scenario you might have many customers who have input into the decision-making process. Each of them needs to be identified, categorized, and understood. Some will have input into the decision but not make the actual purchasing decision. In larger companies that decision is made by a purchasing agent in a department dedicated to purchasing everything the business needs.

Imagine two retail businesses. One is located in a downtown area, while the other is located in suburban area. Even if they are selling the same products, the way they advertise, promote, and position the business could be substantially different because of differences in geographic, demographic, psychographic, behavior variables as well as other characteristics.

Determining your customer profile will require that you prepare a complete market segment analysis to identify each group. Then choose the most desirable groups or those with the greatest potential. Are you selling to the end user or is there an intermediary? If there is an intermediary, then you will need to do two profiles: one for the end user and one for the intermediary.

TIP

Right now simply record the broad market segments. Later on in the market analysis, you will work on a more detailed analysis to create the customer profiles.

Customer Preferences

This is a good time to review the definition of *marketing*. It is the process by which information about a product or service designed to meet a need—real or otherwise—is communicated to those who have the need. The process can take place on the spur of the moment or be planned. However, the goal is always the same. To get people to consider the merits of whatever is being sold.

The strategy is to position your business at the same level as the majority of the buyers. When done well, they will want to investigate further or acquire your item or service. Try to look at yourself as being employed by your customers. If they are your boss, you will let them tell you what they want to buy, how they want it, and how much they are willing to pay as well as where and when they want it. Plus you will also want to learn more about their expectations.

It is critical that you figure out where you want to be positioned in the marketplace. You can go just as broke positioning your product or service above the market as below the market. Remember, look for the biggest bulge of buyers for your specific product or service and then package your product or service to meet the needs of those buyers head-on.

Create a Customer Needs and Preferences Profile

A focused and accurate customer profile will help you zero in on your target market, build marketing momentum, and eliminate lost opportunities. The purpose is to associate your product or service with positive or desired values, which have little or nothing to do with the product itself that are highly sought after by your target market. Brand image transcends facts.

To accomplish this, you need to be able to put yourself in your customers' shoes. Do your best remove your own biases, because customers today have an incredible ability to detect insincerity, and they are looking to do business with companies that understand their needs, wants, emotions and perceptions (NWEP). Understanding your customers' NWEP removes personal bias and helps form a strong foundation for other parts of your business plan.

TIP

Direct all your company resources toward your best prospects by communicating in such a way that all your communication vehicles (brochures, Web site, logo, ads, etc.) clearly mirror your targeted audiences' needs and desires.

With an NWEP profile of your ideal customer, you will be able to create brochures, a Web site, and a business model that is in alignment with the customers' point of view. This valuable information can then be used to speed and simplify the design and development of your positioning strategy. Plus, it reduces the need to reengineer your business model because your marketing and sales plan did not achieve its goals and objectives.

Customer Needs

Your customers' needs are the most urgent or essential feelings they have. First, recognize that something has happened that has created or prompted a new awareness of a specific need in the customer. Once customers or prospects identify the need, they move quickly to satisfy themselves. It will usually be something the customer does not have or a need that is not currently being met. Identify those unmet needs.

TIP

Describe why customers need your product or service. What is the unmet need that the product satisfies?

At this point the prospect is seeking information to meet a specific need. When the need is left unsolved, it transforms into a problem; an unsolved problem creates tension and, by its nature, seeks resolution. People buy things to resolve the pain or pleasure they perceive.

Wants

The difference between a need and a want is that, when someone wants something, it takes the form of a desire or wish and fills some sort of deficiency.

What problem(s) does your product or service solve? No problem = No Desire = No sale. Continue to work on this until you uncover a specific problem that your product or service resolves.

TIP

Be sure to include in your plan what desire your service fulfills for your customers or clients.

Emotions

Every major purchase is made based on emotions and then justified with logic. What emotions do you observe in your customer during the decision-making process? Identify them and evaluate how emotions help or hinder the customer in evaluating the alternatives. Remember, the larger the purchase, the greater amount of the emotion that enters into the picture, which is quickly followed by logic to justify the purchase.

TIP

Identify the emotional factors in customers' behavior when they are purchasing your product/service.

Perceptions

What are the negative and positive perceptions that customers have about you, your company, and its services? How do these perceptions affect the purchasing and decision-making process?

When your customer has specific perceptions about your business or industry, you need to identify which are positive and work in your favor and which are negative. By isolating the negative perceptions, you free the customer to seriously consider the merits of your product. If you fail to deal with negative perceptions, you end up preparing the customer for a competitor who was able to transform those concerns into an opportunity.

TIP

Describe the different attributes of each product or service that adds value for each target market. To some degree the demographics, psychographics, and geographics of your primary, secondary, and tertiary segments will dictate preferences for a specific product or service.

In the markets you have chosen, what do customers want? For example, they might want:

- Less stress.
- To save money.
- To experience a smooth transition on move-in day.
- More safety.
- Simplicity.

Some of the information on customer preferences will come from the industry analysis. Some of it must come from speaking directly with your potential customers.

Proprietary Rights

Describe any legal means you might have to take to protect your ideas, products or services from being used by your competitors. Describe any special skills or abilities you have that give you a competitive advantage. Do you have special skills or knowledge that is not easily obtainable by the competition?

TIP

Record any proprietary rights, information, or patents that make you competitive.

Sample Services Section

Following is the services section of a business plan. The complete business plan can be found in Appendix A.

Services

JOE'S has a fleet of seven units and relationships with hundreds of carriers throughout North America. JOE'S provides clients with excellent equipment coverage. The transportation services business evolves and changes to suit client needs. The sales mix is best defined through understanding the types of commodities and destinations JOE'S expects to serve. The services mix is:

- 50 percent of our loads are related to industrial construction.
- 25 percent are lumber or related products.
- 25 percent are miscellaneous.
- 65 percent of our loads are transborder.
- 35 percent are to Western Canada (in November a series of large industrial construction contracts will begin).
- The majority of our loads are requested by Canadian companies, with freight to move either to the United States or from the United States to Canada.

Services

- Dimensional and overweight shipments.
- Permit and escort setup.
- Job site pickup and delivery.
- Centralized dispatch.
- Expedited (hotshot) service.
- $250,000 cargo insurance.

Equipment   All equipment is air ride:

- *Flatbeds and stepdeck trailers:* 48 ft and 53 ft. Aluminum and steel combo and all steel trailers.
- *Double-drop trailers:* similar to flatbeds except they have a drop deck closer to the ground. Drop decks are used for oversized, overweight, wide, and heavy equipment loads. 48 ft and 53 ft with well dimensions from 25 ft to 45 ft, and these can go to a 10-axle combo set up to 110,000 lb.

Expansion Costs   The cost to add a new lease operator is $4,500 to cover unit start-up costs and the first two months of unit operating expenses. These include:

(Continued)

(*Continued*)

- Two months of U.S. fuel (pay cash via fuel cards).
- $250 for decals.
- $100 for drug and alcohol testing.
- $800 for cash advances (petty cash for drivers for toll roads and incidental expenses).

The lease operator expansion costs are then recovered through a 5 percent holdback on each lease operator's gross monthly revenue.

Average monthly revenue per unit is $16,000 per month or approximately 10,000 miles. When our fleet averageper unit is consistently at or about $20,000 per month, purchase of a new unit or the addition of a lease operator should be considered in order meet increased customer demand, maintain service levels, and prevent driver burnout or lost production.

Service Costs   Revenue and costs are calculated by the mile. Our numbers are:

- Breakeven is $1.04 Canadian (CDN) per mile
- Selling price minimum is $1.65 CDN per mile and up. *Note:* some jobs in western Canada are sold at $2–$2.50 CDN per mile. Canadian freight generally runs at a 20 percent higher margin than transborder trips (United States–Canada) and is easier to dispatch and manage because it is easier to get return trips.

Revenue per Running Mile Experience   The last three months average revenue per running mile (including empty and loaded miles) is:

- June 2000 average: $1.46 per mile.
- July 2000 average: $1.52 per mile
- August 2000 average: $1.72 per mile

Service/Customer Life Cycle   Typically a good client will have a life cycle of 12 months, where a strong relationship and high degree of trust exists. It is typical for clients to conduct a thorough review and competitive tender every 12 months to verify that they are getting a fair price.

Expansion and Redesign   After three years it is expected that continued growth will be dependent upon building a fleet of company-owned vehicles to service the western Canadian market. Also, the integration of satellite, computer, and telephone technology will make the communications and management of the fleet far more effective and efficient.

Changes in Costs and Profit   Other than fuel costs, the company does not anticipate any major changes in costs. Today's tractors are much more fuel-efficient and durable than they used to be. The company will maintain tight sales tracking systems and cost controls on a unit-by unit-basis. Profits are also expected to remain stable. As fuel costs rise, the company will add a fuel surcharge to existing rates.

Customer Profile   The majority of JOE'S customers are mainly industrial or manufacturing companies, such as:

- Industrial construction.
- Fabrication.
- Lumber companies.
- Produce (potatoes, onions, or watermelons).
- Manufacturing.
- Oil fields.

6

Business Description

In describing your business, imagine that you are writing for a reader who knows nothing about it. Describe its personality and purpose, and document the direction of the business, its history, and what it does. The reader should be able to understand how you plan to operate your business, which staff will help you do it, and how your business is unique. The business description should answer the following questions:

- Why will your goods or services appeal to customers?
- What are the primary differences between your company and your competitors?
- What are the main factors that lead customers to choose your business over another?
- Who are your competitors?
- What role will technology play in helping you achieve your business goals?
- What events contributed to the current situation?
- Will the business be profitable?
- What is the financial condition of the business?
- How is the business operated now, or how will the business be operated in the future?
- Who will lead and manage the day-to-day affairs?
- What is your positioning statement (a list of satisfied needs)? Or, if you asked your customer(s) to define your company using ideas, concepts, or words, what would they feel describes the company? Another way of defining your positioning statement is to answer the following questions:

What is the underlying reason a customer would do business with your company? How does it define the scope of your business and identify with the needs of the market? What is the driving need that will be satisfied when customers do business with you?

What will you achieve by answering these questions? The answers will provide you with a point of reference and the basic information you need to begin to write a description of your business. It will also provide readers the answers they need to get a good overview of the business.

Investors, bankers, and business professionals are busy and may not be able to read your entire plan, but, by reading the business description, they will be able to get a good understanding of the business background, goals, and how you plan to go about operating the firm.

If you are unable to describe your business on paper, how can you hope to be able to express it to other important people, such as your bankers, customers, suppliers, and staff? The business description is a vital part of the business plan.

When you're answering the questions posed throughout this book, use clear, convincing statements to make your point. This will be the best evidence that, as an entrepreneur, you have a good sense of what it will take to succeed.

TRAP

If you give short shrift to the business description, you will end up telegraphing that you do not understand the business. This will create doubt in the reader's mind—the last thing you want. Pay attention to the tone of your writing. While it is important to speak with conviction, beware of overstating, overpromising, and hyping your goals. Be real—include a healthy dose of reality in what you say and how you say it.

Define Your Vision

A clear, compelling, and exciting vision can make a substantial difference in helping you achieve your objectives. It should be used to express what is important to you, and it can become the driving force behind your business.

Here is a list of questions to help you guide you in writing your vision statement:

- As the owner of this business, what do you want to achieve?
- How large or small do you want this business to be?

- Do you want to include family in your business?
- Do you desire to provide employment, or, perhaps, you feel strongly about not wanting to manage people?
- Is there some cause or charity that you want the business to address?
- How will the quality, quantity, and/or service meet or exceed customer satisfaction levels?
- How would you describe your primary competitive advantage?
- How do you see the business making a difference in the lives of your customers?

Your vision statement should express how you see the business developing, growing, and what the business will become over the next three to five years. Here are a few examples:

Oilfield manufacturer: "To be recognized as the premier manufacturer of oilfield blowout preventers and valves."

Retiring business owner: "To pay off the mortgage on the plant in three years and to train two managers to run the business in my absence."

Consulting business: "To provide consulting services to the dental community and generate adequate profits to hire and train a junior consultant."

Law firm: "To establish a recognized brand as the premier attorney for retiring business owners in Houston."

Your vision should be short. Although you might initially take as much space as you need to write it, you will ultimately need to edit it down to no more than one or two sentences and definitely no more than one paragraph.

If you are having problems writing the business description, it might be a good idea to write it as your second to last part. Some people find it easier to compose this part after they have most of the business plan complete. Personally, I find the business plan easier to write if I have a clear and compelling vision. However, I often edit it later because of what I learned while working on the rest of the plan.

TRAP

Entrepreneurs often struggle with creating a vision and mission statement. The easy way to remember the difference between them is that a vision statement tells the reader where you want to end up, whereas a mission statement reveals how you plan to get there.

Draft a Mission Statement

Your mission statement explains how you are going to fulfill your vision. While you keep your vision statement private, you will share your mission statement with customers and employees. Your mission statement should answer the following questions:

- Who is the customer?
- What business are you in?
- What do you sell (product/service)?
- What is your plan for growth?
- What is your primary competitive advantage?

To be of practical value, a mission statement must be brief enough to instill confidence and be remembered. Therefore, it should be 25 words or less. For example:

Oilfield manufacturer: "To provide the zero-defect valves and blowout preventers using leading edge ISO Quality Management systems (TC67) and processes for offshore drilling platforms."

TIP

Eventually, you will shorten your mission statement to three to five words, and then you can use that phrase as a promotional tag line to position and promote your business.

Ethics Statement

The ethics statement expresses the basic values that you as the business owner have identified as essential to building the business. These values can become the operational framework for making decisions, dealing with growth, and serving customers. This statement should attempt to capture something of importance for everyone connected with the business.

Start by answering the following questions to reveal your values:

- Are your basic values ethical and fair?
- Do they represent how you would want to be treated?
- Are these values you believe in?
- Have you adopted any that you should discard?

Compile a list of values and then create a short paragraph or two that adequately expresses your business ethics. Here is an example:

"Our customers best interests always come first. We avoid conflict with our clients by conducting a through needs analysis before beginning client work."

Explain Your Business Goals

Identify the goals and objectives of the business by explaining, as specifically as possible, what you want to achieve. Most goals can be expressed as numbers, for example, sales, percentage of income, or expected return on investments. However, other legitimate goals can be:

- Provide better quality service.
- Ensure fast delivery.
- Reduce costs.

Your goals can be general, but they should be measurable. Start with your personal goals. Then list your business goals. Examine both to be sure that they are in alignment. Compare them to your vision and mission statements. Are they in alignment and complementary? If not, rework them and remove the conflicts.

Create two sets of goals—short term and long term. Short-term goals can range from 6 to 12 months while long-term goals can range from 2 to 5 years. Create a list of each kind of goal, beginning with a brief description of action items.

If your business is a start-up, you will want to put extra effort into your short-term goals. Often a new business concept must go through a period of field testing or research and development before it can accurately predict the outcome for longer time frames. Table 6.1 offers an example of these short-terms goals.

Some other goals worthy of including in your business plan are:

- Explaining the current status of operations.
- Explaining the management structure.
- Explaining how the business will be organized.
- Identifying key personnel (include yourself).

If you plan to hire additional staff at certain points, identify the time frame, rationalization, and expected costs.

Table 6.1   Sample Short-Term Goals

Income	Expenses	
0	$10,000	Finish business plan, test market
0	$10,000	Revise business plan, review marketing results, hire management or staff
$50,000	$25,000	Hire and train staff, launch major marketing promotional campaign

TIP

Create a spreadsheet to help you organize your business goals.

TRAP

This is not the time to set detailed financial goals. Anticipated expenses and income are explained in other parts of the business plan.

Operations

The way a business operates is how it converts resources (labor, raw materials, good location, market timing, etc.) into value-added outputs. This is known as *business operations*.

The course the business takes and how it gets things done should also be summarized in the business description.

However, do not write a novel or include every one of your 456 steps in manufacturing your product. Break it down into big pieces. For example, if you are manufacturing a product, you should describe the product (sketch, drawing, or photograph) and list the production work flow and how your manufacturing process provides you with a competitive advantage, if this is the case.

TRAP

Don't be put off by terms, words, or concepts you do not understand. Check the business dictionary in Appendix B. If you do not find what you are looking for, send me an e-mail (see Appendix G).

As a service provider your task is slightly different. Focus on the "activities" that produce the service, the people who provide it, and how your management provides your company with an edge, if any. Some questions to ask yourself include:

- What are the keys to success in your production or service delivery process?

- Are there any specific differences in the way you manage your operations that provide you with a competitive advantage?

- How do you plan to exploit technology to improve your product or service delivery?

- What are the gross profit margins (revenue minus cost of sales)?

- What is the major product line your merchandise fits into? How is that important?

- As a service business what are the steps involved in delivering your service?

- What are your purchasing procedures? How do your procedures provide an advantage to the business?

- How do you plan to manage inventory? How will this reduce your operating costs, if at all?

- In manufacturing your product, what contribution does quality control play in providing your firm with a competitive advantage?

- Do you have an ISO certified quality management system? When was the last time your management system was audited and what were the results?

- What are your planned hours of operation?

- Who are the key employees, and what abilities do they have that make them vital to the success of the business? You might decide to devote a separate section to employees, especially if you think they are key to your success.

- What type of employees do you plan to have and how many?

- What will be the management or organizational structure (attach a table showing who is responsible for what)?

TIP

Do not forget to include yourself when you think about key employees, particularly if you are starting a new business. No need to include your résumé here, simply include it as an appendix in your business plan.

When explaining your own function in the business, you should present your educational background and prior business experience in a way that establishes confidence in your ability to succeed. While you probably will not include a copy of your résumé, much of the information that appears on your résumé will appear in the plan. Do not be afraid to present yourself in the most favorable light that you can honestly and objectively portray.

Type of Facilities

Name the facilities (e.g., retail establishment, manufacturing plant, etc.) you will need to run your business. For example, if you are a manufacturer and you are seeking financing for a building, you will want to devote a separate section to this subject. Include images, architectural renderings, and floor plans along with a budget.

TIP

If part of your purchase includes renovations (i.e., a retail location) make it easy for the reader to visualize the renovations by including drawings, photos, or artist renderings including common areas.

Remember, you are communicating with the reader what is important for your business in terms of the facility. Take nothing for granted and explain everything—as succinctly as possible.

Legal Structure

At this point in your business plan, document the date of incorporation or when you first began operations. This should also include information about the structure of your business (proprietorship, partnership, or corporation). Identify any anticipated changes, for example if you are considering initiating a partnership or taking on new shareholders.

TIP

If you are buying a business, it will be especially important at this point to trace the history of the business and point out any specific or outstanding legal issues.

Some questions to consider when writing this section are:

- Will you incorporate or run as a proprietorship or partnership?
- If you are taking on investors, what is the share structure?
- How much equity are you willing to give up to get the financing?

If your business is incorporated, list the date of incorporation and the business's location, directors, and officers.

Be sure to keep this portion of the business description brief and businesslike.

TRAP

Don't fall into the trap of trying to include everything listed in this chapter or book for that matter. Some of the information should be kept confidential depending on who is reading the business plan. For example, the Ethics statement is best kept for internal use (partners, key employees, staff, etc.).

Sample Business Description

Following is the business description section of the business plan. The complete business plan can be found in Appendix A.

Business Description

JOE'S is a full-service, 24-hours-a-day, seven-days-a-week, open-deck trucking company. It provides FTL and LTL transportation services to industrial companies across North America.

Vision   Our company vision is to be a steady moneymaker with an annual net profit of 5 percent. We do not want to be the largest—just consistently profitable.

Mission Statement   Joe's Trucking Systems, Inc., is a reliable and trusted business partner that works with customers to achieve on-time delivery, throughout North America.

Ethics Statement   Joe's Trucking Systems, Inc., is dedicated to open, honest communications with all customers, suppliers, and staff members. Whenever necessary, we take the time to educate and explain to our customers the reasons behind our systems, processes, and decisions.

Goals—First 30 Days

- To make a smooth transition from To and Fro Transport to JOE'S.
- To confirm that all major customers will continue doing business with JOE'S.

(Continued)

(*Continued*)

Goal—First 60 to 90 Days

- To increase our western Canadian sales volume and reduce the use of brokers for reload opportunities.

Goals—First Year

- To increase revenue through the addition of two new lease operators.
- To focus on the development of sales, dispatch, and administrative systems in order to increase efficiency. We will accomplish this through the use of computer software and technology to improve productivity in sales/dispatch and administration (accounting, fuel tax tracking, etc.).

Legal JOE'S is an operating and marketing company and is owned 51 percent by Sue Switch and 49 percent by Joe Sample.

Sue & Joe Transport is the holding company that owns and leases equipment (four trucks, four trailers, and pilot car) to JOE'S. The majority shareholder is Joe Sample. The benefits of this strategy include reducing potential legal liability in the United States and lowering insurance costs. It will also provide additional tax planning options to the owners.

7
Marketing and Sales Strategy

To build a really effective market strategy, you first need to set your personal agenda aside and let your customers teach you what, when, where, and how they want to do business with your firm. Anyone can jump in and spend a bunch of money on marketing, but that does not translate into a marketing strategy. Unless you do your research and create a plan, all you may end up doing is spending money on something that totally fails to generate any leads or new business for you.

The key to putting together a great marketing strategy is to start thinking like a customer. Ask questions, get involved, and find out why people choose your business instead of the competition.

The Five-Step Marketing Strategy

Before we proceed, let me share with you my definition of *marketing:* the process by which information about a product or service designed to meet a need—real or otherwise—is communicated to those who have the need. The goal of marketing is always to get people to seriously consider the merits of your products or services.

There are five steps to creating a marketing strategy for your business plan:

1. Identify all target markets.
2. Qualify the best target markets.

3. Identify tools, strategies, and methods.

4. Test market strategy and tools.

5. Execute marketing strategy.

Step 1: Identify All Target Markets

First define who your ideal customer or target market is. It makes sense to direct your time and energy toward those customers who are most important to you and to really get to know them and understand their buying patterns, interests, tastes, attitudes, and hot buttons.

Once you have your ideal customer in mind, position your business at the same level as the majority of buyers (majority of revenue) you are targeting. It is critical to figure out where you are positioned and where you would like to be positioned in the marketplace.

TRAP

You can go just as broke positioning your product or service above the market as below! Target the largest and most affluent buyers for your product or service. Always go after people with money on your goods or services versus having to build market recognition and create the budget. It can be done, but is more expensive and time consuming.

To position your product or services to meet your customers' needs, you must understand and identify the key characteristics of your prospects. Make a list of the following data, traits, and characteristics of your potential customers:

- *Demographics:* location, age, sex, occupation.
- *Lifestyle:* interests, attitudes.
- *Buying cycles:* identify any cyclical trends.
- *Psychographics:* what is the intrinsic motivation that is driving your customer?

Your target market is made up of:

1. *Primary target market:* These are your best and most profitable customers. They have a strong interest in your product or service and are highly motivated.

2. *Secondary target market:* Determine what other markets show good potential.

3. *Tertiary markets:* Determine other additional markets that exist for your products or services. They could be new or emerging users or people who are using a totally different product or service.

TIP

Make a list of the customer characteristics you identified. Identify as many unique characteristics as you can think of. Work hard at it. Ask your friends and relatives for ideas. Document and group the characteristics of the buyers by primary, secondary, and tertiary market. Your ideal customer is always your primary market.

Step 2: Qualify the Best Target Markets

In the first step, you defined your ideal customer or target market. The purpose of the second step is to further qualify and determine which customer profile offers you the best odds of success.

TIP

To have any chance at targeting your best customers, you must know them well. You must understand their needs, wants, emotions, and perceptions. Do not give short shrift to this part of your business plan.

You want to make sure that your products or services and business systems are in alignment with the customers' point of view. To do that successfully, you need to create a customer needs and preferences profile, which is covered in Chapter 5. Remember to address your customers' needs, wants, emotions, and perceptions (NWEP) in your marketing plan, as these are the criteria your customers use to make a purchasing decision. By understanding these criteria better, you will be able to make sure your business, marketing, and advertising to be in alignment with your customers.

Sales and marketing are not only a battle between companies, products, and services, but they are a battle between perceptions. There is no real right or wrong product or service, but customers have different perceptions about the value of certain products. You need to uncover your customers' perceptions about your product versus a competitor's product. The only reliable way of uncovering these perceptions is through the consistent application of *probing questions* which cause the prospects to explain and reveal what they really think.

TRAP

Your customers do not care about you. They care about themselves and their needs. The single biggest reason most advertising and marketing plans fail is because the message is out of alignment with the customers' perspective. Every advertisement, brochure, and marketing tool must reflect your customers' needs, wants, emotions, and perceptions; otherwise you are wasting your money.

Interview as many potential or real customers as possible and explain to them that you are trying to improve your business and how you operate. Ask them to help you by answering a series of questions.

Questions to Determine Customer Needs   The purpose of using these questions is to discover how customers first became aware of their need for your product or service, and to understand what it was that caused them to become aware of their need. You can use this information to capture their imagination and get their attention by reflecting this need in your marketing and sales strategy.

1. If you had the opportunity to create the ideal _____ (company, salesperson, product, etc.) what would be the characteristics that you feel would be absolutely essential for you to feel comfortable doing business?

2. What do you look for in a _____ company? What do you see as valuable in _____(product/service)?

3. What problem (need, want) do you see that _____ (product/service) is actually filling? Why is that important to you? How does that make you feel?

4. What are your perceptions about the _____ (industry)?

5. Who have you dealt with before? What do you like about their product, service, people, etc? What could be improved?

6. What is your perception of what you are really buying when you buy _____ (your product service)?

7. How specifically does _____ (what the customers say they are really buying) meet your needs?

8. How do you know that _____ (what they are really buying) is actually meeting your needs?

TIP

Feel free to modify the questions to fit your situation, but be sure that they remain open-ended questions. Then create a worksheet to record their answers to these questions.

To gauge whether you are getting the information you need, ask yourself these questions: Have I uncovered what the prospects think their most urgent needs are? What is this prospect feeling? As it relates to what I am selling, have I uncovered a need I can fulfill?

Questions to Determine Customer Wants Any major purchase is made with emotion and justified with logic. Uncover what the prospect wants in your product or service by asking the following questions:

- Where do you feel is the greatest problem or opportunity is for a business like mine to really serve you well?
- What do you use or buy now? How does that solve your problem or meet your needs?
- What is great about that?
- What could be improved?

The goal of these questions is to identify and understand the role of emotion in the purchasing process. Ask yourself these questions:

- Have I uncovered a specific, legitimate problem that our product or service can solve?
- Do I understand what the prospect wants? What he or she desires?
- Is there a deficiency that our products or services can help the prospect overcome? Can I personally help the prospect overcome the deficiency?
- Have I uncovered something specific that the prospect is dissatisfied with concerning the current supplier, situation, or solution?

Questions to Uncover Customer Emotions The questions at this stage are designed to get at the customer's *emotions*. Watch for any strong outward expression about a specific topic:

1. As it relates to _____(need from previous questions), how does that affect you, your staff, your company, and so on?
2. Of the all the things we talked about, what is the most dominant (or recurring) problem in operating your _____? What are you doing about it? (If nothing is being done about it, ask why.)
3. If this problem were not resolved, what would the implications be? How does that affect you?
4. What would the cost be (money, time, energy, reputation, dissatisfaction)? How would you feel? What would _____ (person) think?

TRAP

These probing questions will make your prospects think and explain their answers. You might feel uncomfortable asking these questions and notice the same with your prospects. Relax. The key in this step is to have staying power and let them form their answers.

If this were a real-world scenario, the customer would be trying to decide whether or not to test your product or service. Look for the things that create *desire* and help him or her evaluate the product or service. Ask yourself these questions:

- What are the implications of the problems I uncovered in the answers to these questions?

- Have I uncovered the most dominant and recurring issue as it relates to my products or services and the customers needs and wants?

- Have I observed specific emotions related to any specific types of questions I've been asking?

- Does this prospect understand the true cost of resolving the problem?

- Is he or she more or less motivated to buy now?

Questions to Determine Customer Perceptions At this stage we want to find out the prospects' perceptions and rules for buying. It's also time to discuss how they've tried to solve their problem before, so that you can alter your approach to address their concerns. Here are some questions to ask:

1. Thinking of _____ (problem), what type of solutions have you explored in the past? What worked and what didn't work?

2. What other solutions are you investigating?

3. We agreed that _____ (problem) comes up because of _____. Left unsolved, the cost would mean _____. What do you feel would have to change, or what do you feel the ideal solution would be?

4. If we had a solution that solved _____ (problem) is that something you would be interested in implementing?

5. What other solutions would you consider?

The purpose of this step is to uncover the buyers' perceptions and rules about how, if, when, and why they would buy your product or service. The best indicator of how buyers make a decision is how they have made purchasing decisions in the past. Probe and ask them what the deciding factors were in making a similar purchasing decision before.

Answer the following questions to make sure that you have the information you need.

- Do you have a clear picture of the prospect's perceptions of the solution(s)?
- Who is your competition?
- Do you have a clear picture of how the prospects make a decision (i.e., what are their rules, ideas of how they would solve the problem, reasons for making a decision to go with the previous supplier or solution, etc.)?

TIP

Review all the answers to your NWEP questions and create a description of your ideal customers' needs, wants, emotions, and perceptions. Write a profile of your ideal customer. When you compare the ideal customer profile to the products or services you plan to sell, determine where there could be a mismatch or where there is a direct match. What do your customers want from the products and services you provide? Determine what is missing. Then make the appropriate adjustments.

Questions to Determine What Product Attributes Customers Want
Identify the primary drivers causing your customers to investigate purchasing your goods and services. To some degree the demographics, psychographics, and geographics of your primary, secondary, and tertiary segments will dictate preferences for a specific product or service. Some information on preferences will come from the industry and market analysis. Some of it will also come from speaking directly with your potential customers. Questions to ask yourself are:

- What is the intrinsic motivation that is driving your customers to buy your product or service? What do they want to learn?
- When customers think of buying your product or service, what thoughts come to their mind?
- What goal do they want to achieve? What do they want to experience more of or less of as a result of doing business with you?

In your business plan, be sure to describe the different attributes of each service or product you offer and how each attribute adds value for each segment of your target market.

Step 3: Identify Marketing Tools, Strategies, and Methods

Now it is time to focus on which strategies to use to reach your target market. I suggest that you build and use as many tools or strategies as you can afford. Choose the tools that best fit your style and business model. For example, if you intend to use salespeople to sell a broad line of products, a printed catalog and a real-time online Web site/catalog would be an essential tool. In fact, if your competitors do not have a real-time database where customers can check inventory and place orders, this might be a significant advantage in certain markets.

Remember, a market you cannot access is a market you cannot serve. Which tools will get your advertising message directly in front of the customer? Choose a combination of tools and strategies that increase your odds of success.

Consider everything. Your location, colors of the interior design, attitude of staff members, products, and services all contribute to creating an "experience" for the customer. Take the time to identify how your marketing and sales process works and then choose the right tools for the job. Keep the following things in mind when you're working on this part of your business plan:

- *Location:* If your business appeals to a certain demographic, then locating your business in an area that has a high density of those potential customers will increase your odds of success.

- *Proximity of your primary competitors:* Depending on the strength and image of your competitors, it may be beneficial to locate near them. You would be able to tap into the traffic they generate with their advertising and promotions. Your presence might encourage comparison shopping.

- *Distribution methods:* These could include wholesale, retail, manufacturers' agents, and strategic alliances.

- *Credit policies:* Easy payment terms such as no upfront payment, deferred payments, or no interest will work well in certain retail sectors that sell large-ticket items.

- *Product and service guarantee or warranty:* Extended warranties or guarantees of performance may help to reduce buyer resistance to trying a new company or product.

- *Sales model:* Members of the direct sales staff will need tools to help them do the job (e.g., a brochure, catalog, or product sample).

- *Pricing strategies:* Using a low price penetration strategy might allow you to win some market share. However, will you be able to maintain the low price strategy over the long term? Another strategy is to gradually raise prices as you become more established and have had an opportunity to build relationships with your customers. If you have established that your customers appreciate quality and have above-average incomes, a high price strategy could be effective. Try combining this strategy with a great ambiance and upscale facility.

- *Special events:* Use this strategy to reward customers and build a sense of community.

TIP

There are a lot of different ways to market and promote your business, but the key is to have at least 10 different marketing strategies working at any specific time. The more tactics and strategies you have tested that work, the more diversified your leads are, the less risk you are exposed to should one of them stop working.

Make a list of the tools you plan to use to market your business. Put them into a calendar format or at least into a spreadsheet with costs and time lines. Then you can use that information when it comes time to create your financial plan.

See Appendix C for more marketing tips, tools, and strategies

Step 4: Test Marketing, Strategy, and Tools

Prepare before you venture out into the world. Test your assumptions. Test your ideas and your pricing. Test your sales pitch. Test your advertising. In a word, *test!*

TRAP

It is very easy to get so wrapped up and committed to achieving a certain goal or result that we miss seeing the errors in our assumptions. Business planning is 50 percent explaining what you know and what you will do and the other 50 percent confirming key assumptions and success indicators.

Before spending your entire budget creating the tools and implementing strategies, first conduct some preliminary market testing. Try selling your products or services to a friend who has a similar profile to your ideal customer. If no friends meet the profile, go out into the marketplace and find someone! Explain that you are in start-up mode and ask for his or her help. One of the best places to find potential customers is in the parking lots, sidewalks, and neighborhood where you would like to set up shop.

Prepare a questionnaire and ask your test candidates a series of questions to get their feedback on your goods, services, and pricing. Interview them and ask them to be honest. Try your sales pitch. Show them sample advertisements or anything else that you plan to use in your promotions-marketing mix. Ask lots of questions! Listen for subtle differences or suggestions in the responses. These are "gold nuggets" that you can study and use to modify your approach to the marketplace.

TRAP

Do not skip confirming your assumptions through market testing. Just because you feel uncomfortable asking people on the street for help, that's not a good enough reason to skip it. Overprepare by making a list of questions and print them out and use it to record answers.

Thank the people you use in your testing! If they expressed an interest in your products or services, ask for their permission to contact them when you are operational.

Direct Mail Let's assume that you were going to rely heavily on direct-mail campaigns. Mail a small number of direct-mail packages to prospects. Try to get the prospects to buy your product or service, just as you normally would try to convince any customer. Then:

- See if you get any responses and, if you do make a note of how many responses you got to the mailing.
- Follow up: do a telephone follow-up to survey and try to quantify the reader's attitude, beliefs, and behavior as they relate to your mailing.

Take the feedback, study it, modify your approach, and test again. You will find that, as you test and modify your approach, your response rates should climb substantially. For example, perhaps you mailed 300 direct-mail packages and you got a 0.05 percent response on your first mailing. For the second mailing of 600, the response was 1.5 percent, and the final test (mailed 1,000) brought in a response of 3.5 percent. This represents a significant increase in revenue and profits. It takes time, but it pays off in the long run.

TRAP

Do not burn up your entire database by using it just in case the direct mail campaign fails or brings in a low response. By holding back some of the database, you to keep your losses low to use the remainder after having made some adjustments. Ultimately, this strategy will increase your revenue, assuming you are able to increase response rates with subsequent tests.

Press Releases After some testing and trial runs, try doing a press release and some inexpensive advertising. Important points to remember are:

- *Media:* The media aren't interested in giving you free promotion. They are interested in providing information that will help the subscriber, viewer, reader. So you must have a unique angle that helps them help the subscriber, viewer, and reader, plus, it has to be newsworthy.

- *Local papers:* Do some test advertising in the classified advertising section of your local newspaper or community newsletter. These ads are text only and low cost. You can afford to run lots of them and test different attention getting headlines.

- *Networking:* Find some networking groups, leads clubs, and mixers to attend. Usually, they allow new members to do an infomercial. This will provide you with an opportunity to test your approach. The infomercial should be full of benefits you are offering and clearly explain what business you are in or what products or services you provide.

The 12-Month Marketing Plan After you have done some initial testing, modified your approach, and confirmed that you are on the right track, create a 12-month marketing action plan. It should include:

- Descriptions of promotions, marketing strategies, and advertising tools.
- Exact costs and budgets.
- Time lines; establish specific dates to prepare and to train you staff, if necessary. Also set campaign launch dates.

TIP

Be sure to include information on how you will test and evolve your marketing strategies.

Pricing Decisions and Strategy

TRAP

If there is one issue that will kill a marketing or advertising campaign, it is not having a well-defined market pricing strategy, which is central to the overall development of a profitable marketing strategy.

Remember, marketing is communicating the benefits of a product or service. If your price is too high or low, your prospects/customers may not take you seriously, or they may dismiss your proposition outright. The entire purpose of marketing is to communicate and create a perception of value! Choosing the correct price is essential to creating the right perception of value.

Create a Market Price Strategy

Every price creates a "perception of value" in the mind of your prospect or customer. Your goal is to find the balance between a price that is low and impossible to maintain and a price that is too high and handicaps sales.

If your products or services do not have enough value in the mind of the customer or your marketing and sales system has failed to communicate the real value of your products or services, they will be perceived as overpriced. On the other hand, a price that is too low could create the perception that the product or service is of poor quality.

The point is that both scenarios create a "perception" problem. An effective market price strategy strikes a balance between real perceived value and the maximum sustainable price for goods and services for a particular market segment.

If your price is too high, you may not be able to achieve adequate market share, and you'll lose important sales and profits. If your price is too low, you may be leaving money on the table, and you will not have enough profit to sustain your business.

The solution? Find a balance between competitive factors, customer perceptions, expectations, and corporate goals. See Figure 7.1.

TIP

Generally, the less personal interaction you will have with a customer, the more accurate you need to be about your pricing strategy.

To make a decision on your market price strategy, you will need to consider the following points:

1. *Determine an acceptable range of prices:* Based upon your corporate values and objectives, do you want to establish a discount image or a quality image? The key is to make sure that your decision is in keeping with your corporate values.

Figure 7.1 Market Price Strategy

2. *Set a target price for a specific target market:* Based upon your understanding of this market and the estimated demand, you next set a price that will maximize sales and profits.

3. *Estimate the demand:* Compared to your competitors, will your price bring you enough market-share to be profitable? If the share is too small either adjust the value in your proposition or select a new price.

4. *Try to determine your competitors' reaction:* If your price and expected market share generate enough volume, you will want to anticipate your competitors' reaction. If your price is too low, a price war could break out. If your price is too high, it might stimulate a new competitor with a lower price.

5. *Compare and test the price against your financial goals:* Can you meet an acceptable level of return on your investment or will the pay back period be too long? It is best to test your price against your financial needs and goals as early as possible.

6. *Is your price congruent?* The price must be evaluated based upon a number of factors, such as comparable products or services, distribution channel, advertising expenses, and any personal selling strategies that will be used.

7. *Develop a profit plan:* Create a spreadsheet that analyzes the cost of production plus the cost of marketing and distribution at the anticipated sales levels. A lack of profit will require your establishing a new price or finding ways to reduce costs or add value.

Finally, set your final price. Take into account the price of competing products or services and adjust your price to fit. For example, you may prefer a price of $91.56, but you may adjust the final price to $89.95 for psychological reasons. If you plan to use a high-price skimming strategy, you may want to be ready to anticipate lowering prices so your market share does not dip significantly. Generally speaking, the more mature your industry the more accurate you need to be in your pricing strategy.

TRAP

A market price strategy that works well in one market segment may fail in another. You cannot assume anything; you must research your competitors' pricing strategy, test your own with real live customers, and then adjust to fit the market.

Want to Avoid Failure? Then Develop a Sales Strategy

Selling is nothing more than exerting influence, building relationships, and communicating effectively. Consider the following questions when you're developing your sales strategy.

Do I have a valuable product or service that people want, and do I believe in it?

If people have a legitimate need for your product or service, you are off to a good start. Nothing is more attractive to a customer than a company or salespeople who really walk, talk, and believe in the product or service they are selling. It gets customers' attention and respect and solves the issue of your credibility.

Am I someone people in business would want to have a relationship with?

The first sale you need to make is to yourself. Are you proud of being a salesperson? Do you believe in your abilities? Would you buy the product or service you are selling? Have you purchased or do you own the product or service yourself?

Being able to put yourself in the customers' shoes is an important ability. It will allow you to understand and respect where the buyer is coming from and will allow you to speak from a position of strength as someone who already owns the product or service.

Is this customer someone I want to have a business relationship with?

You might as well have *no* business rather than have bad business. An example of bad business would be customers that don't pay their bills, waste your time, and do not appreciate or understand the value of your product or service.

Sit down with your potential customers and ask them a series of questions. After all, if you are going to sell to someone, sell to your best candidates first. Probe for the prospects' values and beliefs. Ask them these questions:

- What is driving them to buy now?
- Have they purchased this in the past?
- What did they like? What could have been improved?

Are the customers' needs, wants, emotions, and perceptions in alignment with your marketing and sales strategy? If not, you may need to realign your sales and marketing strategy.

Sales = Influence

Whether consciously or unconsciously, as humans, we analyze each other's demeanor, style, manner, habits, methods, and customs all the time. Using this information, we make decisions and judgments and form biases toward people, events, products, and services.

Depending who or what we judge (perceive) as being superior, right, better, or stronger, we sometimes change our positions or opinions. There is a word for this—*influence!* The way in which influence can be used for the good of both parties involved is called *sales.*

TIP

Get a piece of paper and a pen. Read the next question. Then stop and write the answer on the piece of paper. When you think of the word "salesperson," what comes to mind? If most of the words you wrote down are negative, the first order of business is to deal with your fear of selling. You cannot worry about what people might think or get distracted by your own emotions about buying and selling.

Remember, in selling, failure is your friend if you learn from it. Do this and you cannot help but improve and succeed.

Creating Your Sales Strategy

Business plans without a sales strategy are doomed to fail. It is the process of "making a sale" where the rubber hits the road and your business succeeds or fails.

TIP

The most overlooked section of business plans is the "sales strategy," because the writers are so focused on getting the loan and financing they need that they forget the most basic of business tactics—making a sale. Also, taking the time to test your sales strategy while writing your business plan allows you to make mistakes on paper and not with time or money.

Create your sales strategy using the following process.

1. Differentiate Specific Buying Habits and Traits

Identify the key traits or indicators of your ideal prospects, including buying patterns, intentions, beliefs, and values. These are identifiable criteria that can be used to "flag" those leads and prospects that have the highest likelihood of buying your product or service (go back to your notes from the marketing strategy and review the NWEP of your ideal customer). Create specific categories in a database that will allow you to search, sort, and identify these customers quickly.

2. Determine "High-Yield" Customers

Those customers that have bought from you and have the potential for continued sales (high yield) are to be singled out for special treatment and privileges, including mailings, gifts, and the like. What are the most prevalent buying patterns or purchasing criteria you can identify and track? Look to your current best customers to determine their high-yield characteristics. Categorize all the other customers and work on creating strategies to pull them into high-yield status.

3. Create Systems to Reach Them

An effective communication system will allow you to turn your inventory of leads and prospects into customers. A successful communication system could include:

- Sales process and questioning strategy.
- Phone strategy.
- Newsletters.

See Appendix C for a list of more than 101 marketing and sales tools.

TIP

In your business plan, be sure to describe how your communication strategy will help boost the profile of the business and fits into your overall business plan.

4. Have Customers for Life

As your customers grow and mature, so should your business systems, products, and services. Create a system to monitor your customers changing needs. Determine how you can reengineer your products or services to extend the business relationship and have customers for life. Ask yourself these questions:

- What ancillary products or services do they buy that are similar or what other related needs do they think about when in the buying cycle?
- Could you sell those products or services too?
- Is there a way you could create a "prepaid" club program that would save them money and lock them into your company for a longer period while making them less vulnerable to the competition?
- Would creating a reminder program help to bring them back to purchase again?

5. Work Actively with Customers

Create an after-sale follow-through strategy such as a satisfaction survey. In this survey:

- Ask customers for their ideas and comments.
- Thank them for their feedback and tell them you will get back to them. Then make sure you keep your promise.
- Advise them of changes and improvements you have made based on their suggestions and feedback. Make sure to communicate with them even if you are unable to incorporate their suggestions right now or ever. It will create trust because they know you are listening.

TRAP

Without an after-sale follow-through strategy you could be missing out on additional revenue or allowing customers to leave for a more aggressive competitor.

The Complete Six-Step Sales Process

Selling is the most fundamental of all entrepreneurial activities and is often misunderstood. Before you can make a penny in profit, someone has to sell and someone has to buy. Customers buy your goods or services to solve a "problem."

To accomplish this, you may need to change the way you think about selling. While you as a business owner think of a narrow list of products or services and how you can bundle and sell them to the customer, customers think only of their own needs and activities.

Your Customer Is Looking for Solutions to Problems

Show your customers that you have a solution to their problems, and they will buy or at least inquire about your products or services. It is your job to show potential customers that you can help them.

Solution (to problem) + (awareness of) Need = (motivation to) Buy

People don't buy anything significant unless they think it solves a problem and unless the price of your solution is perceived to be cheaper than the "cost" of not solving the problem.

The Six Steps in the Buying and Sales Cycle

Understanding the stage your customer is at in the buying and selling cycle will allow you to respond with appropriate information, tools, and strategies (see Fig. 7.2).

1. The approach In the beginning we first try to understand our prospect or the customer's current situation. Our goal is to build rapport with the person and to understand and uncover his or her beliefs patterns and preferences as they relate to your company and its products or services. I call this a sales interview.

The thing I like to ask in the beginning is, "Why did you decide to meet with me? What got your attention?" The answer will reveal the prospects' cur-

Figure 7.2 The Complete Buying and Sales Cycle

rent thinking and their perceptions as to why they think they might need my products or services. As a result of asking these questions and listen to the answers, I will have gathered enough information to help me create a needs profile of my customer or prospect.

2. Uncover the problem   Every purchase must solve a problem. No problem = no sale. If customers do not see how your goods or services can help them solve their problem, they have no reason to buy from you. Therefore, you must uncover a specific problem that the customer is motivated to solve *by* purchasing one of your products or services.

The way to uncover the customers' problem is to ask probing, honest, and well-intentioned questions. Also, they are a powerful way to create rapport and to get the prospect to trust and respect you. Everyone likes and respects a good listener and trust is the foundation of making a sale.

TIP

If you need some good questions, you can find them at: http://www.sbishere.com/category/sales-selling/.

3. Identify consequences   There is always a consequence, pain, or cost for customers if they do not solve their "problem." The consequence or cost could be something like a desire being unfulfilled. For example, if a person were considering using the services of a professional organizer, the consequence of not using this service would be a lack of productivity. When buying a home, the consequence of not being able to enjoy the close proximity of the house to my place of work would mean increased travel costs and time spent in traffic.

Making the connection between the customers' problem and consequences is what I call the *golden key*. Finding the golden key will help you to unlock and uncover the customers' true motivation and help them buy your product or service.

TRAP

The greatest mistake you can make when selling is to assume that the customer understands the consequences of not buying from you. When you do not to get your prospects emotionally involved (identify consequences and costs), they will buy from the next salesperson who helps them understand the consequences, gets them more excited, or communicates more effectively about the value of their product(s) or service(s).

4. Demonstrate capabilities   Rookie salespeople often lead with the capabilities of their products and services. Capabilities should never be discussed until you have identified a problem that the customer is motivated (via consequences) to solve. Discussing can disengage the customer because they do not perceive how your solution solves their problem.

If you lead too soon with capabilities, benefits, and features, you might never find out the customer's true motivation for buying. Remember, at this stage it is your role to help customers connect the dots between the issues, problems, and solutions that they stated earlier in the sales process.

5. Make it easy to buy   Be prepared! If you use contracts, have a contract prepared, ready to be signed. If you accept credit cards, be prepared to take the credit card information. Do whatever it takes to make it smooth, simple, and easy to complete the transaction.

6. Customer service   This is probably the most overlooked area of selling. It can be as simple as saying thank you via e-mail. Make sure you have a customer service plan that addresses the following questions:

- What happens after your customer makes a purchase? What is your next step?
- How will you provide support?
- How are you going to provide value after the sale?

Be sure to congratulate the customer on making a good decision!

What are your plans to contact customers again to make that second or third sale?

Repeat Customers Generate Substantial Profits

I read in *Business 2.0* magazine that 98.7 percent of visitors do not return to a Web site, even if they buy something. Getting that first sale is important, but even more important is getting existing customers to make additional purchases. Why? Because repeat customers will generate more than three times the revenue of new customers.

TIP

It is easier to get a repeat order from an existing customer than it is to find a new customer.

Creating a flawless customer experience is essential for getting that first sale. After that, be sure to utilize a number of strategies that develop the customer-vendor relationship. Send customers updates, notices, and special offers. Keep in touch! What about providing an incentive for repeat orders or encouraging word-of-mouth advertising? When the repeat purchase cycle is spread out over a long period of time, it proves that building a solid customer relationship is crucial for maximizing future selling opportunities and profits.

TIP

Be sure to include an explanation of how you will bring customers back again and again.

Sample Marketing and Sales Strategy

Following is the marketing and sales strategy section of the business plan. The complete business plan can be found in Appendix A.

Marketing and Sales Strategy

JOE'S will focus its sales and marketing efforts on moving LTL and FTL open-deck freight in two primary geographic areas:

- Western Canada.
- Canada to the United States and the United States to Canada.

The highway transportation industry is a fast-moving business. Load and equipment availability change quickly throughout any given day. The ability to respond quickly to customer requests for price is essential. Therefore, we will utilize the latest database marketing, telemarketing, and Internet tools to communicate with our customers. Other marketing tools to support the sales and marketing efforts will include:

- Telephone, fax, direct marketing, and sales.
- Internet and Web site.
- Driver distributed flyers (select locations).
- Networking and leads from customers.

(Continued)

(Continued)

One of JOE'S best methods for acquiring new leads and potential customers is through a combination of:

- Capital projects announcements.
- Observations of and networking by drivers.
- Dispatcher supervision of local loading: provides an opportunity to get to know operations staff and fosters an atmosphere of a little extra care and attention as well as seeing what customers have in the yard that may need to be transported somewhere.
- Networking with existing customers: listening to which bids they lost and to whom, upcoming work, and industry and competitor news.
- Announcements in newspaper.

Existing Sales Volume JOE'S sales assumptions are based upon past sales history of To and Fro Transport and that all major customers have agreed to continue business with JOE'S. There are 22 major accounts that did a total of $1,110,917 of business with To and Fro Transport in the last 12 months.

In a recent survey, 13 of those accounts expect to do more business with JOE'S in the next 12 months. Of the remaining nine, all intend on continuing doing business with JOE'S. The exact amount of sales that can be expected varies and cannot be confirmed at this time. (For a detailed list of accounts and volumes see "Assumptions").

Upcoming Contracts JOE'S has confirmed four new contracts:

- Starting in October 2000, JOE'S has been awarded a $108,000 transportation contract from WE Do It All Industrial (Clear Creek project).
- $74,200 Looking For More, September–November 2000, moving pump jacks.
- $55,000 from Jumble, moving pre-engineered buildings when returning from Clear Creek.
- May 2001 to May 2004/2005, a $650,000 transportation contract with Anywhere Industrial.

Customer Profile The company's primary target market is industrial companies that have the type of freight that will not fit into a van trailer and that requires an open deck. This type of freight includes:

- LTL
- Machinery

- Metals and fabricated products
- Wood, paper
- Electrical cable tray
- Oil field equipment: pump jacks, vessels, etc.
- Produce: potatoes
- Tubing, pipe
- Vessels
- Preengineered buildings
- Mining equipment
- Cranes

Database Marketing and Telemarketing Survey For the first six months the customer service representative will conduct a survey to further qualify and segment our database. As a result we will:

- Know which customers ship to which lane ways (destinations).
- Determine what types of commodities they ship or receive.
- Know the contact name of shipper, project manager, or decision maker.
- Determine how often they ship (number of loads per week or month).

The database will allow us to quickly communicate via fax, e-mail, or telephone and find more productive reloads.

Pricing JOE'S's pricing strategy will be to maximize profit margins through close monitoring of bids and administrative and operations expenses.

- Average gross revenue per mile: $1.52 per mile CDN (includes empty miles).
- Minimum selling price: $1.65 per mile CDN.

As mentioned elsewherein this plan, western Canadian freight has three main advantages:

- Generally sells for a higher price per mile.
- Generally paid round trip.
- Runs lower cost capital equipment.

Depending upon the job, the selling price per mile in western Canada runs between $1.75 CDN to $2.50 CDN.

(Continued)

(Continued)

Competition Analysis

Name	Market Area	Size	Reputation
Three-Way	Canada and U.S.	Same	Respected, good competitor
Cancer	Western Canada	Larger	Respected, good competitor
First Guy	Western Canada	Larger	Unreliable and sloppy
So Many More	Western Canada	Larger	Unreliable and sloppy
First Time	Canada and U.S.	Larger	Unreliable, poor business practices
Next Line	Canada and U.S.	Larger	Cheap, big, poor business practices
Hangon	Canada and U.S.	Larger	Respected, expensive
Big Bird	Canada and U.S	Broker	Excellent competitor
Four Bros.	Canada and U.S	Small	Poor business practices
Needs Help	Western Canada	Small	Poor image and business practices

Competitive Strategy JOE'S's objective is to provide consistent JOE'S, on-time delivery. The company's policy is to always be honest when a delay or mishap occurs, offering both an explanation and a solution whenever possible.

JOE'S's experience has proven that being accountable, open, and honest in communications and dealings not only creates trust but also builds relationships. Customers routinely call JOE'S to help them out of a tight spot because they know they will get an honest answer and that JOE'S delivers on its promises.

8

Operations and Management

The main reason for business failure is inexperienced management. Managers of bankrupt firms did not have the experience, knowledge, or vision to run their businesses. Even as the firms' age and management experience increases, knowledge and vision remain critical deficiencies that contribute to failure.

As a surviving business grows, new sets of problems arise that are associated with the increased complexity of running an older and often larger firm. Managerial issues such as the poor use of outside advisers, lack of emphasis on quality, an unwillingness to delegate responsibilities, departure of key personnel, and "personal" problems associated with the owner-manager become important factors that contribute to the possibility of failure as a business ages.

Why Operations and Management Plans Are Taken for Granted

In my experience, operations and management are the most ignored areas of business planning, even though they are the areas in which business owners spend the majority of their time.

TRAP

It is your familiarity with your business that can cause you to be lulled into a false sense of security and this is where the problem begins.

Operations and Management as a Marketing Tool

A well-run operation has structure, controls, and quality checkpoints throughout the business. Such businesses are a wonder to behold because they do such a great job of serving the customers' needs. In Chapter 17 I mention that restaurants provide examples of some of the best and worst managed businesses.

The owners of well-run businesses have spent a lot of time, effort, and energy improving and refining their operations. They exhibit a passion for meeting the customers' needs and an eagle eye for modifying their procedures, educating employees, and maintaining the appearance of the business to align with those needs. The one thing that all great businesses have in common is that they create a great customer experience, and it shows.

TRAP

It is the operation and management of your business that creates a great or a poor experience. Never take it for granted because if you cannot explain how you will manage your operation in the business plan, you will not be able to implement it in real life.

Your Financier Will Take a Critical Eye to Management and Operations

Investors, bankers, and financiers will pay special attention to your operations and management plan because it will tell them how you intend to run the business. As they read this part of your business plan, they will be making an assessment of your abilities to manage the business and achieve the objectives you detail. Your operations and management plan is a tool that not only helps you run your business better but also showcases your management philosophy: It is the best indication of your management skills.

TIP

Your operations and management plan is especially important when you need a large business loan, because the loan committee will have only your business plan to represent you and your interests.

Uses of an Operations and Management Plan

The level of detail you include in your operations and management plan will depend on whether your business plan is for an internal or external audience.

When writing for an internal audience, the purpose of the operations and management plan is to provide enough detail so that your superiors and subordinates can read it and understand it. In the case of subordinates, your operations plan should have sufficient detail to allow them to understand your expectations, changes that may need to be made, and how to go about implementing the plan.

When writing for an external audience, include an overview of the entire operations and management plan and its components. Flow charts, facility layout, renderings, and graphics and photos all help to demonstrate how you will implement your plan.

Components of the Operations and Management Plan

Depending on the type of business you have, what you actually include in this part of your business plan will vary. The plan for a service or retail business would not need to include information on production, quality control, or distribution, but it will need to pay special attention to location. A service business must place more importance on the customer experience and service blueprint. Following are the components of the operations and management plan.

Current Situation

Write a paragraph or two explaining how the business currently operates. In the case of a start-up, provide an encapsulated version of what has been accomplished to date. Be sure to include a summary of your efforts to get started, covering your market research, if you have negotiated a lease for office or shop space, product development, and market testing, if any. You should also include a list of equipment you have purchased, staff you have recruited, and anything that shows how you have been working on getting the business up and running.

For an established business you would write a few paragraphs to provide insight into the major issues and challenges the business is coping with and what needs to change. For example, a jobber machine shop experiencing an increase in demand as a result of acquiring new long-term contracts should explain and quantify how current equipment needs to be replaced to increase capacity and meet the demand. Detail any other circumstances, changes to processes, staff, facility, equipment, location, and renovations that also need to be included in making changes to the operation of the business.

Location

Choosing a location for the business directly influences the viability of the business because you are setting roots in a community whose environment will have a direct impact on the business. Therefore, the first step is to complete your market analysis (Chapter 4) before choosing a location.

Seldom will any location be a perfect fit. The purpose in writing about the location of the business in the operations and management plan is to identify the business's needs for a specific facility with easy access to customers, suppliers, and labor. Then clarify community amenities including transportation, taxes, and how business-friendly municipal regulations do or do not work to the advantage of your business. Your description of the business location should answer these questions:

- Does the business require easy access to major transportation hubs? If so, how will this location affect the viability of the business?

- Is the facility of adequate size to meet current needs and still offer some opportunity to grow and expand? What would be involved in expanding? How much growth in inventory could the current location absorb? Do you have an option to lease or acquire space nearby?

- Where will the business be located? How does this specific site provide a competitive advantage, and how does it contribute to the business achieving its goals and outcomes?

- What is the history of rental, leasing costs, and real estate (land and commercial buildings) prices? How do they compare to other areas nearby? Is there an opportunity to save on fixed costs while still having access to the market?

- Have you spoken to local economic development authorities, and do any of the county, municipal, or neighborhood authorities offer support, financial incentives or tax breaks?

- What are the growth prospects for this community? How will the local infrastructure (transportation, government, educational institutions, labor utilities, etc.) inhibit or enable business growth?

- Is there enough pedestrian and vehicular traffic to sustain operations? What is the population density of the area? What is the outlook for the next five years? Are the demographics of the area in alignment with your business concept?

- How would you rate the cost of construction and the availability of trades in this area?

- How do the cost of living and business overhead costs (transportation, local taxes, energy, etc.) for this area compare with nearby competitive areas? Will there be extra costs involved in delivering products or services to customers from this location?

- Will access to suppliers and major customers be an advantage or a detriment? If a detriment, how do you plan to deal with this weakness? Is the location difficult to find or is your location off the beaten track, which could make transportation and shipping more challenging and expensive?

- When compared to similar markets, how does customer demand compare in this location? How visible is the business? Does the developer have plans to build additional buildings? If so, would there still be adequate parking?

- What is the perception of the community? Is it considered safe and pleasant?

Facility

A well-planned facility makes an important contribution to enabling the business to serve, deliver, and process client orders. The purpose of describing your facility is to help those who read your business plan get a sense of how you intend to use the facility to serve your customers.

TIP

If the main reason for writing a business plan is to get the financing to buy, renovate, or expand your facility, then this portion of the operations and management plan should get extra attention.

Using a combination of text, drawings, renderings, and flowcharts, your goal is to illustrate how the space, building, and/or property will be utilized to maximize work flow, efficiency, and output.

Depending on the magnitude of investment in the premises, your facility plan should increase in size accordingly with respect to the level of detail it contains; it should include space plans, processes, and product layout diagrams.

TIP

When seeking construction financing, it is common practice to include a picture of the architect's rendering, construction bid summaries, and Gantt charts showing construction time lines in your plan.

Here are some questions to consider when you're writing about your facility:

- What is the age of the equipment and the expected life cycle and condition of the assets?

- Is there enough space for the equipment, furniture, and storage to produce the projected volume? If not, what needs to change? What will the cost of the change be? How will the new or expanded space improve work flow and productivity? Do you plan to lease or own the equipment? What are the terms of the lease, costs, and buyback options, if any?

- How do the layout and setup of the facility provide a competitive advantage? Would changes to the facility provide a competitive advantage? If so, what specifically needs to be changed or improved? Include drawings, floor plans, and process work flows to justify the changes.

- Are there changes or modifications that need to be made to the facility to make it more efficient and effective? Is the building energy-efficient? Has there been an energy audit? If so, what were the findings? What investment will be required and what is the payback to making the improvements?

- Do you plan to lease or own the facility? If leasing, identify the lessor, track record, and the terms of the lease including significant caveats or restrictions. If you are buying the facility, when was the last time the building and property were inspected? What are the EPA (Environmental Protection Agency) implications? Will any cleanup of the site or building be required to conform to EPA standards?

Process and Procedures

The methods, processes, and procedures used to deliver your goods to market are the areas in which you have the single greatest opportunity to create additional value. This section of your operations and management plan covers how you compete in the marketplace and is at the core of your brand.

Perhaps one of your business's most important processes is the steps involved in creating the customer experience. This chain of specific events is designed to provide value to the customer, and from this point on I refer to this as your *value-added chain.* Your value-added chain encompasses everything from concept through to customer service follow-up. If your business plan is for an internal audience, make sure to include enough detail and information so that executives, managers, and employees can understand and implement the processes in the business operation. For an external audience, focus on a document that explains the value-added chain on a higher level. The five parts of every value-added chain are:

1. *Development:* Provide a brief description of your efforts to develop the processes and procedures. This should include product design, prototyp-

ing, and testing. In a service business include the implications of your market analysis on the value-added chain.

2. *Manufacturing and preparation:* Explain how your product or service is created, built, or prepared. For a manufacturing business this component should be fairly detailed since this is where most of the added value occurs. Make sure to include all steps involved in the preparation of your product or service. For example, a new car dealer will prepare a new car for delivery by checking fluid levels and by washing and detailing the vehicle.

3. *Marketing and sales:* The promotion of its products and services are important for every business. For example, the marketing and sales process will have a large impact on customer expectations. Make sure to include how your industry or business tends to approach marketing and sales differently from other businesses or industries, if there are any differences.

4. *Delivery and consumption:* Detail specific requirements for the delivery and/or consumption of your service or product. In the case of a product that requires installation, explain how the product is to be installed and the qualifications of the installers. If you are selling a service, the delivery and consumption phases will directly affect the customers' experience. Provide an explanation of the experience, how it will be delivered, and by whom. Include a few sentences about your plans for measuring customer satisfaction and maintaining quality control.

5. *Customer service and follow-up:* As much as this is an opportunity for an up-sell, it also represents an opportunity to check the quality of your service and customer satisfaction. The more people and steps between your customer and the receipt of your product or service, the greater opportunity for something to go wrong. Spell out your customer service and follow-up strategies.

TIP

Every business plan should include a description of its value-added chain. Process flowcharts, diagrams, and pictures should be included with the business plan of a manufacturer. For service businesses your value-added chain will become your service blueprint.

People reading your business plan will want to read about your approach to striking a balance between the costs and benefits of creating value. (See Fig. 8.1.)

$$\text{The Value of a Deliverable} = \frac{\text{Information and Intangibles}}{\text{Mass and Tangibles}}$$

Figure 8.1 Value-Added Formula

Purchasing

Manufacturing and distribution businesses require the purchase, control, and handling of incoming materials and goods. Document your purchasing procedures and how you make decisions to add additional products. Is there an opportunity to increase income by adding complementary products? If so, identify the products and how they can be added to your product mix without diluting sales of existing product lines.

If your business uses raw materials, explain the purchasing process, procedures for handling, and storage requirements of those raw materials. In addition, consider the following questions:

- What system do you use to track inventory?

- Do you participate in any buying groups, alliances, or exclusive relationships that provide a competitive and price advantage?

- How do you control purchasing costs? What is the percentage of revenue expended on purchases?

- Who are your suppliers and how reliable are they? How long have they been in business? What type of support do they or will they provide?

- Who provides warranty or service for the products? What is the percentage of returns? Is the defective rate is normal?

- What are the items in your inventory that turn over the fastest? How do you buy those items? Do you buy them in bulk, at a discount, or with special payment terms?

- How much of your product line is seasonal? Explain what you do to minimize the carrying costs.

- Are you required to carry a significant inventory because of lengthy delivery schedules?

The equivalent of purchasing procedures for a service business is the outsourcing of labor or services. Explain how, when, who, and where services will be outsourced. Will the vendor have contact with the customer? If so, what measures are in place to protect your relationship with the customer?

Inventory Management

The effective, efficient, and aggressive management of inventory can be one of the most important management and control functions for a manufacturer or distributor. Therefore, include an adequate description of your inventory management strategy.

Most goods distributors and resellers handle only finished goods, whereas a manufacturer will have goods in various stages of production. As the manufacturing process moves along, products move from raw materials to components or a semi-finished state to the finished product and then on to packaging and storage. For many consumer goods the last two steps are really one final step.

How goods move from one stage to the next and your production schedules affect the amount of inventory your firm may need to carry. If you produce the finished product on a frequent basis and the supply of raw materials is stable, you can afford to inventory less finished goods. The more efficient you are at managing the movement of product from raw state to delivery to the customer, the lower your overall costs will be.

TRAP

Without access to a reliable supply of raw materials you will have to keep a greater inventory of raw materials or finished goods on hand, which will raise your handling costs and lower your profit margins.

Accurate sales forecasting, inventory control, calculation of reorder points, and an account of the time it takes to ship and transport the raw materials or goods should all be included in your calculations to maintain adequate inventory levels. Consider the following questions:

- What systems and processes will you use to count, manage, and control inventory levels?

- What software or system do you use to automate inventory management?

- How do you track and communicate information about the status of inventory levels, transportation time lines, production schedules, balance on hand, age of inventory, and turnover rates?

- Do you use any handheld computers to count and manage inventory? How often is the count done?

- What measures are in place to prevent employee theft and fraud?

Distribution

Sales distribution is very important for any business whose end user buys the product or service from a reseller. This would include wholesale distributors, manufacturers, and inventors. In this part of the business plan, describe your distribution policies and strategy. Who sells your product or service? What qualifies them to sell it? What training and support will you provide? Include a breakdown of your suggested selling price as well as price lists for each distribution level. Show your profit on the sale to your customer as well as the markup and profit margins for resellers.

TIP

In a retail business, instead of distribution, discuss the impact that your location has on your business.

Quality Control and Customer Service

Quality control is as much a customer service function as it is part of the process of manufacturing a product. Competition dictates management of the customer experience, and customers; perception of the level of quality is one of the most important key performance indicators (KPI) that tends to be ignored. Most firms I work with fail to measure the effectiveness of this important outcome. In this section of your business plan, include answers to the following questions:

- What are the quality standards you maintain?
- What variables do you measure? At what point do you measure them in your process?
- How do you communicate your quality and customer service standards to employees and management?
- How you will take action to improve quality and customer service standards?
- What checks and verification systems do you use to ensure accurate filling of customer orders?
- How do you plan to correct mistakes and errors in order processing?

TRAP

Quality cannot be assumed. Failure to implement a system to measure and track quality is a management failure, and faulty products can make it into the field, causing delays, damage, and customer dissatisfaction. It is always cheaper to remove faulty products or employees that do not perform up to standard than to replace a customer.

Human Resources

Most people start a business with an idea of a product. But to build an organization, you must think one level above the idea/problem/pain that your business solves and focus on how to attract really great people (technicians) who can deliver a great service or build a great product. Include answers to the following questions in your plan:

- How important is the ability to supervise, organize, plan, and lead subordinates?

- What is your plan for hiring staff with a warm and sociable attitude toward customers?

- What are your policies regarding your employee's personal appearance?

- What type of personality characteristics and communication skills are required for the jobs in your organization?

- What is your policy toward ongoing education training and long-term growth of employees?

- How will you monitor employee compliance with policies, procedures and business structure?

- Which positions in your company require employees with excellent leadership and communication skills? What specific traits, experience, skills, and knowledge are expected?

- Define your ideal employee. Build a profile and provide details of employees' ability to adapt to change as well as their leadership and communication skills. How important is it for them to cooperate with other employees and build a team? Do they have a personal drive and desire for personal achievement, do they show initiative, and are they dependable?

Take an appropriate amount of space to explain your procedures and policies for checking references.

TRAP

A lack of clear expectations and standards leaves employees to determine their own level of performance and effort. This is an abdication of your leadership role. Define and communicate performance expectations.

Management and Organizational Structure

If you are a one-person company, you can ignore this section. However, if you plan to add staff as you grow and for the time period the business plan covers, provide a brief overview of your management and organizational structure.

In this section, define how communication takes place in your organization. Who reports to whom? Provide an overview of job descriptions, titles, and duties. If you have a number of staff members, a flowchart can easily communicate the structure and reporting relationships.

Key Management and Staff

The smaller the organization, the more important a section describing the background and experience of management becomes. Answer the following questions in this section:

- Can you run this business? What is your background, experience, and training that qualifies you to run this business?
- Have you been in business before? If so, tell the story.
- Do you have a reasonable chance of achieving your goals? Explain your rationale and justification.

Provide a brief overview of any key staff and management members. List their qualifications, experience, and a brief job description. Put a detailed version of the job description in the appendix. Do not forget to include yourself! Include a personal résumé for each key management and staff member.

TIP

If you have a key manager (other than yourself), answer the questions above based on his or her experience and background and add it to your business plan.

Advisory Board and the Board of Directors

If you are a solo entrepreneur, you will want to show that you have access to a group of advisers or professionals who can help you grow your business and make decisions.

Your business plan is based on certain assumptions. Some of these assumptions will prove to be correct, and others will not. The key in any successful enterprise is the owner's ability to learn and then quickly apply that new knowledge. This will require making certain strategic and tactical decisions to ensure your success. Provide an overview of your decision-making process and how you will consult with outside advisers and professionals to help offset the risk of making decisions, omissions, and expensive errors.

If you plan to incorporate, list the names, addresses, and phone numbers of your directors. List their terms of office and areas of expertise. How often will the board of directors meet?

Professional Services

Identify the consultants who will support your business and add overall strength to the management team. Also note costs for using their services in your financial statements. Some of these professionals may include:

- *Marketing research firm:* If you plan to use a market research firm, identify the company, services to be performed, and all costs.

- *Advertising agency:* If you plan on using an agency, list the agency, the services it provides, and the associated costs.

- *Attorney:* If you plan to incorporate and are anticipating any type of partnership, additional directors, or shareholders a lawyer can make sure that things are set up properly.

- *Accountant:* A certified public accountant (or a chartered accountant or certified general accountant in Canada) will be used to set up your books and prepare year-end financial statements and tax returns.

- *Any other professionals:* Detail any other consultants or business professionals you plan on using and explain what they will do and identify any associated costs.

Sample Management, Operations, and Organization Section

Following is the management, operations, and organization section of the business plan. The complete business plan can be found in Appendix A.

Operations and Management

All major decisions that have the potential to negatively affect the company's ability to maintain a 5 percent net profit must pass a case study and be reviewed by the owners and the company's professional advisers. The goal will be to always maintain a 5 percent net profit.

Administration and Office Manager (Sue Switch) Responsible for all administration, office management, and financial record keeping and reporting. Her jobs will include:

- Cash flow management: tracks and analyzes financial performance.
- Internal control systems: budgets, purchase orders, credit approval and collection.
- Weekly and monthly ratio reports and analysis reports.
- Accounts receivable collections: maintains average receivables aging 51 to 52 days.
- Job costing.
- Payroll.

(Continued)

(*Continued*)

- Accounts payable (A/P) and accounts receivable (A/R).
- Overseeing of shop expenses.
- Handling of bank reconciliations.
- Forecasting of A/P and A/R on a weekly basis with Operations manager.
- Individual case studies for major purchases, as needed.

Operations Manager—Dispatch and Sales (Joe Sample)
Management of the day-to-day operations, which include:

- Procuring loads and quoting rates for Canada and U.S. at a minimum of $1.65 per running mile.
- Maintaining on-time pickup and delivery schedules.
- Maintaining daily drivers' logs.
- *Lease operations:* Achieving a minimum $16,000 gross revenue per month per unit and maintaining a positive mood and working environment.
- *Sales:* Maintaining contact with all major accounts (weekly) and actively establishing relationships with new customers (two per week).
- Completing dispatch and billing orders.
- Compiling weekly management reports.
- Being available for work Monday to Friday 8:00 a.m.–5:00 p.m. (starting 7:00 a.m. on Mondays) and being on call 24/7.

Customer Service Representative (Sara Kale)   Reporting to the operations manager, she keeps all office- and dispatch-related procedures running smoothly, including:

- Completion and tracking of all paperwork: preparation of bills of lading for invoicing purposes.
- Maintaining customer database: updating all customer lists and broker contact lists.
- Assisting dispatcher to find loads, when required.
- Maintaining dispatch production sheets.
- Preparing and submitting via fax or theInternet rate quotes once completed by dispatcher.
- Preparing dispatch sheets for all hired units.

Credit Policy   All accounts will be required to complete and sign a credit application. Administration will check credit references and check with Equifax/Creditel. Credit terms are:

- Terms net 30 days.
- Collection follow-up on the 31st day.
- Any accounts at 60 days aging will be reviewed by the dispatcher, and services will be provided at his discretion. At 90 days dispatcher will hold shipment until payment is received.
- The operational goal is to maintain a 51 to 52 day average aging on A/R. (Cash flow projections based upon 60 days.)

Office Hours   The office will be open 8 a.m. to 5 p.m., with 24/7 after-hours service via pager and cell phone.

Owner-Operators   The key to attracting and retaining good owner-operators is to treat them with respect, recognize that they have a small business, and help them build and grow their business.

Equipment Maintenance   JOE'S has an agreement with a customer (Tony's Equipment) to do all major service and repairs.

Maintenance Facilities and Office Space   JOE'S is remaining in the TO AND FRO location. Included in our rental agreement is the use of an office including photocopier, fax machine, and lunch room. Also included is a heated indoor truck parking bay, parts and inventory storage, and the use of the wash and service bay.

Office Equipment   For an additional $2,700 JOE'S is purchasing computer equipment and office furniture (see the appendix for a complete list).

Organizational Structure

Joe Sample—Operations Manager, Sales, Dispatch, and Operations

Sara Kale, Customer Service Representative

Sue Switch, Administration and Office Manager

Professional Advisers

Legal: Three Guys & Company
John Smith
Barrister and Solicitor

(*Continued*)

(*Continued*)

123 Main Street
Northern AB
HOH OHO
Phone: 555-555-1234
Fax 555-555-1692

Accountant: Everyday Accounting, Chartered Accountants LLP
Accounting Way
Northern AB
A3G 9H6
Phone: 555-555-1578
Fax: 555-666-3918
E-mail: hismail@signuphere.com

Business Consultant: The Company Way
Greg Jones
47 Sweet Street
Northern, AB
K7T 9H6
Phone: 555-725-1232
Fax: 555-982-2492
Services include: marketing, business development support, graphic design, Web site design, and Internet marketing.

Computer Hardware

It's Broke Computers
Mr. Fix It
Northern, AB
Phone: 555-333-1686

9

Pro Forma Financial Plan

A business plan without a financial plan is like a car without wheels: It won't be going anywhere. The purpose of this chapter is to lay a foundation of the concepts and structure required to build a pro forma financial plan for your business. A solid financial plan is a key indicator of a well-rounded business owner as it demonstrates that you understand the factors that contribute to success and failure, the importance of financial management, and the skills required to operate the business.

TIP

Pro forma financial statements show what you plan to do with the businesses finances in the future. Past financial statements show everything that happened in the past.

Once you are operating, the pro forma financial statements become an important tool for benchmarking and comparing the actual results of operating the business to your plan. They become a way to maintain accountability and remind you of the commitments made to the bank and investors.

Drive to the Finish Line

Anyone who has run a marathon knows that at about the 20-mile mark you "hit the wall" where you begin to experience significant pain. To finish the race, you have to push through the pain. The same thing is true in writing a business plan.

By the time you decide to draft a financial plan, the planning and writing process has been underway for quite some time, and you may start to feel like you're hitting a wall. Push forward!

Creating your financial plan is a process of translating your plans and strategies into financial terms. A strong financial plan is a reflection of the owner and his/her ability to manage the company's financial resources. Putting your financial picture together will require you to spend a fair amount of time at your computer entering your data. Expect to do a fair amount of adjusting, tweaking, and changing to get your financial plan just right.

Persist Because Practice Makes Permanent

I had a tennis instructor who would often say that, "Practice does not make perfect, practice makes it permanent." She would go on to say that our "Muscles have a memory and, once trained, playing tennis will come as natural as breathing." The first few times we try anything new, it is stressful, challenging, and may feel awkward. Those feelings disappear if you persist and practice.

Anytime You Feel Confused, Dig Deeper

If something in your financial plan does not add up or make sense go back and check your data entry, as it could simply be a transposition error or typo. If all your data entry looks correct, then you need to make a decision to leave it the way it is or change your plan(s).

TRAP

Do not fall into the trap of estimating expenses. Make sure you are using accurate numbers and get actual prices to plug into your spreadsheet.

Showing a loss is not the end of the world just so long as the financial statements show a trend toward profitability. If you are showing nothing but a loss each and every year and that is not what you expected, either there is an error in your data entry or in the plan itself.

Be a Detective—Investigate

I can tell you from experience that it takes time to identify what is out of whack with a spreadsheet. As your financial plan grows, it becomes more complicated, and finding errors will require more investigation and persistence on your part.

When things do not add up, I have found that the best strategy is to review the appropriate chapter, review my work and, if I am still stuck, set it aside and come back to it on another day. Often what I could not see yesterday suddenly becomes clear today. You can always get some professional support from your accountant, business coach, or a friend. Remember, I can be reached at my Web site www.sbishere.com.

TIP

View the financial planning process as an opportunity to see how much you can learn and absorb. In the process you could quite literally discover an opportunity you had not previously considered.

The Purpose of Your Pro Forma Financial Plan

Your financial plan, market analysis, and marketing strategy are the most important sections of your business plan. The purpose of the pro forma financial plan is to show the financial resources that are required to carry out your intentions as laid out in the business plan.

TIP

Building your pro forma financial plan is a great way to test your ideas on paper for viability and feasibility.

The Pro Forma Financial Plan Must Answer Four Questions

There are four questions that your pro forma financial plan must answer:

1. Is the Business Viable?

The pro forma financial plan details how will you realize you goals and the levels of revenues and expenses required to achieve those goals.

2. How Much and When Will Financing Be Needed?

Following the time line of the business plan the cash flow portion of the pro forma plan reveals when cash shortfalls will occur, how much they will be, and the amount of financing required for the firm to remain current with its obligations.

3. What Type of Financing Is Required?

You need to give serious consideration in your business plan to how the firm will strike a balance in its capital structure using debt, equity, and the owner(s) investment and/or equity in the firm. Deciding on the makeup of your capital structure will be based upon the firm's ability to borrow, ability to repay, the amount of risk, and the quality of the assets.

TRAP

Avoid the trap of considering only your financing needs during the term of your business plan. Think beyond the typical three years and anticipate what type of financing will be needed in the long term. You need to leave yourself enough flexibility in your capital structure to meet the business's financial needs in the future.

Seed Capital *Seed capital* is the amount of capital needed to develop your concept, design and build a working prototype, and prove your business model. Most often seed capital is provided by the entrepreneur because of the high risk in investing in a business that is simply a figment of the imagination of the entrepreneur.

TIP

In some cases, a sophisticated investor can provide seed capital, especially if the opportunity for growth is significant. For example, an invention may require a lot of engineering, design, and development to get to the prototype stage.

Start-up Capital *Start-up capital* is the amount of money needed for the business to get up and running. Because of the short time it takes for a business to start up, these loans are short term and are repaid quickly. Most banks and financial institutions will not provide start-up capital because of the risk. If they do provide financing, it is usually because they have a personal guarantee or a direct lien on the entrepreneur's personal assets to guarantee repayment of the loan. Funding a start-up is usually the position taken by private investors or venture capital firms. You can get funding only when your business plan can confirm that your management team is made up of capable and experienced administrators, when a strong possibility of outstanding success is evident, when you can prove widespread acceptance of the business in the market, and when you can provide a large rate of return on their investment.

Working Capital *Working capital* is a form of short-term financing that is used to support the increase in your firm's need for inventory, accounts receivable, and cash. Building your inventory levels to meet seasonal demand, increasing the amount of sales sold on credit, and using the company's cash to increase capacity (i.e., staff, equipment, fixtures) are common uses for working capital financing. Most often banks and other financial institutions use the assets themselves to guarantee the business loan.

Long-Term or Growth Capital *Long-term or growth capital* is typically used when purchasing land or buying or building the physical plant or assets of the firm. This kind of capital is referred to as long term because the maturity of these loans typically exceeds the term of the business plan and will be used by the business over an extended period of years. To obtain this kind of financing requires a profitable business, the owner having sufficient equity to use in lieu of the standard 20–30 percent down payment required and adequate collateral to guarantee the loan.

TIP

In some areas of the United States there are SBA (Small Business Administration) funded programs that are administered by the Community Development Corporations (CDC), which will guarantee up to 90 percent financing. Similar programs in Canada are delivered through the Business Development Bank of Canada and use a Seed and Commercialization Funds Initiative.

4. Who Will Provide the Financing?

Two sources of financing exist: internal and external. Internal financing is the available cash within your company (residual profits) remaining after normal operations or increased investment of the existing owner(s) (from the purchase of additional shares). External financing comes from using debt or selling equity in your company to someone outside the company.

Research and Study Sample Financial Statements

Locate your financial statements if you have an existing business. As a start-up you can obtain sample financial statements based upon industry averages. In Canada you can get them online for free at www.strategis.ca (search for "benchmark your business"). For a U.S. business the best source I have found is at www.bizminer.com.

Both these sources will provide data from corporate tax returns that have compiled and averaged based on industry and business type. Whether you are in start-up mode or run an existing business, these reports will provide data in dollars and percentages that can be used to compare to your own projections.

Building Your Business Financial Plan

Creating a financial plan is a process. Figure 9.1 provides a flowchart to illustrate the steps involved with creating the pro forma financial statements for your business plan. The five steps start with gathering and organizing your financial information.

TIP

In Figure 9.1 notice that we start with a sales forecast, personnel plan, and then the cash budget for all other expenses. Do not confuse these with your financial statements (balance sheet, income statement, or cash flow projections). These are worksheets used for gathering the information needed to build your financial plan. If you are using my spreadsheet (www.sbishere.com), as you enter your information into the worksheets note that they are also linked to the appropriate area within the financial statements.

Gather, Organize, and Enter Data

To build your financial plan, you will need a spreadsheet software program. I use Excel by Microsoft. You can build your own or visit my Web site to download a sample that I built for this purpose. Go to www.sbishere.com, search for "companion spreadsheet," and then register (it is free). I will send you a password so that you can open the page where you can download the spreadsheet.

If you are going to build your own spreadsheets, set up a 14-column sheet (from left to right) like the one displayed in Figure 9.2.

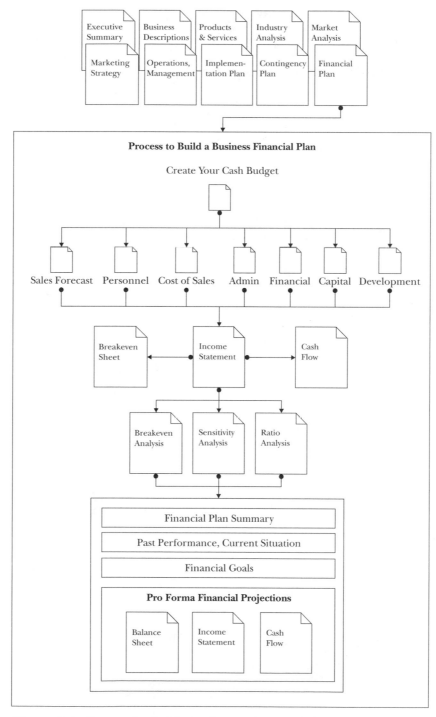

Figure 9.1 Process for Building a Business Financial Plan

	Month 1	Month 2	Month 3	Month 4	Month 5	Month 6	Month 7	Month 8	Month 9	Month 10	Month 11	Month 12	Total
Office Supplies	$102	$90	$66	$22	$150	$30	$50	$600	$180	$268	$775	$60	
Rent	$5,000	$5,000	$5,000	$5,000	$5,000	$5,000	$5,000	$5,000	$5,000	$5,000	$5,000	$5,000	
Travel	$500	$500	$500	$500	$500	$500	$500	$500	$500	$500	$500	$500	
Training			$300			$1,500			$290				
Mktg. & Promo													
Stationary		$540											
Brochures		$900											
Website	$1,500	$10	$10	$10	$10	$10	$10	$10	$10	$10	$10	$10	
Promotional Items				$400			$500				$600		
Advertising	$785	$785	$785	$785	$785	$785	$785	$785	$785	$785	$785	$785	
Dues & Subscriptions	$89						$89						
Consulting	$1,500	$1,500	$1,500	$1,500	$1,500	$1,500	$1,500	$1,500	$1,500	$1,500	$1,500	$1,500	
Accounting												$2,000	
Payroll	$4,888	$4,888	$4,888	$4,888	$4,888	$4,888	$4,888	$4,888	$4,888	$4,888	$4,888	$4,888	
Payroll Burden/Taxes	$2,478	$1,506	$1,645	$1,460	$1,414	$1,414	$1,645	$1,784	$1,876	$2,015	$2,108	$2,200	
Owners Draw	$5,000	$5,000	$5,000	$5,000	$5,000	$5,000	$5,000	$5,000	$5,000	$5,000	$5,000	$5,000	
Group Benefits	$1,483	$1,483	$1,483	$1,483	$1,483	$1,483	$1,483	$1,483	$1,483	$1,483	$1,483	$1,483	
Interest	800	800	800	800	800	800	800	800	800	800	800	800	
Bank Service Charges	100	100	100	100	100	100	100	100	100	100	100	100	
Licenses & Fees	$500												
Utilities & Telephone	2000	2000	2000	2000	2000	2000	2000	2000	2000	2000	2000	2000	
Other				500		500		500		500		500	
Repairs & Maintenance		500											
Insurance	10000												
Total Gen. & Admin	$24,225	$23,103	$22,077	$21,948	$21,630	$23,010	$22,350	$22,450	$22,413	$22,349	$23,549	$24,326	

Figure 9.2 General and Administrative Expenses (Operating Budget)

This is where you detail item by item and month by month the costs associated with running your business.

Cash Budget

The cash budget is created by combining budgets from seven areas:

1. The sales forecast
2. Personnel
3. Operating or cost of sales (COS)
4. Administration
5. Financial
6. Capital
7. Development

Sales Forecasts Using the Customer-omatic Method

Think of your business as a machine that manufactures customers. It looks a lot like a large funnel or a hopper where you load your marketing, sales, and customer service strategies into the top and what comes out the bottom is a customer and the resulting profit. Figure 9.3 illustrates the concept and is a good model for how a business actually operates.

TRAP

Avoid estimating revenues by assigning arbitrary gross dollars per month. In my experience this method is prone to exaggeration and inaccuracies. When a banker or investor asks you how you came up with your revenue projections, the last thing you want to say is that you just picked a number and plugged it in. In doing so, you will only expose your lack of experience and naïveté because there is no way to justify or explain your logic or approach about how you came up with your sales forecast. Plus it is too easy to overstate your revenues.

Using the Customer-omatic method to generate your sales forecast is the only method that mirrors how your business actually works. Generating your sales forecast using the Customer-omatic method is a simple three-step process.

Step 1: Start by listing the number of leads from existing and past customers and add your leads from new customers (leads you will generate

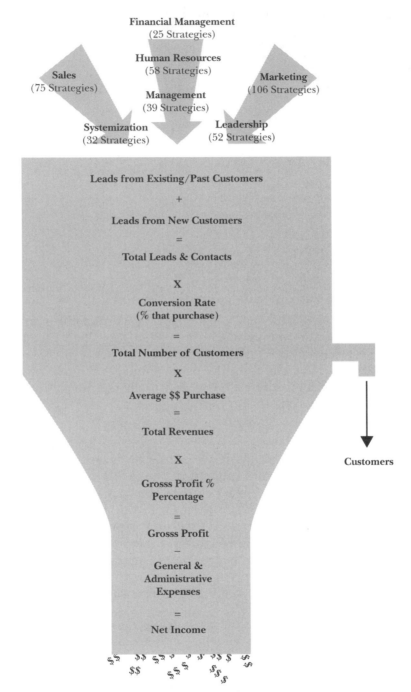

Figure 9.3   The Customer-omatic Machine

from marketing and sales activities). This gives you the *total leads* and contacts to whom you can sell your products or services.

Step 2: Next, multiply your number of total number of leads and contacts by the conversion percentage (percentage of those who actually buy), which will provide the *total number of customers.*

Step 3: The last step is to come up with your revenue number. Multiply the *total number of customers* by the average dollar amount per sale to get your revenue. See Figure 9.4 for an example.

Your sales forecast is an estimate of sales (in dollars, units, etc.) for a specified future period. Remember, your estimate is a guess or what you believe your gross revenues will be for a specific period. To help make your best guess, use the following questions to help you apply a critical eye to reviewing your sales forecast:

- Is there a seasonal demand that you will need to take into account? What selling strategies can you use to boost revenues in the off-season?

- Based upon the location of your business, how large is the local market?

- How much of a factor will competing with similar businesses in the area affect your sales volumes?

- What are the specific demographic, economic, and social trends in your market area and how will they affect attaining your revenue goals?

- What is your competitive advantage and how could that affect your sales forecast?

- How do you plan to compete in the market to sell your products or services? What competitive strategies do you plan to use (price, delivery, selection, service, unique proposition, loyalty, and advertising)?

- What market share is required to meet your sales forecast?

- What alternative strategy will you use to build revenues if you miss your sales forecast?

Projections for expense categories are easily quantified; creating accurate revenue projections requires insight, experience, or research. Experienced entrepreneurs may rely on their personal experience, whereas new business owners have to rely on solid research.

TIP

The best way to build your revenue projections is to mirror what actually happens in the business. Sales are made one customer at a time, and your sales projections can easily be configured to reflect this using the Customer-omatic method.

Sales Forecast Year 1   ABC Example Manufacturing Co.

Conversion Rate
50.00%

Average Unit Sale
$950

	Month 1	Month 2	Month 3	Month 4	Month 5	Month 6	Month 7	Month 8	Month 9	Month 10	Month 11	Month 12	Total
Leads													
Existing & Past Cust.	15	10	15	15	10	10	15	20	20	25	25	25	205
New Leads	200	100	110	90	90	90	110	120	130	140	150	160	1,490
Total Leads	215	110	125	105	100	100	125	140	150	165	175	185	1,695
Total No. New Cust.	107.5	55	62.5	52.5	50	50	62.5	70	75	82.5	87.5	92.5	$ 847.50
Total Revenue	$102,125	$52,250	$59,375	$49,875	$47,500	$47,500	$59,375	$66,500	$71,250	$78,375	$83,125	$87,875	$805,125

Figure 9.4   Sales Forecast—Sample Calculation

Alternative Sales Forecast Methods

There are two alternatives to the customer-omatic method for calculating the sales forecast:

1. *Actual sales results from past financial statements:* This process is used primarily for existing businesses. If you have access to the company accounting program, export the sales records to an Excel spreadsheet. Most current accounting programs allow exporting of data to a spreadsheet. I highly recommend using the most recent (last three years) statements to extract your data. If the information is available, I would go back as far as five years. The longer the period, the more data you have available to spot trends, cycles, and seasonal patterns.

2. *Sales per employee:* There are a number of sources where you can get sales data per employee, including the local library (see the reference librarian), bizminer.com (for the United States), or strategis.gc.ca (for Canada).

Personnel Plan

Identify the human resources needed to attain the objectives of your plan. Place new hires on the time line—when they will begin work as well as the amount they will be paid including bonuses, employer tax, and insurance. As a general guideline add 15 percent as payroll burden.

TIP

If your business is seasonal and you lay off staff during the off-season, explain how you plan to recruit and rebuild your staff levels.

General and Administrative Budget

Document all the costs associated with supporting your products and services. These will include office, travel, training, advertising and marketing, sales and administration compensation, and owner draws, dividends, and salaries.

- *Office:* Provide all the costs associated with maintaining your office including the salaries of administrative personnel. Take into account phone systems, long-distance service, fax, and Internet access costs. Include janitorial staff or out-sourced janitorial service if you use it.

- *Travel:* If you pay for or supplement the travel costs of your sales staff, include them here. Include travel costs of a company-owned vehicle and costs associated with traveling to training events.
- *Training:* Include costs of any staff meetings, sales training, and staff indoctrination and/or training.
- *Owner compensation package:* Include salaries, benefits including private insurance policies (death and disability), and retirement plans.
- *Sales staff:* This will be calculated by adding any draws, salaries, or commissions.
- *Marketing, advertising, and promotion:* Expect that this list will be fairly long. I like to organize these expenses in a calendar format. It serves a dual purpose because it can also be reused in the marketing strategy section. Review this list and mark the items you are planning to implement during the term of the business plan.
- *Print:* This includes letterhead, business cards, brochures, postcards, newsletter, envelopes. Remember to include newspapers, yellow pages, flyers, or catalogs you produce.
- *Promotional items:* Include T-shirts, jackets, caps, uniforms, key rings, golf balls, and client gifts.
- *Signs:* Include exterior, interior, and architectural signs.
- *Promotions:* Include on-hold messaging, press releases, TV and radio advertising, barter, contests, costs of free trials, gift certificates (include them as prepaid revenue if you sell them), trade-ins, point of sale, logo design and development, and layaway.
- *Events:* Include trade shows, demonstrations, closed-door sales events, customer appreciation.
- *Customer service:* Include follow-up surveys, call center, service contracts and delivery costs.
- *Internet:* Include Web site hosting, design, maintenance, search engine optimization, pay-per-click, e-zine distribution, and Internet marketing consulting fees.
- *Consulting:* Include any fees paid to consultants including coaching, marketing, or public relations services.
- *Rent:* Include rent for facilities and/or office.

Cost of Sales

Cost of sales is also known as the "operating budget." Its purpose is to keep track of everything required to put your product or service together. This

includes labor, utilities, materials, supplies, services, facilities, accounts payable, and inventory.

TIP

In a manufacturing business, materials refer to the raw materials that you need to make your products. In a services business, you can omit raw materials from your plan.

- *Labor:* Include all costs associated with maintaining an adequate workforce to achieve your objectives. Make sure to include health benefits, worker's compensation, vacation pay, uniforms, profit sharing, recruiting costs, and payroll taxes.
- *Utilities:* This category includes natural gas, hydro (electric) power, telephone, water, and waste management.
- *Services:* In a manufacturing setting include any outsourced or subcontracted services and quality control and management. Janitorial services are often overlooked as an expense.

  If you are a services business this section will likely be your single largest expense item because it reflects the staffing levels required to deliver the service. If you plan to use independent contractors, make sure to include the amounts you expect to be invoiced. Do not calculate payroll taxes on independent contractors because they are responsible for remitting their own taxes.
- *Facilities:* If you own real estate, make sure to include amounts for building and grounds maintenance.
- *Supplies:* In a services business your supplies could be just office related items or it could also include items that are part of the total service package that you purchase elsewhere

  Manufacturing companies should include additional shop supplies or items that become part of the finished product.
- *Inventory:* As a distributor you will purchase a product at a wholesale or jobber price that you resell to your customers. Therefore, an accurate tally of the costs and inventory levels you plan to maintain is required.
- *Raw materials:* Include the costs of the raw materials that are used to produce a component or the finished product. Break down the cost to a per finished unit. Make sure to include incoming shipping costs (if you pay the freight bill) as part of the calculation.

Financial Budget

Make a list of all the expenses you have for managing your assets, including loans, investments, interest, taxes, bookkeeping services, professional services, and accounts receivables.

- *Accounts receivable (AR):* This is money owed to you by customers who have purchased your goods or services on credit. It can also include loans or credit extended to employees. (AR is calculated on the income statement)

- *Bookkeeping:* If you outsource your bookkeeping and records management, this is the place to record the fees you pay for the service. Remember to include any software or supplies you've purchased.

- *Professional services:* The fees you pay your accountant, lawyer, consultants or business coach should be included.

- *Taxes:* Recording taxes paid or payable should include sales tax and payroll tax as well as any state or local taxes.

Capital Budget

This category of expenses covers funds for large expenditures and purchases. Assets to include are company vehicles, land, buildings, equipment, and computers.

TIP

Take into account replacement of obsolete equipment, facilities expansion, and major repairs during the term of your business plan.

Development Budget

Track the money set aside for developing new products or services. Include research, design, and other development costs related to the development of the company and its products or services. Think of intangible assets too, including intellectual property like the cost of registering a trademark, obtaining a patent, or documenting trade secrets or business processes.

- *New products or services:* Product, competitive, and customer research for things like focus groups, surveys, product design, cost of building a working prototype, and market testing.

- *Intellectual property:* legal, search and associated costs for developing and protecting your intellectual property. Can include trademarks, service marks, patents, and legal costs to protect trade secrets.
- *Expansion:* The costs to develop or build in a new area, including land, buildings, and legal costs. Include any money spent to develop new markets, including expenses like market research.

How to Build the Income Statement

The income statement displays your financial results of operating your business for a specific period. (See Fig. 9.5.) It records the company's sales, cost of sales, and other expenses that lead to the company's net profit.

Structure of the Income Statement

Between the sample income statement (Fig. 9.5), the sample available from my Web site (www.sbishere.com), and the instructions that follow, you should be able to build a valid income statement that calculates your net income. The calculation is quite simple:

Net Profit = Sales – Cost of Sales and General and Administrative Expenses.

TRAP

Do not get caught making promises, guarantees, or representations of your income statement to investors or bankers. Remember, the income statement is part of your pro forma financial statements, which are hypothetical financial projections based on a set of assumptions. When the assumptions change, so will the financial results.

Make a list of the important assumptions that could have an impact on the financial performance of the company.

Sales

Starting at the top of your spreadsheet, the first numbers you will list are the sales for the period. If you have separate divisions or specific product lines, list them separately so that those reading the statements can identify trends, calculate market mix, and see the results of your planned sales activity.

	Month 1	Month 2	Month 3	Month 4	Month 5	Month 6	Month 7	Month 8	Month 9	Month 10	Month 11	Month 12	Total
Revenue from Sales	$102,125	$52,250	$59,375	$49,875	$47,500	$47,500	$59,375	$66,500	$71,250	$78,375	$83,125	$87,875	$885,125
Loan Proceeds		$80,000											
Revenue from Investing													
Revenue from Equip Sold													
Total Income	$102,125	$132,250	$59,375	$49,875	$47,500	$47,500	$59,375	$66,500	$71,250	$78,375	$83,125	$87,875	
Expenses													
Cost of Goods Sold	$43,484	$22,248	$25,281	$21,236	$20,225	$20,225	$25,281	$28,315	$30,338	$33,371	$35,394	$37,416	$342,814
General & Admin	$24,225	$23,103	$22,077	$21,948	$21,630	$23,010	$22,350	$22,450	$22,413	$22,349	$23,549	$24,326	$273,430
Total Expenses	$67,709	$45,350	$47,359	$43,185	$41,855	$43,235	$47,632	$50,765	$52,750	$55,721	$58,943	$61,743	$616,244
Net Income	$34,417	$86,900	$12,017	$6,691	$5,645	$4,265	$11,744	$15,735	$18,500	$22,655	$24,183	$26,133	$268,882

Figure 9.5 Income Statement for ABC Example Manufacturing Company, December 31, 2005

Cost of Sales

Cost of sales immediately follows sales on the income statement. Cost of sales is any expense including raw materials, components, or other expenses that is part of the product being produced and sold.

For example, if you manufacture screwdrivers, the cost of the plastic to form the plastic handle, the steel shank, and the labor cost of the employees running the machines contribute to the final product and therefore become part of the cost of sales calculation. See Figure 9.6 for a sample cost of sales calculation.

The cost of sales calculation starts at the beginning of the period the statement covers, by counting the inventory of raw materials, parts, components, and all purchases made during the time period. At the end of the period the remaining inventory is deducted to arrive at the actual cost of the product inventory that was used.

Accurate cost of sales is the foundation for running a profitable firm because the final calculation of the selling price is based on the true cost of the final product.

TIP

To arrive at the true cost of your final product will require doing detailed calculations and estimates of all costs of production.

For example, including the depreciation attributable to the machines used in manufacturing, labor used, and even a percentage of the utilities used in the shop could be categorized as a cost of the final product. The more accurately you are able to attribute costs, the more accurately you can determine your true gross profit.

Gross Profit

Sales minus cost of sales gives you your gross profit. This is the amount left before you subtract selling, administrative, and other expenses.

$$\text{Sales} - \text{cost of sales} = \text{Gross profit}$$

The more accurate this number is, the more accurately you can predict the impact of increases or decreases in sales on your bottom line.

Cost of Sales   ABC Example Manufacturing Co.

	Raw Material Cost/Unit $150			Labor/Unit $185		Packaging/Unit $10		Inbound Freight $12		Sales Commissions 5.00%			
	Month 1	Month 2	Month 3	Month 4	Month 5	Month 6	Month 7	Month 8	Month 9	Month 10	Month 11	Month 12	Total
Raw Materials	$16,125	$8,250	$9,375	$7,875	$7,500	$7,500	$9,375	$10,500	$11,250	$12,375	$13,125	$13,875	$127,125
Labor	$19,888	$10,175	$11,563	$9,713	$9,250	$9,250	$11,563	$12,950	$13,875	$15,263	$16,188	$17,113	$156,788
Packaging	$1,075	$550	$625	$525	$500	$500	$625	$700	$750	$825	$875	$925	$8,475
Inbound Shipping	$1,290	$660	$750	$630	$600	$600	$750	$840	$900	$990	$1,050	$1,110	$10,170
Sales Comm.	$5,106	$2,613	$2,969	$2,494	$2,375	$2,375	$2,969	$3,325	$3,563	$3,919	$4,156	$4,394	$40,256
Total Cost of Sales	$43,484	$22,248	$25,281	$21,236	$20,225	$20,225	$25,281	$28,315	$30,338	$33,371	$35,394	$37,416	$342,814

Figure 9.6 Cost of Sales

144

Calculating Net Profit

Gross profit less selling, administrative, and other expenses gives you your net earnings or net profit before income taxes:

Gross profit – general and administrative expense
+ other (income/expense) = Net profit (net income)

Another way of calculating your net profit is:

Net profit = sales – all expenses (before taxes)

TIP

If you arc a C-corporation, this is your *earnings before interest and taxes* (EBIT). Other types of entities do not pay their own taxes and, therefore, income tax is not recorded.

Selling expenses and general and administrative expenses follow gross profit on the income statement.

General and administrative expenses (G & A), commonly referred to as overhead, is the amount that it would cost each month (or whatever the period) to keep the doors open regardless of the sales volume and is not directly associated with production.

As the business grows, you can expect to see your G & A expenses grow as you hire more staff and increase your marketing and sales spending. Generally your G & A expenses are considered fixed since items like rent, utilities, office payroll, professional fees, and other costs do not change often. Other income and expenses are those expenditures that are non-recurring.

Building Your Pro Forma Statement of Cash Flows

Pro forma statement of cash flows shows how you expect to see money move in and out of your company. The amount of cash left over at the end of the month can be used later, when you run a cash flow deficit. This shows how much you need to borrow to be able to pay your bills for the period.

TRAP

Do not get confused between profit and cash flow. It is not unusual to see cash flow deficits in a profitable company, especially if the business experiences strong seasonal fluctuations in business activity. You could have a profitable month but still run a cash-flow deficit as a result of purchasing inventory the month before that has now come due. Deficits in your pro forma cash flow are an indication of how much money you need to borrow to keep your accounts payables current.

How to Prepare Cash Flow Projections and Determine Required Financing

This section of your financial plan will help you determine how much money you will need to borrow to sustain operations (pay your bills on time). Your statement of cash flows records specific transactions that affect the amount of available cash and demonstrates how the cash will be used over a specific period of time. It will show when you have excess cash and when a deficit occurs.

Positive cash flow occurs when cash received exceeds debts that are due at the time. A deficit occurs when the debts that are payable within a specific period exceed your cash receipts. For a sample statement of cash flows, see Figure 9.7.

TIP

In writing your financial plan, I recommend using monthly cash flow projections for the first year and annual projections thereafter.

Cash In

The first entry on your income statement is your cash balance. This represents the cash that comes into the business as cash from sales and operating activity. If you have other sources of income from corporate-owned investments and financing activity, such as loan payments from money you loaned to others, include those cash amounts as well.

Cash Out

Cash outflow occurs when money moves out of the business to pay bills and employees and to make purchases. By now you should have your general and

Receivables 30 days 40.00% Receivables 60 days 60.00%

	Month 1	Month 2	Month 3	Month 4	Month 5	Month 6	Month 7	Month 8	Month 9	Month 10	Month 11	Month 12	Total
Beginning Cash Balance	$100,000	-$68,120	$4,881	$19,207	$19,163	$15,133	$4,293	-$11,350	-$25,965	-$34,240	-$41,101	-$45,843	
Cash In (income)													
Accounts Receivables Collection 30 days		$40,850	$20,900	$23,750	$19,950	$19,000	$19,000	$23,750	$26,600	$29,500	$31,350	$33,250	$286,900
Accounts Receivables Collection 60 days			$61,275	$31,350	$35,625	$29,925	$28,500	$28,500	$35,625	$39,900	$42,750	$47,025	$380,475
Loan Proceeds		$80,000											
Cash Sales & Receipts	$100,000												
Other													
Total Cash Inflows	$100,000	$120,850	$82,175	$55,100	$55,575	$48,925	$47,500	$52,250	$62,225	$63,400	$74,100	$80,275	
Available Cash	$100,000	$52,731	$87,056	$74,307	$74,738	$64,058	$51,793	$40,900	$36,260	$34,160	$33,000	$34,432	
Cash Out													
Raw Materials	$16,125	$8,250	$9,375	$7,875	$7,500	$7,500	$9,375	$10,500	$11,250	$12,375	$13,125	$13,875	$111,000
Production Labor	$19,888	$10,175	$11,563	$9,713	$9,250	$9,250	$11,563	$12,950	$13,875	$15,263	$16,188	$17,113	$136,900
Packaging	$1,075	$550	$625	$525	$500	$500	$625	$700	$750	$825	$1,050	$1,110	$7,400
Inbound Shipping	$1,290	$660	$750	$630	$600	$600	$750	$840	$900	$990	$875	$1,110	$8,880
Sales Commissions	$5,106	$2,613	$2,969	$2,494	$2,375	$2,375	$2,969	$3,325	$3,563	$3,919	$4,156	$4,394	$35,150
Office Supplies	$102	$90	$63	$22	$150	$30	$50	$600	$180	$268	$775	$60	$2,291
Rent	$5,000	$5,000	$5,000	$5,000	$5,000	$5,000	$5,000	$5,000	$5,000	$5,000	$5,000	$5,000	$55,000
Travel	$500	$500	$500	$500	$500	$500	$500	$500	$500	$500	$500	$500	$5,500
Training	$0	$0	$300	$0	$0	$1,500	$0	$0	$290	$0	$0	$0	$2,090
Mktg. & Promo													
Stationary	$0	$540	$0	$0	$0	$0	$0	$0	$0	$0	$0	$0	$540
Brochures	$0	$900	$0	$0	$0	$0	$0	$0	$0	$0	$0	$0	$900
Website	$1,500	$10	$10	$10	$10	$10	$10	$10	$10	$10	$10	$10	$110
Promotional Items	$0	$0	$0	$400	$0	$500	$500	$0	$0	$0	$600	$0	$1,500
Advertising	$785	$785	$785	$785	$785	$785	$785	$785	$785	$785	$785	$785	$8,635
Dues & Subscriptions													$0
Consulting	$1,500	$1,500	$1,500	$1,500	$1,500	$1,500	$1,500	$1,500	$1,500	$1,500	$1,500	$1,500	$16,500
Accounting													$2,000
Payroll	$4,888	$4,888	$4,888	$4,888	$4,888	$4,888	$4,888	$4,888	$4,888	$4,888	$4,888	$4,888	$53,768
Payroll Burden/Taxes	$2,478	$1,506	$1,645	$1,460	$1,414	$1,414	$1,645	$1,784	$1,876	$2,015	$2,108	$2,200	$19,067
Group Benefits	$1,483	$1,483	$1,483	$1,483	$1,483	$1,483	$1,483	$1,483	$1,483	$1,483	$1,483	$1,483	$16,315
Interest	$800	$800	$800	$800	$800	$800	$800	$800	$800	$800	$800	$800	$8,800
Bank Service Charges	$100	$100	$100	$100	$100	$100	$100	$100	$100	$100	$100	$100	$1,100
Licenses & Fees	$500	$500	$0	$0	$0	$0	$0	$0	$0	$0	$0	$0	$0
Utilities & Telephone	$2,000	$2,000	$2,000	$2,000	$2,000	$2,000	$2,000	$2,000	$2,000	$2,000	$2,000	$2,000	$22,000
Other	$0	$0	$0	$0	$0	$0	$0	$0	$0	$0	$0	$0	$0
Repairs & Maintenance	$10,000	$500	$0	$500	$0	$500	$500	$0	$0	$500	$500	$500	$3,000
Insurance	$785	$785	$785	$785	$785	$785	$785	$785	$785	$785	$785	$785	$8,635
Sub-Total	$75,120	$42,850	$44,359	$40,685	$38,855	$40,735	$44,543	$48,265	$49,750	$53,221	$55,943	$59,243	$518,446
Other Cash Outflows													
Capital Purchases	$5,000												
Building Construction	$65,000												
Decorating	$8,000												
Fixtures & Equipment	$10,000												
Install Fixtures & Equip.													
Remodeling													
Lease Payments													
Loan Principal	$5,000	$5,000	$5,000	$5,000	$5,000	$5,000	$5,000	$5,000	$5,000	$5,000	$5,000	$5,000	$40,000
Owner's Draw			$5,000	$5,000	$5,000	$5,000	$5,000	$5,000	$5,000	$5,000	$5,000	$5,000	$50,000
Accounts Payables (60 days)			$18,490	$9,460	$10,750	$9,030	$8,600	$8,600	$10,750	$12,040	$12,900	$14,190	$114,810
Other:													
Sub-Total	$93,000	$5,000	$23,490	$14,460	$20,750	$19,030	$18,600	$18,600	$20,750	$22,040	$22,900	$24,190	$204,810
Total Cash Outflows	$168,120	$47,850	$67,849	$55,145	$59,605	$59,765	$63,143	$66,865	$70,500	$75,261	$78,843	$83,433	$680,406
Ending Cash Balance	-$68,120	$4,881	$19,207	$19,163	$15,133	$4,293	-$11,350	-$25,965	-$34,240	-$41,101	-$45,843	-$49,001	

Figure 9.7 Statement of Cash Flows—ABC Example Manufacturing Company

administrative expenses spreadsheet complete. Include the amount(s) from the "total general and administrative expenses" into the "cash out" portion of the cash flow projection (Figure 9.7).

There are two types of cash outflows:

1. *Cash used by operating activities:* This is money you spend to do business. This is the non-cash, income-producing (or using) operating activities.

2. *Cash used by investing and financing activities:* This includes purchases of fixed assets and payments made on loans.

Calculating Net Cash Flow

To calculate your net cash flow, simply calculate the difference between cash in and cash out. When a negative number is displayed, this is the amount of financing you will need in that time period to meet the obligations of the business.

The Difference between Cash Flow and Profitability

Do not confuse profitability with a cash flow (positive or negative). There is a significant difference between cash flow and profit.

TIP

You can be profitable and yet have a negative cash position. It is very common for a new business to be in a negative cash flow position for a limited period of time.

Remember, cash flow is the change in your cash balance over a specific period of time. This results from the difference between the amount of bills you have to pay and how much cash you have collected from customers and have on hand. Remember, anything you buy on credit in one month is usually payable next month and needs to be included in your cash flow projections.

For example, when you're starting a business, you will most likely spend more money setting up the business than you would normally. This is because you have to purchase inventory and raw materials, pay annual insurance premiums, and make other expenditures which require that you either purchase in bulk or prepay.

Dealing with Negative Cash Flow Projections

Negative cash flow cash flow projections simply indicate how much money you will need to pay your bills on time. From a practical perspective your options are to arrange in advance with your bank to grant you a line of credit to cover the shortfall or negotiate deferred or longer payment terms with your suppliers for your start-up expenses or other special situations.

Balance Sheet

Your balance sheet depicts your company's financial condition at a specific moment in time. It identifies what your company owns and owes and what the company is worth. From an accounting perspective the formula is:

$$Assets = Liabilities + Equity$$

As a business owner, I like to think of it this way:

$$Equity = Assets - Liabilities$$

Everything the company owns (its assets) comes from the money you invested in the company and any money you borrowed, or from net profit that was left over and used to purchase something.

Structure of a Balance Sheet

Figure 9.8 shows a sample balance sheet.

Assets		Liabilities	
Cash	-$49,001	Current Liabilities	
		Accounts Payables	$12,470
Current Assets			
Accounts Receivables	-$667,375	Long-Term Liabilities	
Inventory	$60,675	Owner's Equity	-$603,171
Fixed Assets			
Equipment	$65,000		
Total		Total Liabilities	
Assets	-$590,701	and Owner's Equity	-$590,701

Figure 9.8 Balance Sheet

Assets

The order in which items appear on the balance sheet is based on a relatively simple concept. All asset listings start with the asset that is most easily "convertible" to cash, and proceeds to the assets that are hardest to convert to cash. Therefore, all balance sheets list cash as the first asset.

Often you will see a few assets listed as current assets. Current assets are assets that will most likely be converted into cash within one year. Therefore, assets like accounts receivable and inventory are typically listed under a subclass called "current assets."

The next class of assets is "fixed" assets; these include machinery, furniture, buildings, land, and so on. These are expenditures that were purchased for long-term use and are therefore not current assets. Since they are purchased for long-term use, the expense gets prorated over the estimated period that they will be used. This is called *depreciation*. For example, if you bought a computer for $1,000 and estimated that you would have it for five years, you would depreciate it at $200 per year.

TIP

Of course, there are many ways to depreciate assets, including allowable amounts by the IRS. See your accountant if you have detailed questions on depreciation.

Most balance sheets list the total expenditure on fixed assets with a separate line for accumulated depreciation, which is just a way of saying, "All of the depreciation taken up to this point." Then that figure is subtracted from the total to give the reader an idea of the residual value of fixed assets. My sample spreadsheet does not include depreciation because the business is a start-up and has not completed a full year of operation. Therefore, in the second year depreciation of assets will begin to accrue.

The last category of assets is "other assets," which can include many different items such as patents, copyrights, deposits, long-term notes receivables, and generally any other expenditure for a product or service that will be held for over one year and has a value.

Liabilities

Liabilities are obligations that the company owes, such as debts to suppliers or vendors. Just like the assets, these are listed in the order in which they will most likely "use" cash. Therefore, current liabilities are those that will be paid within one year. Current liabilities include trade accounts payable, payroll taxes payable, accruals for payroll and other expenses (if you are reporting on an accrual basis), short-term notes payable, and the current portion of your long-term debt that will be paid within a year.

The next category is long-term liabilities, which are those that will take more than a year to be paid. This would include notes to the bank, stockholders, and other lenders.

Equity

Equity includes the initial investment you made purchasing company stock, as well as any other shares purchased by the company by way of a treasury stock. Also included in equity is an account called "retained earnings." It is the portion of net income that was reinvested or retained by the business rather than being paid out as dividends to the owners. Another way to look at it is the total accumulated net profits of the company since its inception.

Putting Your Balance Sheet Together

The purpose of the balance sheet is to show the financial condition of the business, which includes a summary of the assets, liabilities, and owner's equity.

Calculating the Value of Your Assets

If you followed my instructions, you should be able to pull together all the information you need for your balance sheet from your cash flow statement:

- *Cash:* Insert the final cash number from your pro forma cash flow statement on the first line of your balance sheet under "assets."

- *Accounts receivable:* This also comes from your pro forma cash flow statement.

- *Inventory:* You can calculate this by subtracting the beginning and closing inventory number from your pro forma cash flow statement.

- *Prepaid expenses:* The unused portion of a prepaid expense would be included here.

- *Equipment, land, buildings:* These are long-term assets.

Calculating Your Liabilities (How Much You Owe)

Liabilities represent the money you owe suppliers, employees, and the IRS that have yet to be paid.

- *Current liabilities:* Under the heading of current liabilities include your accounts payables (trade debts). These are debts that will be paid within the year.

- *Long-term liabilities:* Include any debt that will still be outstanding after one year.

Calculate Your Equity

In a start-up situation your equity will show up as a negative number. This is the amount of financing you will require. For owner's equity and retained earnings, subtract total liabilities from total assets. This will provide you with the amount of equity you have in the business.

Using the Balance Sheet to Determine Profit or Shortfall

Working on building your pro forma balance sheet will show you how much external financing you will require. Take the projected results from the operating activities of the business (taken from the income statement) including profit, purchase of assets, and any additional debt incurred, and, using the following simple formula, estimate excess profit or shortfall:

$$\text{Equity} = \text{Assets} - \text{Liabilities}$$

TRAP

A shortfall can happen quite easily as sales increase. To continue to grow, the company will need to increase its asset base in order to make additional purchases (inventory, equipment, etc.), and, without adequate internal cash to fund the purchases, the money will have to be borrowed.

Breakeven Analysis

The breakeven analysis depends on four specific variables:

1. The fixed production costs for a product.
2. The variable production costs for a product.
3. The product's unit price.
4. The product's expected unit sales (sometimes called projected sales).

Variable Unit Cost	$170.00	Total Variable Costs	85000
Fixed Cost	$14,000.00	Total all costs	99000
Expected Unit Sales	500	Total Revenue	$200,000.00
Price Per Unit	$400.00	Total Profit	$101,000.00
Profit/Unit	$230.00		
Number of Units to Break Even	**61**		

Figure 9.9   Sample Breakeven Analysis

The breakeven calculation is the number of units that must be sold in order to produce a profit of zero (but recover all related costs). See Figure 9.9 for a sample breakeven analysis.

$$\text{Breakeven} = \text{Fixed cost}/(\text{unit price} \times \text{variable unit cost})$$

You can download a free copy of my breakeven analysis spreadsheet at www.sbishere.com.

Understanding Breakeven

While your breakeven can vary from month to month, this tool can be used to calculate the sales volume required to recover the total variable and fixed costs associated with producing your product or service.

After you reach your breakeven point, you begin to earn profit. This tool is a great aid when you're trying to make strategic decisions, including setting price levels and determining the most favorable combination of fixed and variable costs.

TIP

Notice that each time you change a parameter in the breakeven analysis, the breakeven unit volume changes, and so does your risk.

Sensitivity Analysis

The purpose of the sensitivity analysis is to gauge the sensitivity of the firm to changes in sales and expenses. This will allow you to see what happens to the financial health of the business when sales drop or costs increase.

What I like to do is create at least three different scenarios. Each scenario uses different assumptions, for example:

1. Sales drop by 10 percent, and costs increase by 10 percent. In this scenario I purposely lower sales by 10 percent and increase costs by 10 percent across the board. If I cannot make a small profit using these assumptions, then the business is quite vulnerable to fluctuations in economic conditions. In a case like this I would review my expenses and see where I could cut costs to provide a little more room to absorb a significant shift in the firm's financial structure.

2. Sales remain the same, and costs increase by 20 percent. This one is similar to the first scenario except that costs have increased a lot more and revenues (sales) have remained the same. Again, this is a quick way to check how delicate my company financial situation is to major increases in costs.

3. Sales increase by 20 percent, and costs increase by 10 percent. In a perfect world I am able to increase sales to offset any increases in my costs of doing business.

You can change these numbers to suit your view of the economic climate, industry trends, and your management skills.

Ratio Analysis—Understanding Your Financial Ratios

Your banker will use financial ratios to make a lending decision. You want to make sure that you understand what your ratios mean. That way, if your ratios in your financial plan are a bit off, you can explain why this is the case.

Liquidity Ratios

Liquidity ratios measure the company's capacity to pay its debts as they come due. Liquidity ratios include the current ratio and quick ratio.

Current Ratio

The current ratio is a way of measuring liquidity of your business:

Calculation Current assets divided by current liabilities.

What It Means A company with a 1:1 current ratio means that the company has $1.00 in current assets to cover each $1.00 in current liabilities.

Look for a current ratio above 1:1 and as close to 2:1 as possible. Another way to look at this is if you had a 2:1 current ratio in any given month, this would mean that you would have an extra month of cash (or assets) to pay the bills.

One problem with the current ratio is that it ignores the timing of cash received and paid out. For example, if all the bills are due this week and inventory is the only current asset but won't be sold until the end of the month, the current ratio tells very little about the company's ability to survive.

Quick Ratio

This is the ratio between all assets that are quickly convertible into cash and all current liabilities. It specifically excludes inventory.

Calculation Current assets less inventory divided by current liabilities.

What It Means The quick ratio indicates the extent to which you could pay current liabilities without relying on the sale of inventory or how quickly you can pay your bills. Generally, a ratio of 1:1 is good and indicates that you don't have to rely on the sale of inventory to pay the bills.

Although this ratio is a little better than the current ratio, the quick ratio still ignores the timing of receipts and payments.

Safety Ratios

Safety ratios are an indicator of the business's vulnerability to risk. These are the ratios often used by creditors to determine the ability of the business to repay loans. There are two kinds of safety ratios you should include in your financial plan.

Debt to Equity Ratio

The debt to equity ratio shows the ratio between capital invested by the owners and the funds provided by lenders.

Calculation Total liabilities divided by total equity (loans to shareholders are treated as equity).

What It Means This makes a comparison of how much of the business was financed through debt and how much was financed through equity. For this calculation it is common practice to include loans from owners in equity rather than in debt.

TIP

From a lender's viewpoint, the higher the ratio, the greater the risk to a present or future creditor. The ideal is to maintain a debt to equity ratio in the range of 1:1 to 4:1.

TIP

Most lenders have credit guidelines and limits for the debt to equity ratio. For example, a ratio of 2:1 is commonly used as the upper limit for many small business loans.

TRAP

Too much debt can put your business at risk, and too little debt may mean you are not realizing the full potential of your business, which can actually hurt your overall profitability. This is particularly true for larger companies where shareholders want a higher reward (dividend rate) than lenders (interest rate). If you think that you might be in this situation, talk to your accountant or financial adviser.

Debt Coverage Ratio

The debt coverage ratio indicates how well your cash flow covers debt and the capacity of the business to take on additional debt.

Calculation   Earnings before interest, taxes, depreciation, and amortization (EBITDA) divided by the current portion of debt + interest.

What It Means   The debt coverage ratio shows how much of your cash profits are available to repay debt. Lenders look at this ratio to determine whether there is adequate cash to make loan payments. Look for a number above 1.

Profitability Ratios

The ratios in this section measure the ability of the business to make a profit.

Sales Growth Ratio

The sales growth ratio is the percentage increase (or decrease) in sales between two time periods.

Calculation (Current period sales × prior period sales) divided by prior period sales.

What It Means Ideally you want to show a steady increase in sales. If overall costs and inflation are on the rise, then you should watch for a related increase in your sales. If you do not see this correlation, then this is an indicator that your selling prices are not keeping up with your costs.

COGS to Sales

The cost of goods sold (COGS) to sales ratio indicates the percentage of sales used to pay for expenses, which vary directly with sales.

Calculation Cost of goods sold divided by sales.

What It Means Look for a stable ratio as an indicator that the company is controlling its gross margins. Compare your business to others in the same industry to see if your business is controlling production costs.

Gross Profit Margin

The gross profit margin ratio is an indicator of how much profit is earned on your products without considering selling and administration costs.

Calculation Gross profit divided by sales.

What It Means Compare your business to others in the same industry to see if your business is operating as profitably as it should be. Look at the trend from month to month. Is it staying the same? Improving? Deteriorating? Is there enough gross profit in the business to cover your operating costs? Is there a positive gross margin on all your products?

Sales, General, and Administrative Costs to Sales Ratio

The sales, general, and administrative costs to sales ratio represents the percentage of selling, general, and administrative costs when compared to sales.

Calculation General and administrative expenses divided by sales.

What It Means Look for a steady or decreasing percentage indicating that the company is controlling its overhead expenses.

Net Profit Margin

The net profit margin ratio shows how much profit comes from every dollar of sales.

Calculation Net income divided by sales.

What It Means Compare your results to other businesses in the same industry to see if your business is operating as profitably as it should be. Look at the trend from month to month. Is it staying the same? Improving? Deteriorating? Are you generating enough sales to leave an acceptable profit? The trend from month to month can show how well you are managing your operating or overhead costs.

Return on Equity Ratio

The return on equity ratio determines the rate of return on your investment in the business. For an owner or shareholder this is one of the most important ratios because it shows the hard facts about the business—are you making enough of a profit to compensate you for the risk of being in business?

Calculation Net income divided by total equity.

What It Means Compare the return on equity to other investment alternatives, such as a savings account, stocks, or bonds. Compare your ratio to other businesses in the same or a similar industry.

Return on Assets

Return on assets (ROA) is considered a measure of how effectively assets are used to generate a return. (This ratio is not very useful for most businesses.)

Calculation Net income divided by total assets.

What It Means ROA shows the amount of income for every dollar tied up in assets. Year-to-year trends may be an indicator, but watch out for changes in the total asset figure as you depreciate your assets (a decrease or increase in the denominator can effect the ratio and doesn't necessarily mean the business is improving or declining).

Owner's Discretionary Profit Dollars

The owner's discretionary profit dollars are the amount of income generated by the company that is available for the owner.

Calculation Officer salaries + net income + income tax.

What It Means Obviously, we want this to be as high a number as possible to provide ownership with ample dollars as well as ample opportunities.

Owner's Discretionary Profit Percentage

The owner's discretionary profit percentage is the percentage of profits in relation to sales before owner compensation or income taxes are paid.

Calculation (Officer salaries + net income + income tax) divided by sales.

What It Means Look for steady or increasing percentages from year to year. The company should be able to pay the owner as well as produce a profit to continue operations.

Efficiency Ratios

Efficiency ratios can also be called asset management ratios and are an indicator of how efficiently the company manages its assets.

Days in Receivables

Days in receivables is a calculation that shows the average number of days it takes to collect your accounts receivable (number of days of sales in receivables).

Calculation (Accounts receivable divided by sales) × 360.

What It Means Look for trends that indicate a change in your customers' payment habits. Compare the calculated days in receivables to your stated terms. Compare to industry standards. Review an aging of receivables and be familiar with your customers' payment habits and watch for any changes that might indicate a problem.

Accounts Receivable Turnover

The accounts receivable turnover is the number of times that trade receivables turn over or paid during the year.

Calculation Sales divided by accounts receivable.

What It Means The higher the turnover (ratio), the shorter the time between sales and the collection of cash. Compare to industry standards.

Days in Accounts Payable

Days in accounts payable is a calculation that shows the average length of time your trade payables are outstanding before they are paid (number of days sales at cost in payables).

Calculation (Accounts payable divided by cost of goods sold) $\times$ 360.

What It Means Look for trends that indicate a change in your payment habits. Compare the calculated days in payables to the terms offered by your suppliers. Compare to industry standards. Review an aging of payables and be familiar with the terms offered by your suppliers.

Accounts Payable Turnover

The accounts payable turnover is the number of times trade payables turn over during the year.

Calculation Cost of goods sold divided by accounts payable.

What It Means The higher the turnover, the shorter the time between purchase and payment. A low turnover may indicate that there is a shortage of cash to pay your bills or some other reason for a delay in payment.

Days in Inventory

Days in inventory is a calculation that shows the average number of days it will take to sell your inventory.

Calculation (Inventory divided by cost of goods sold) $\times$ 360.

What It Means Look for trends that indicate a change in your inventory levels. Compare the calculated days in inventory to your inventory cycle. Compare to industry standards.

Inventory Turnover

Inventory turnover is a calculation that shows the number of times you turn over (or sell, then replenish) inventory during the year.

Calculation Cost of goods sold divided by inventory.

What It Means Generally, a high inventory turnover is an indicator of good inventory management. But a high ratio can also mean there is a shortage of inventory. A low turnover may indicate overstocking or obsolete inventory. Compare to industry standards.

Sales to Total Assets Ratio

The sales to total assets ratio indicates how efficiently your business generates sales on each dollar of assets.

Calculation Sales divided by total assets.

What It Means This ratio is a volume indicator that can be used to measure the efficiency of your business from year to year.

Sales Per Employee

The sales per employee calculation yields the dollar amount of sales for each full-time employee.

Calculation Sales divided by number of employees.

What It Means You want to maximize your sales per employee. This shows the amount of sales generated per employee. Compare your number to industry standards.

Gross Margin Return on Fixed Assets

The gross margin return on fixed assets ratio indicates how efficiently you used your fixed assets.

Calculation Gross profit divided by net fixed assets.

What It Means This shows the amount of gross profit dollars generated by every dollar of fixed assets (net of depreciation). Caution: major fixed-asset purchases can appear to have a negative impact on a current year.

Formatting the Financial Plan

Use Excel or another spreadsheet software program to format your financial plan.

Financial Plan Summary

Create a brief overview for readers so they can understand the thrust of the initiative. You should include the type and amount of financing required.

Give readers who are busy an executive summary of what you are trying to accomplish. When they want more detail, they will go inside the plan. Explain how your financial plan is going to improve the effectiveness, efficiency, and operations of the business. Connect the dots between your cash management philosophy and specific improvements that will stimulate growth.

Past Performance and Current Situation

Provide the readers of your business plan with a snapshot of your current situation and past performance to provide context to your financial plan. Include any significant changes in your financial position, major market or competitive changes, and other issues that impacted the business.

For Existing Business Most owners have developed a feel for how the company is doing. Remember, this is your subjective perception and should play a part only in planning ongoing operations. For example, you may feel that you are not being compensated at a level that is appropriate when compared to the amount of time you put in. A plan that calls for you to continue working long hours must establish, in your mind, that the benefits derived from implementing the plan are worth the effort. This is where a financial plan begins to make sense because it will allow you to quantify the results of your efforts in operating the business.

For an existing business include at least the past three years' financial statements (in the appendix of the business plan) plus a selection of graphs, charts, key performance indicators (KPIs), and financial ratios that show where the business has been, the current position, and where the business is headed. Restrict your comments to the financial portion of the business because the reader can get the rest of the information within the business plan.

For New Businesses If you are not currently operating, you do not have a history to examine or talk about. However, you likely have a general working knowledge of the type of operation that you are considering. If you are striking out on your own in the same line of products or services that you dealt with for your former employer, what you learned as an employee will help you to assemble your financial picture.

TIP

If time is short, you could use an industry balance sheet and income statement as a comparative sample (available from www.bizminer.com). However, if you do have the time, doing a complete set of financial projections will only help solidify your financing request. Plus you get the added benefit of using them as a management and administrative tool.

When starting a new venture you could use an industry sample from bizminer.com, but the best option is to always build your own financial plan. I suggest that a start-up include both because the industry sample will provide you with guidelines that will provide you with a starting place in preparing your own plan. These samples will provide you with averages in dollar amounts and percentages and provide readers of your plan with something to compare your projections and plans to. Finally, including an industry sample will instill confidence in the reader because it demonstrates the depth or research and effort you have invested in preparing the business plan.

TRAP

A business plan without financial projections is a dream. Do not get caught in the trap of writing a business plan without mirroring your plans in financial form with no way for the reader to know whether or not you will be profitable. In my experience this is the one of biggest mistakes businesses that go bankrupt have in common—no financial plan.

Financial Goals

To maintain viability, a business needs to be meeting its financial objectives. The financial goals set the benchmark that will be used to measure the business's progress and make sure it remains viable.

The financial goals to include are the costs associated with carrying out planned activities (marketing campaigns, expansion, new product lines, etc.), rate of return for the owners of the business, debt obligations, how you will meet out-of-pocket expenses and replacement of computer, equipment, or real estate.

Profit Margins Be clear about the gross and net profit margins you expect to achieve. This is where a well-prepared pro forma financial statement comes in handy as a planning tool. Once you have your data entered, you can change the variables, which will allow you to experiment with different scenarios before you publish your expected profit margins.

Debt State the amount of financing you will need, interest rate, terms, and repayment plan.

Equipment, Fixtures, and Real Estate Make sure to include a budget for maintenance, repair, and replacement of obsolete or worn equipment, and for real estate for the time period covered by the business plan.

Return on Investment for the Owners Document any management fees, salaries, or dividends that will be paid to the owners.

Implementation Costs   Include expenditures that will be required to implement your plans, including advertising, marketing, training, and any other items.

Unexpected Expenditures   Include considerations of how you will meet out-of-pocket expenses and replace computers, equipment, and other fixed assets as they come to the end of their life cycle.

Realty Check—Revise and Make Final Adjustments

In my experience it is always a good practice to take a short break away from the financial planning process. It will give your mind a break and will allow you to look at the spreadsheets from a fresh perspective.

Pro forma from a business planning perspective assumes that the events have already happened. Pro forma statements follow the same format and style as regular financial statements; this allows for easy comparison to past financial statements or an industry sample.

TIP

You can modify certain items in your cash budget and sales forecast and then use the ratios analysis (in this chapter) as a tool to examine the impact of the changes on the viability of the plan. This will allow you to make necessary changes that will improve your chances of getting a business loan.

You can then print your financial statements and take them to your accountant to review and check your work.

Review Your Work with an Accountant

One of the best ways to get a reality check is to get your CPA to check your work and help you understand what your projections mean. Taking the time to have your accountant review your work and your sensitivity analysis will increase your understanding of your financial plan and increase your confidence in it.

If there are errors, your accountant will point them out, and then you can make the corrections. Further, he or she can explain the impact of the various scenarios in your sensitivity analysis. Another good thing to review with your accountant is your financial ratios.

TRAP

Do not skip reviewing your projections with your accountant. He or she may find mistakes. If you skip a formal review and errors are found, you may be found liable by investors or shareholders if the business is in distress or fails, because it could appear that your material misstatement was the underlying cause of the business failing.

After conducting your informal review and meeting with your accountant, make the final changes and then print the income statement, balance sheet, and cash flow statement.

TIP

Remember to revise your business plan to reflect any changes!

Financial Planning Tools

Probably the greatest challenge my clients have in completing a business plan is the financial section. This book was written to provide you with a basic working knowledge so that you will be able to prepare, read, and interpret your financial statements.

If you would like to speed the process of creating your financial projections, I recommend purchasing Business Plan Pro (https://secure.paloalto.com/store/checkout_line.cfm?affiliate=sbisheresm&item=bpp5st) because it has amazing financial tools. It is worth buying just for the integrated financial tools.

All you do is input your income and expense projections month by month, your personnel plan, and so on, and Business Plan Pro assembles the financial statements including sales forecast, personnel plan, breakeven analysis, income statement, pro forma cash flow projections, and a balance sheet.

The other powerful part of the tool is the ratios analysis. It analyzes your financial data and creates a table that illustrates the various financial ratios. Ratio analysis is what banks and investors will use to judge the viability of your business plan.

Conclusion

If your knowledge of financial statements is nonexistent, you might feel intimidated by this task. Do not worry.

The financial side of your business is not boring; it is exciting! I hope that the information provided here is helpful and empowering. I will be dedicating a section on my Web site to answering your questions and posting updates and clarification. Visit www.sbishere.com if you have any questions, beefs, or bouquets. I answer all inquiries.

Sample Pro Forma Financial Plan

Following is the pro forma financial plan section of the business plan. The complete business plan can be found in Appendix A.

Pro Forma Financial Plan

Finance Request For the first year of operation Joe's Trucking Systems, Inc., will require a $100,000 line of credit based upon the following:

- Schedule of start-up costs.
- Forecasted financial statements—year ended September 30, 20XX.

See the attached forecasted financial statements for the year ended September 30, 20XX, as prepared by Everyday Accounting.

Schedule of Start-Up Costs

Start-Up Costs

Telephone system	$ 1,250.00
Telephone connection	447.00
Insurance	5,950.00
Prorate/authorities	7,695.90
Fuel (U.S. prepaid)	5,000.00
Driver testing	750.00
Benefits	700.00
Rent	1,300.00
Printing	1,200.00
Office supplies	300.00
Business consultant	3,500.00
Web page, domain name, etc.	450.00
Decals on units	1,750.00
Parts stock inventory	2,500.00
Total	$32,792.90

(Continued)

General and Administrative Expenses (Operating Budget)

	Month 1	Month 2	Month 3	Month 4	Month 5	Month 6	Month 7	Month 8	Month 9	Month 10	Month 11	Month 12	Total
Office Supplies	$102	$90	$66	$22	$150	$30	$50	$600	$180	$268	$775	$60	
Rent	$5,000	$5,000	$5,000	$5,000	$5,000	$5,000	$5,000	$5,000	$5,000	$5,000	$5,000	$5,000	
Travel	$500	$500	$500	$500	$500	$500	$500	$500	$500	$500	$500	$500	
Training									$290				
Mktg. & Promo			$300			$1,500							
Stationary		$540											
Brochures		$900											
Website	$1,500	$10	$10	$10	$10	$10	$10	$10	$10	$10	$10	$10	
Promotional Items				$400			$500				$600		
Advertising	$785	$785	$785	$785	$785	$785	$785	$785	$785	$785	$785	$785	
Dues & Subscriptions	$89						$89						
Consulting	$1,500	$1,500	$1,500	$1,500	$1,500	$1,500	$1,500	$1,500	$1,500	$1,500	$1,500	$1,500	
Accounting												$2,000	
Payroll	$4,888	$4,888	$4,888	$4,888	$4,888	$4,888	$4,888	$4,888	$4,888	$4,888	$4,888	$4,888	
Payroll Burden/Taxes	$2,478	$1,506	$1,645	$1,460	$1,414	$1,414	$1,645	$1,784	$1,876	$2,015	$2,108	$2,200	
Owners Draw	$5,000	$5,000	$5,000	$5,000	$5,000	$5,000	$5,000	$5,000	$5,000	$5,000	$5,000	$5,000	
Group Benefits	$1,483	$1,483	$1,483	$1,483	$1,483	$1,483	$1,483	$1,483	$1,483	$1,483	$1,483	$1,483	
Interest	800	800	800	800	800	800	800	800	800	800	800	800	
Bank Service Charges	100	100	100	100	100	100	100	100	100	100	100	100	
Licenses & Fees	$500												
Utilities & Telephone	2000	2000	2000	2000	2000	2000	2000	2000	2000	2000	2000	2000	
Other													
Repairs & Maintenance		500		500		500		500		500		500	
Insurance	10000												
Total Gen. & Admin	$24,225	$23,103	$22,077	$21,943	$21,630	$23,010	$22,350	$22,450	$22,413	$22,349	$23,549	$24,326	

Sales Forecast Year 1 — ABC Example Manufacturing Co.

Conversion Rate 50.00%
Average Unit Sale $950

	Month 1	Month 2	Month 3	Month 4	Month 5	Month 6	Month 7	Month 8	Month 9	Month 10	Month 11	Month 12	Total
Leads													
Existing & Past Cust.	15	10	15	15	10	10	15	20	20	25	25	25	205
New Leads	200	100	110	90	90	90	110	120	130	140	150	160	1,490
Total Leads	215	110	125	105	100	100	125	140	150	165	175	185	1,695
Total No. New Cust.	107.5	55	62.5	52.5	50	50	62.5	70	75	82.5	87.5	92.5	847.50
Total Revenue	$102,125	$52,250	$59,375	$49,875	$47,500	$47,500	$59,375	$66,500	$71,250	$78,375	$83,125	$87,875	$805,125

Income Statement for ABC Example Manufacturing Co.
31-Dec-05

	Month 1	Month 2	Month 3	Month 4	Month 5	Month 6	Month 7	Month 8	Month 9	Month 10	Month 11	Month 12	Total
Revenue from Sales	$102,125	$52,250	$59,375	$49,875	$47,500	$47,500	$59,375	$66,500	$71,250	$78,375	$83,125	$87,875	
Loan Proceeds													
Revenue from Investing		$80,000											
Revenue from Equip Sold													
Total Income	$102,125	$132,250	$59,375	$49,875	$47,500	$47,500	$59,375	$66,500	$71,250	$78,375	$83,125	$87,875	$885,125
Expenses													
Cost of Goods Sold	$43,484	$22,248	$25,281	$21,236	$20,225	$20,225	$25,281	$28,315	$30,338	$33,371	$35,394	$37,416	$342,814
General & Admin	$24,225	$23,103	$22,077	$21,948	$21,630	$23,010	$22,350	$22,450	$22,413	$22,349	$23,549	$24,326	$273,430
Total Expenses	$67,709	$45,350	$47,359	$43,185	$41,855	$43,235	$47,632	$50,765	$52,750	$55,721	$58,943	$61,743	$616,244
Net Income	$34,417	$86,900	$12,017	$6,691	$5,645	$4,265	$11,744	$15,735	$18,500	$22,655	$24,183	$26,133	$268,882

Cost of Sales
ABC Example Manufacturing Co.

	Raw Material Cost/Unit $150	Labor/Unit $185	Packaging/Unit $10	Inbound Freight $12	Sales Commissions 5.00%								
	Month 1	Month 2	Month 3	Month 4	Month 5	Month 6	Month 7	Month 8	Month 9	Month 10	Month 11	Month 12	Total
Raw Materials	$16,125	$8,250	$9,375	$7,875	$7,500	$7,500	$9,375	$10,500	$11,250	$12,375	$13,125	$13,875	$127,125
Labor	$19,888	$10,175	$11,563	$9,713	$9,250	$9,250	$11,563	$12,950	$13,875	$15,263	$16,188	$17,113	$156,788
Packaging	$1,075	$550	$625	$525	$500	$500	$625	$700	$750	$825	$875	$925	$8,475
Inbound Shipping	$1,290	$660	$750	$630	$600	$600	$750	$840	$900	$990	$1,050	$1,110	$10,170
Sales Comm.	$5,106	$2,613	$2,969	$2,494	$2,375	$2,375	$2,969	$3,325	$3,563	$3,919	$4,156	$4,394	$40,256
Total Cost of Sales	$43,484	$22,248	$25,281	$21,236	$20,225	$20,225	$25,281	$28,315	$30,338	$33,371	$35,394	$37,416	$342,814

Statement of Cash Flows - ABC Example Manufacturing Co

Receivables 30 days 40.00%
Receivables 60 days 60.00%

	Month 1	Month 2	Month 3	Month 4	Month 5	Month 6	Month 7	Month 8	Month 9	Month 10	Month 11	Month 12	Total
Beginning Cash Balance	$100,000	-$68,120	$4,881	$19,207	$19,163	$15,133	$4,293	-$11,350	-$25,965	-$34,240	-$41,101	-$45,843	
Cash In (income)													
Accounts Receivables Collection 30 days		$40,850	$20,900	$23,750	$19,950	$19,000	$19,000	$23,750	$26,600	$28,500	$31,350	$33,250	$286,900
Accounts Receivables Collection 60 days			$61,275	$31,350	$35,625	$29,925	$28,500	$28,500	$35,625	$39,900	$42,750	$47,025	$380,475
Loan Proceeds		$80,000											
Cash Sales & Receipts													
Other													
Total Cash Inflows	$100,000	$120,850	$82,175	$55,100	$55,575	$48,925	$47,500	$52,250	$62,225	$68,400	$74,100	$80,275	
Available Cash	$100,000	$52,731	$87,056	$74,307	$74,738	$64,058	$51,793	$40,900	$36,260	$34,160	$33,000	$34,432	
Cash Out													
Raw Materials	$16,125	$8,250	$9,375	$7,875	$7,500	$7,500	$9,375	$10,500	$11,250	$12,375	$13,125	$13,875	$111,000
Production Labor	$19,888	$10,175	$11,563	$9,713	$9,250	$9,250	$11,563	$12,950	$13,875	$15,263	$16,188	$17,113	$136,900
Packaging	$1,075	$550	$625	$525	$500	$500	$625	$700	$750	$825	$875	$925	$7,400
Inbound Shipping	$1,290	$660	$750	$630	$600	$600	$750	$840	$900	$990	$1,050	$1,110	$8,880
Sales Commissions	$5,106	$2,613	$2,969	$2,494	$2,375	$2,375	$2,969	$3,325	$3,563	$3,919	$4,156	$4,394	$35,150
Office Supplies	$102	$90	$66	$22	$150	$30	$50	$600	$180	$268	$775	$60	$2,291
Rent	$5,000	$5,000	$5,000	$5,000	$5,000	$5,000	$5,000	$5,000	$5,000	$5,000	$5,000	$5,000	$55,000
Travel	$500	$500	$500	$500	$500	$500	$500	$500	$500	$500	$500	$500	$5,500
Training	$0		$300						$290				$2,090
Mktg. & Promo													$0
Stationary		$540											$540
Brochures		$900											$900
Website		$10	$10	$10	$10	$10	$10	$10	$10	$10	$10	$10	$110
Promotional Items				$400			$500				$600		$1,500
Advertising	$785	$785	$785	$785	$785	$785	$785	$785	$785	$785	$785	$785	$8,635
Dues & Subscriptions													$0
Consulting	$1,500	$1,500	$1,500	$1,500	$1,500	$1,500	$1,500	$1,500	$1,500	$1,530	$1,500	$1,500	$16,500
Accounting												$2,000	$2,000
Payroll	$4,888	$4,888	$4,888	$4,888	$4,888	$4,888	$4,888	$4,888	$4,888	$4,838	$4,888	$4,888	$53,768
Payroll Burden/Taxes	$2,478	$1,506	$1,645	$1,460	$1,414	$1,414	$1,645	$1,784	$1,876	$2,015	$2,108	$2,200	$19,067
Group Benefits	$1,483	$1,483	$1,483	$1,483	$1,483	$1,483	$1,483	$1,483	$1,483	$1,433	$1,483	$1,483	$16,315
Interest	$800	$800	$800	$800	$800	$800	$800	$800	$800	$830	$800	$800	$8,800
Bank Service Charges	$100	$100	$100	$100	$100	$100	$100	$100	$100	$130	$100	$100	$1,100
Licenses & Fees	$500												$0
Utilities & Telephone	$2,000	$2,000	$2,000	$2,000	$2,000	$2,000	$2,000	$2,000	$2,000	$2,030	$2,000	$2,000	$22,000
Other													$0
Repairs & Maintenance		$500		$500		$500		$500		$530		$500	$3,000
Insurance	$10,000												$1,500
Sub-Total	$75,120	$42,850	$44,359	$40,685	$38,855	$40,735	$44,543	$48,265	$49,750	$53,221	$55,943	$59,243	$518,446
Other Cash Outflows													
Capital Purchases	$5,000												
Building Construction	$65,000												
Decorating													
Fixtures & Equipment	$8,000												
Install Fixtures & Equip.	$10,000												
Remodeling													
Lease Payments													
Loan Principal					$5,000	$5,000	$5,000	$5,000	$5,000	$5,000	$5,000	$5,000	$40,000
Owner's Draw	$5,000	$5,000	$5,000	$5,000	$5,000	$5,000	$5,000	$5,000	$5,000	$5,000	$5,000	$5,000	$50,000
Accounts Payables (60 days)			$18,490	$9,460	$10,750	$9,030	$8,600	$8,600	$10,750	$12,040	$12,900	$14,190	$114,810
Other:													
Sub-Total	$93,000	$5,000	$23,490	$14,460	$20,750	$19,030	$18,600	$18,600	$20,750	$22,040	$22,900	$24,190	$204,810
Total Cash Outflows	$168,120	$47,850	$67,849	$55,145	$59,605	$59,765	$63,143	$66,865	$70,500	$75,261	$78,843	$83,433	$680,406
Ending Cash Balance	-$68,120	$4,881	$19,207	$19,163	$15,133	$4,293	-$11,350	-$25,965	-$34,240	-$41,101	-$45,843	-$49,001	-$49,001

169

Balance Sheet to Dec 31 20XX

Assets		Liabilities	
Cash	-$49,001	Current Liabilities	
		Accounts Payables	$12,470
Current Assets			
Accounts Receivables	-$667,375	Long-Term Liabilities	
Inventory	$60,675	Owner's Equity	-$603,171
Fixed Assets			
Equipment	$65,000		
Total		Total Liabilities	
Assets	-$590,701	and Owner's Equity	-$590,701

10

Implementation Plan

Think of your business plan as a small book. If you take the time to write it, take the time to reread it on a regular basis. After all, if the information is important enough to include in the plan, it is important enough to implement, track, and manage.

TRAP

Following through on your business plan may seem evident, but I have personally witnessed well-intentioned entrepreneurs short-circuit themselves by not implementing, testing, or executing a well-thought-out strategy. It is easy to get distracted and forget about the commitments you made in your business plan!

Write It, Then Read It

There are two ways to prevent yourself from getting off track:

1. Reread your business plan periodically and compare it to how you are doing.

2. Create an implementation project plan.

TIP

The trick is to think ahead to the implementation phase while you are writing the business plan. Decide how you will actually implement and use the ideas, concepts, and strategies you come up with in the planning stage. Then write these implementation strategies directly into your plan or as a separate document (see below) to use later.

Track Implementation Ideas as You Write

To track your implementation ideas, create a separate spreadsheet or table in your word processor. It should have at least four columns: task, description of the task, date it needs to be completed, and who is going to do it.

1. *Task:* Name the task using action words like; create, build, set up, and start.

2. *Description:* Describe in a sentence or two what the end result will look like. For example, "design advertisement for Yellow Pages that focuses on our pick up service."

3. *Date:* The reason I like to use a calendar format is that I can place the task into the date it needs to be started or completed.

4. *Who:* Whenever possible, assign responsibility to a specific person. Remember, you cannot do everything.

Integrate your business plan into the way you work. If you put a date to a task and then decide to delay or postpone doing it, at least you have made a conscious decision. If you do not hold yourself accountable by assigning who, what, and when priorities, tasks are easily forgotten.

Identify Tools Required

When it comes to writing about business tasks, concentrate on the tools you will need. For example, if you were going to create a new brochure, you might need some new photographs of staff and the facility, a new logo design, and, most importantly, the copy and content for the brochure. The same thing applies whether you are working on your Web site, press release, direct mail, or e-mail campaign.

Identify Systems and Strategies

Some of the tasks outlined in your business plan will be strategic and may include describing projects like staff training or creating human resource systems or a customer service blueprint. The important thing is to identify and develop these strategies in order to successfully implement them.

If your system or strategy does not exist, you will have to create it before you can use it. Therefore, your first task on a project like staff training is to write a small project plan. Start with identifying the training focus and end result. Identify the issues and concerns that prompted you to identify the need for staff training. Next, one by one, address each of the issues and concerns you identified and provide any information necessary to understanding the need and purpose of the training. Then break down the training project into small steps.

Special Considerations for Start-Ups

The implementation plan for a start-up should carry a lot of detail. This can include plans for renovation(s), store set up, and the specific projects and tasks that will need to be completed to open for business.

Plan to spend a few weeks working out the kinks and fine-tuning your operations before your official "grand opening."

New Management

The management of new firms face a substantial learning curve. Most bankruptcies occur in the early stages of a business's life when internal deficiencies are often prevalent. Management must master the basic internal skills—general and financial knowledge, control, communications, supervision of staff, and market development—or the business will fail solely from the weight of these problems.

The antidote for management deficiencies is training, structure, and planning, all of which should be a part of your implementation plan. Make a list of areas in which you need training and support, and then create an action plan to fill those gaps. Create your own professional and personal development program. The areas to look closely at are:

- *Human resources:* Develop a plan for the recruiting, selecting, training and managing your human resources so that you have the right people in the right places at the right time.

- *Marketing and sales:* Develop a plan to roll out your marketing and sales tactics slowly so you have an opportunity to build a lead generation system to supply the company with qualified leads of prospects interested in your products or services.

- *Product or service development and selection:* It is relatively easy for any small business to identify new opportunities. The real issue is whether the opportunities are worthy of your time, energy, and money. Keep an eye on industry trends and opportunities. Engage your new and long-time customers in a conversation to gauge their support of your ideas before you invest the time, effort, and resources.

- *Technology:* This means more than just using computers and having a Web site. Read, investigate, and work to find new ways to apply existing technology to revitalize your business. Look for technology to improve your operations, accounting systems, and financial management.

- *Raise additional capital:* By taking steps early (creating a financial plan) to identify the amount of capital you need to sustain operations—in the form of equity—you will create a balanced financial structure and, by following your plan, minimize costly errors and missteps.

TRAP

Without adequate equity coping with sudden changes in costs or revenues put the business at risk. Equity is the residual liquidity within the business that is available to be invested in the business or the dollar amount left after paying all liabilities.

Experience, Partners, and Home-Based Businesses Are Positive Factors

Owning a business previously, having multiple owners, and being home-based at start-up seem to increase a business's survivability. A stay-at-home business owner enjoys the work-at-home lifestyle and is more likely to continue to operate a struggling business.

TRAP

On the downside, relatively younger owners (service and retail businesses), not having start-up capital, and being in an urban or suburban area can lead to a higher rate of business closings.

Young Owners Should Start Small

Because young owners in urban or suburban areas are more likely to have better business or job opportunities, owning a business comes with a higher opportunity cost for them. In my experience those who start small and go after a business that is easy to start and easy to close seem to fare much better than entrepreneurs who bet the whole farm on one idea.

Implementation for Established Firms

Established firms should concentrate on competition analysis because this has proven to have the greatest impact on improving the firms' profitability. Follow the procedures listed in the market analysis chapter (Chapter 4). Identify the changes you feel you need to make and then create a project plan with time lines and costs. Then incorporate the changes into your marketing strategy, operations plan, and financial plan.

Use of Funds

Every implementation plan should include a description and time line for the use of funds. With respect to funds, your financier will need to know:

1. Amount.
2. Intended use.
3. When the money will be needed.

On larger projects like construction of a building, renovations, or expansion, a Gantt chart provided by your project manager is important to include.

TIP

Your contractor can provide you with the documentation you will need. In addition photos, renderings, floor plans, and layouts should be included in the appendix of your business plan.

Three-Part Implementation Plan

When you're writing your implementation plan, it helps to divide it into three parts:

1. First 30 days following start-up or following funding.
2. 60 to 90 days.
3. The first year.

Sample Implementation Plan

Following is the implementation plan section of the business plan. The complete business plan can be found in Appendix A.

Implementation Plan

Marketing Campaign and Announcement Formal announcement of the start-up and acquisition of To and Fro Transport:

First 30 Days

- *Furniture and fixtures:* As part of the purchase agreement with To and Fro Transport, we will be purchasing computers, desks and chairs, and so forth.
- Fax flyer to all customers.
- Phone campaign to ask former To and Fro Transport customers (763) to confirm their patronage.
- Distribution of business cards and printed flyers via drivers to existing and new customers.
- *Staff training:* Further train Sarah Sunset as customer service representative:
  - Sales and telemarketing.
  - *Software:* use of ACT! 2000 (database), Dispatch 2000.
  - Trucking industry.

60 to 90 Days

- *Part-time/spare driver:* Hired an experienced, semi-retired driver on an as-needed basis to:
  - Provide relief to other drivers.
  - Do in-town work.
  - Pilot car and hotshot.
  - Train new drivers.
  - Increase operations efficiency.

The First Year
- *Dispatch systems and software:* JOE'S plans to use dispatch and truck load management software as well as an onlinc load-matching service.
- *Communication:* In order to offer 24/7 service and keep in touch with our drivers, customers, and suppliers, we will use a combination of:

- E-mail.
- Phone.
- Fax.
- Cellular phones.
- Pagers.

- *Bookkeeping:* All bookkeeping and accounting will be done with Quick Books Pro 2000 accounting software.

- *Research and development:* As part of our continuing development, we will have a database of customers and potential customers, with types of loads, lane ways, and destinations.

11
Contingency and Emergency Plan

Contingency and emergency planning is not a new concept. What feels new is the number of major crises we have witnessed in North America, from the ice storm that hit parts of Quebec including Montreal, Canada, to the World Trade Center attacks in 2001, to the devastation from Hurricane Ivan in 2004, and Hurricanes Rita and Katrina in the southern United States in 2005.

Every business needs an emergency and contingency plan to reduce the risk and lessen the potential impact on employees, customers, and the financial health of the business in the case of an emergency.

Business Planning Evolves

The field of business planning continues to evolve. Crisis and contingency planning are the survival tools of the new millennium. For example, in the early 1970s few people thought to create a contingency plan to deal with the impact of skyrocketing gas and diesel fuel prices, and all of them felt it in lower profit margins.

In the 1980s few would have thought that interest rates would climb above 20 percent—but they did. Because of changes in the energy, business, and political climate, it is now standard practice to include a contingency plan to compensate for fluctuations in fuel, energy, and interest rates.

No one could have predicted the disaster inflicted by terrorists on the World Trade Center. You can bet that business plans for office buildings and towers in New York City now contain contingency plans to prepare them to deal with the crisis, damage, and business interruption should another act of terrorism, or a natural or human-created disaster, occur.

What Is the Purpose of a Contingency and Emergency Plan?

The purpose of your contingency and emergency plan is to think ahead about the potential risks and plan how you will respond, manage, and act when specific events occur. Taking the time to conduct a risk assessment in advance allows you and your management teams to think through possible scenarios, define the implications, and plan a response.

What Is an Emergency Plan?

An *emergency plan* is a specific response to a disaster. It defines what you will do when it (the event) happens. It details a specific tactical and practical response to deal with the problems, issues, and confusion after a major emergency. Your emergency plan can focus on just the business, or it can also include employees, customers, and suppliers. It involves the creation of specific strategies, organizational issues, and a structured response to provide an opportunity for members of your team to discuss the issues, train, and prepare.

What Is a Contingency Plan?

A *contingency plan* is the portion of your business plan that examines the underlying assumptions in your business plan. Every business plan is based upon specific assumptions—such as certain facts, projections, and market trends—that you believe are true. The process of writing your contingency plan will help you examine the viability of the business when assumptions prove not to be correct.

TIP

Review the assumptions you have made in your business plan. Then select those that have *not* been verified for accuracy and write a plan for what you will do to compensate for the changes to minimize the impact on business viability. Take a notebook and walk around your business to identify potential threats to the business.

Examine and Verify All Assumptions

When writing your business plan, it is very important to examine all your major assumptions and seek to get them confirmed using information from a third party for accuracy. Your contingency plan should answer the following questions:

1. *Drop in revenue:* What would you do if you do not reach your sales and revenue targets? How much of a difference would need to occur before you reexamine your marketing and strategies?

2. *Borrowing costs increase:* If you are borrowing heavily and interest rates suddenly increase, what would you do to compensate for the increased costs? How much of an increase in interest rates would the business be able to absorb before it the viability of the business is affected?

3. *Customer bankruptcy:* What is your contingency plan if your business suffers a sustained interruption to cash flow resulting from a major customer going out of business?

4. *Disaster:* In case of a major accident, event, or disaster, what would happen to your business based on your current level of preparedness? Is your business at lower/higher risk than others?

5. *Loss of a key staff member:* What will you do if a key staff member suddenly becomes ill, quits, or dies? How would that affect you? How easy would it be to replace the person? How much would it cost?

6. *Regulatory restrictions:* What is your plan if the health board closes your business? Are there any real estate or development caveats that could negatively affect the business? Are you compliant with all health, safety, and employer laws?

7. *Increase in costs:* What is your plan if utility, fuel, or raw materials suddenly increase in cost? Are any of your products dependent on energy? If so, how can you mitigate the impact of a steep increase in energy costs?

8. *Lose a major supplier:* What is your plan if a supplier goes out of business? What would happen to your business if a supplier loses the right to continue to sell or distribute a product that is important to your business?

9. *Accident on premises:* How will you respond if a customer gets injured, falls ill, or creates a disturbance? What would need to change to ensure an appropriate response from you, your staff, and the business?

10. *Robbery or violent act:* How vulnerable is your business to theft from employees, customers, and third parties? What is your data backup routine? What would be the impact of an act of vandalism or theft on your computer systems? Would you be able to restore operations on another system? How long would it take? How much would it cost? What is your insurance coverage? What is covered and what is not?

Key Performance Indicators

Key performance indicators (KPI) are well-known management and accounting measurement tools used to monitor the performance of the business. KPIs are expressed as ratios when two or more totals from your financial statements are calculated. For example, one of the KPIs that many entrepreneurs are familiar with is called *current ratio.* It is one way of expressing liquidity in your business by calculating the ratio between all current assets and all current liabilities. The actual calculation is current assets divided by current liabilities = current ratio. You can read more about these ratios in Chapter 9, "Pro Forma Financial Plan."

An example of a common KPI is sales per employee. In 1996 Toyota Motor Corporation had $604,346 sales per employee and $14,489 after tax earnings per employee. In 2005 sales per employee was $578,005, but after tax income rose to $36,493 per employee. Compare that performance to $650,000 sales per employee for Microsoft; Google has $1,500,000 sales per employee. To give some perspective, I calculated the sales per employee for some other businesses (US NAICS 2002):

- *Software publishers:* $293, 635 per employee per year.
- *Crude oil and natural gas extraction:* $905,632 per employee per year.
- *Natural gas liquid extraction:* $3,016,321 per employee per year.
- *Motion picture and video production:* $408,347 per employee per year.
- *Videotape and disk rental:* $62,439 per employee per year.
- *Internet service providers:* $152,427 per employee per year.
- *Web search portals:* $274,711 per employee per year.

What I want you to notice is that KPI values can vary widely from industry to industry. Sales per employee is just one example of a KPI measurement. You need to know the ratios for your industry because they will provide you with something with which to compare the performance of your business.

TIP

Compare your operation to that of your competition to see how you are doing. When there is a difference that is not in your favor, you can ask yourself some questions to begin to investigate whether a problem exists and what you need to do about it.

From a contingency planning viewpoint Google (comparing 2005 results to 2002 industry statistics) is doing almost sixfold above industry averages. Even in 2004 it was doing four times the industry average. So in that situation

Google's main strategy is to focus on what to do to maximize revenues. Whereas, a smaller Web search portal that was averaging less than $274,711 per employee and that needed to get more funding to reinvent itself would need to develop a turnaround plan and a set of KPIs and an appropriate contingency plan to deal with shifts and changes in the company's KPIs.

Identify and Define Your Own KPIs

There are numerous assumptions made in every business plan. I would suggest that you sit down and make a list of all the key assumptions that underlie and support your business plan. What are the changes, trends, or events that could have a significant negative impact on the business and disrupt revenues, profits, and the viability of your operation? Look to identify the underlying trend(s) that would have to change in order for it to negatively affect your business. Here are some suggestions I would make to a wholesale distributor:

- Number of phone calls taken per day per employee.
- Number of orders to the number of calls.
- Number of new customers or accounts opened each month.
- Amount of returns per customer. Average dollar amount per invoice.
- Percentage of customers ordering a new product.

Create your own list of key performance indicators that you will track on a regular basis. It is just a matter of establishing a relationship between two known values and then calculating the value or ratio. As you track them over an extended period, you will get a feel for what is a normal level of activity so that when activity levels drop, change in the KPIs will bring it to your attention so you can investigate and take corrective action.

Here are some examples of the most common financial KPIs you can also use to monitor the health of your business:

- *Liquidity ratios:* current ratio, quick ratio.
- *Safety:* Debt to equity, debt coverage ratio.
- *Profitability:* Sales growth, COGS to sales, gross profit margin, net profit margin, return on equity, return on assets, owner's discretionary profit dollars.
- *Efficiency:* Accounts receivable turnover, accounts payable turnover, days in inventory, inventory turnover, sales to total assets, and sales per employee.

You can learn more about these KPIs in Chapter 9.

Write a Six-Step Emergency/Disaster Plan

Take the time to review your preparedness according to these six steps. Depending on your business and where you are located you will likely need to adjust this plan to meet your specific needs. Many states and large counties have a disaster plan and tools to help you prepare.

Step 1: Assessment and Mitigation

To reduce the impact and cost of a natural or human-created disaster, advance planning will help you to determine the level of risk and allow you to think through the impact disasters common to your area could have on the business. Creating a written disaster plan can not only reduce the cost and impact of a disaster but it can also be used as a guide to direct the preparations and the training of management and staff. Your disaster recovery plan should anticipate how to deal with these possible events:

- *Power:* An energy disruption is a short-term loss of power that can damage equipment when power resumes. This applies especially to hospital equipment, data centers, and manufacturing facilities. Describe the procedures that will be followed to protect your equipment when power resumes.

- *Computer software or hardware failures:* Damage to this equipment can also damage, delete, or corrupt your information. Describe the measures that will be followed when computer software or hardware fails.

- *Network and computer crime:* Network security is an ongoing concern. When hackers and viruses gain access to your network and/or computer, the damage can range from a serious interruption to outright loss or theft of data. Describe your plan to protect your data and make backup copies of all data in a secure offsite location.

- *Labor strife:* While a labor dispute (walkout, shutdown) might not be considered a disaster, it is certainly disruptive to business operations. Create a written list of procedures for equipment shutdown and storage.

- *Natural disasters:* These events include earthquakes, fire, flood, and storms. You need to plan for the type of natural disaster that is common to your area. Find out what type of disasters you should anticipate and create your plan based on guidelines provided by your city, county, and state.

- *Terrorist acts:* These include the use of violence for the purpose of creating fear in order to achieve political, religious, or ideological goals. They may include weapons of mass destruction or smaller threats. Follow similar preparations as for other disasters and check with local, state and federal authorities for suggestions on preparation.

Make sure that you take the time to examine all of the potential events and scenarios. Think through the impact each would have on the business and prepare a plan to recover and restore business operations. By taking the time to identify the most likely scenarios, you will be better equipped to cope with the recovery and restoration of the business.

Step 2: Response and Recovery Plans

Once you have identified the potential threats, it is time to focus on writing your plan for responding to the emergency and then the recovery plan. Stop and think about the components that make your business run; then these are the areas that you will want to concentrate your planning efforts around, for example:

- *Financial:* Depending on the severity and type of disaster, access to financial institutions could range from being restricted to total shutdown. Areas to concentrate on include preserving records (paper and digital), a supply of alternative invoices, purchase orders, checks, and banking documents.

- *Facility and equipment:* Accurate records of equipment—serial numbers, make, model and manufacturer, including the suppliers' contact information—will be important when it comes time to making an insurance claim. Include an overview of your procedures to secure and shut down equipment. Then create a subset of documents for specific instructions and procedures for specific pieces of equipment. Describe your training process. If damage to the building or plant is severe, you will need to find an alternative location, and your plan should include a list of options and alternatives that can be used as a guideline when needed.

- *Insurance:* Make an appointment with your commercial insurance carrier. Make sure you understand your policy—what is covered by the policy and what your options will be at claim time. Record contact information for your broker and the company's head office, and keep a copy of your policy with your plan.

- *Customers:* Create a procedure for contacting your customers to let them know about what happened to the business. I recommend creating a sample agenda that outlines what the customer needs to know about the company's plans for recovery and resumption of operations and what will be done to meet the customers' interim needs.

- *Employees:* Every employee will be dealing with his or her own family situations when a widespread disaster hits an area. In the case of a fire limited to your building, you may have to write paychecks to bring employees' pay up to date, and, if the rebuilding downtime is extended, you may need to temporarily layoff your staff until the building gets to a point where you can call them back to work. Call the local unemployment office to find out more about how you should handle the layoffs to make sure the employees get their benefits.

- *Government:* Your plan should include names and contact information of all relevant local, state, and national offices and officials. This should include police, ambulance, and hospitals. Make sure to include a directory of government departments and assistance programs.

- *Communication:* Service disruptions can range from periodic to total shutdown of regular communications systems. Create a communication plan to get the word out about the status of the business. Make sure to include alternative communication devices including handheld radios, CBs, and cell phones. Another option is to locate a local ham radio operator in your area.

Step 3: Damage Assessment Process

Your plan should include preformatted worksheets to help you document the damage so that you can get a handle on it and make an appropriate and accurate claim to the insurance company. Worksheets should include inventory, equipment, and assets.

Step 4: Salvage Procedures

Part of coming to a settlement with your insurance company will be documenting your efforts to salvage inventory, equipment, components, and building. Describe your plan, which should include a camera and inventory or equipment control sheets to record the type of damage. In some cases, the insurance company will want to repair instead of replace items when possible.

Step 5: Rehabilitation Plans

Depending on the breadth of damage from the disaster, there will be certain restrictions that could prevent you from getting started with the rebuilding and rehabilitation process. You will need to wait for local authorities, utilities (water, power, gas, phone), and other infrastructure to get back up and running before you can really get started rebuilding your business. Your plan should describe the level of support for physical, emotional, and psychological needs your staff and their families.

Step 6: Disaster Recovery Plan

The biggest issue after a disaster is to be able to resume business operations to ensure continuity of the business. This will include the information, facility, and supply infrastructure of the business, including computer systems, equipment, furniture, and buildings.

It is fairly difficult to write a lot about your disaster recovery plan when you have no idea what the level of damage will be. What you can do is assign responsibilities to various management and staff members to help organize the disaster recovery plan.

TIP

I recommend that you assign areas of responsibility for the rebuilding process based upon how the business was organized prior to the event. Employees and managers are most familiar with their departments and will be able to bring that perspective to the recovery and rebuilding process.

Archive of Business Data

Be sure to include the following information in your contingency plan:

- *Contact sheet:* This includes a list of people and the actions to be taken to contact customers, staff, suppliers, and staff family members in case of an emergency.

- *Plan members and organization:* The plan should include a list of the members of the planning team and their roles and responsibilities. It should also include specific instructions for maintaining the plan and keeping it accurate and current.

- *Responsibilities:* The plan should include a clear description of the responsibilities of managers, staff, and department heads. Make sure to include human resources, administration, facilities, and information technology.

TIP

Don't forget to routinely update the various notification lists and other items such as the names and numbers of employees and suppliers that will need to be contacted; office and home numbers; family members to contact; and a list of local authorities and recovery teams.

TIP

Make sure to include drawings of your building as well as a list of inventory, emergency supplies, and third parties who can provide support.

What's Missing from the Sample Contingency and Emergency Plan

The sample contingency and emergency plan that follows is missing a disaster plan. It should include plans for dealing with

- employee accidents.
- traffic accidents.
- payload damage.
- fire, storm, and water damage.

You may find you need to get your business plan finished before you have a chance to put together a comprehensive Contingency and Emergency Plan. When this happens make sure to include an item in your Implementation Plan (see Chapter 10) to indicate when you will have your Contingency and Emergency Plan complete.

Sample Contingency and Emergency Plan

Following is the assumption and potential risks section of the business plan. The complete business plan can be found in Appendix A.

Assumptions and Potential Risks

Rising Fuel Costs A typical load of a little over 20 tons could be handled for about 6 gallons of fuel per thousand ton-mile in 1975. Today, a typical load of 30 tons (trucks are larger now) can be handled for about 3 gallons per thousand ton-miles. And this is considering "typical" loads. There are a lot of big trucks that do considerably better than this today. In our cash-flow projections fuel costs are estimated based upon a historical average as 20 percent of revenue. While fuel costs can be expected to rise, we will compensate by adding fuel surcharges to existing rates.

Aging Driver Population The average age of a truck driver is two to three years older than that of average workers in general. Starting in 2005, a large number of drivers will be either retiring or considering retirement within a few years. The industry has not been successful attracting workers under 25 years of age to consider trucking as an occupation. The biggest factor in driver retention is a fair wage, respect, and making the job easy with the right type of truck and equipment (i.e., chains, straps, etc.). Our driver recruiting strategy will include creating a strategic alliance with a driving school and finding drivers who are willing to apprentice and be trained. The other method will be to keep an eye out for good experienced lease operators.

Private Fleet Growth Many private carriers believe that their fleet costs are comparable to or lower than those of for-hire carriers, and the visibility they receive from using their own trucks is considered to be a positive factor. Private trucking accounts for 28 percent of truck movements. This market share decreases to 10 percent on longer-distance transborder trips. JOE'S will focus on longer highway trips, where for-hire fleets have 90 percent of the market share.

Sales Assumptions Our sales assumptions are based upon previous revenue experience with To and Fro Transport. The customers identified below have been contacted and all have agreed to continue business with JOE'S.

JOE'S Major Accounts

Customer	$ YTD	Next 12 months
Right Here Products	$39,321.06	Increase
Next Door Logistics	$147,208.46	Varies
Hard Steel	$19,689.28	Increase
We Know the Way Transportation Ltd	$17,151.90	Varies
No One Knows Metals	$44,481.42	Varies
Black White & Gray	$20,534.96	Increase
Canadian Imitation Products Co.	$53,921.95	Increase
Edmonton Growers	$63,484.54	Varies

(*Continued*)

(Continued)

Oilfield Tubes	$63,464.17	Increase
Big Tanks & Equip Ltd.	$28,833.72	Increase
ABCD	$125,786.90	Increase
To and Fro Transportation (TO AND FRO)	$34,500.00	Varies
Big Guy Industries	$40,006.17	Increase
Metal Buildings Inc.	$37,154.50	Increase
Heavy Equip. Sales	$17,840.00	Increase
Big Bird Transportation Inc. (Sunpine)	$85,980.34	Varies
Both Sides Intl. Transport Inc.	$11,520.00	Varies
Transportation Company	$9,100.00	Varies
Always On Time Logistics Ltd.	$43,928.00	Varies
Three Small Men Holdings Ltd.	$88,991.99	Increase
The Weather Is Bad Here	$46,675.00	Increase
Oilfield Welding & Overhead Cranes	$105,843.21	Increase
Total business YTD	**$1,145,417.00**	

12

Executive Summary

The executive summary provides the reader with a high-level overview of your entire business plan. Remember, this is only supposed to be a snapshot: if the reader wants additional information, he or she can refer to the details elsewhere in the document. (See Fig. 12.1.)

Customize the Executive Summary for the Person Reading Your Business Plan

Generally, a business plan communicates the viability of a business idea for the purpose of obtaining financing.

When the business plan is mostly complete it is time to write the Executive Summary. Once you have a rough draft of it, you should then modify it for a specific reader.

Keep in mind who will read it and what they expect to learn from it. A banker will look for different information than an investor or a supplier. There are basically two groups of people you will need to tailor your business plan for: an internal and external audience.

Internal Audience

Your internal audience is made up of people such as your partner and key employees who are a part of your business. An executive summary written for an internal audience should include:

- Goals and purpose of the business plan.

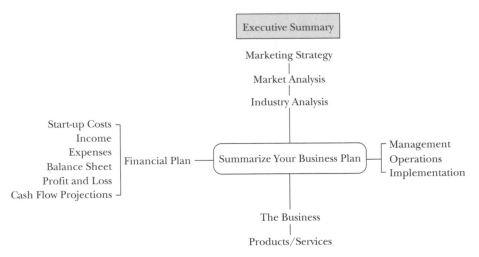

Figure 12.1 Visual map of an executive summary

- Table of contents.
- List of resources required to accomplish the business plan.
- Identification of potential roadblocks and barriers and how you plan to overcome them.

External Audience

The external audience includes people outside the business who will want to see certain documents and your business plan before they decide if they want to invest in, contract with, or otherwise have a relationship with your business. This group includes such people as your banker, venture capitalists, credit rating firms, and vendors. An executive summary written for an external audience should include:

- A brief description of your business and products or services.
- Amount of financing required.
- How the money will be used.
- How the money will be repaid.
- Summary of annual sales, profits, and cash flow needs.
- Security offered, terms, and explanation of any unusual conditions or business circumstances.

TIP

Remember, you do not have to provide a full copy of your business plan until you get an indication of interest from a financier. In some cases you could use a financing proposal before you release your entire business plan and confidential information it contains.

Similar in format to an executive summary, a financing proposal will include:

- Type of financing requested.
- Security offered.
- Terms of loan or credit, interest rate, and repayment terms.

Using a financing proposal is a way of prequalifying lenders based on their level of interest before you disclose all the pertinent details, such as a full business plan and financial statements.

Customizing the Executive Summary for Your Bank

When you're ready to approach your bank with your business plan, first ask the loan officer if the loan you're seeking is within his or her scope of decision-making. Do not be surprised if you are told that your request will have to go to the branch manager or loan committee. In these cases the loan officer will check your credit history and credit report, the business plan, and your financial projections to make sure your request falls within the bank's profile.

TRAP

Every lending institution has its own guidelines and policies concerning risk and markets. For example, some banks will not finance restaurants, while others do not touch transportation, trucking, or courier companies. Check with your local branch manager to find out more about your particular situation.

If you have a good relationship with your personal loan officer, you can start with him or her, but be prepared to have this person pass you on to someone else in the bank more familiar with business financing.

TIP

Think of your executive summary as your silent salesperson. It should provide enough detail to educate the readers about your request and point them to the table of contents where they can find more information.

The final decision to grant the loan will most likely be made by your loan officer's boss or a loan committee. That is why it is so important to do a good job on your business plan, and especially on the executive summary, because the business plan document becomes your advocate with the "invisible" loan committee or boss.

Confidentiality

Use good judgment and exercise caution when giving out a copy of your business plan. For example, when providing a copy to a prospective business partner or senior employee, insist on a nondisclosure agreement, since you are likely sharing competitive and perhaps proprietary information that could hurt your business if it got into the wrong hands.

When you provide people with a full copy of your business plan, or if they have seen an excerpt, ask them to sign a confidentiality, nondisclosure agreement.

TRAP

Experienced investors and active venture capitalists will often refuse to sign a confidentiality or nondisclosure agreement. Do not be surprised. This is not an indication of their lack of interest or professionalism. They see so many business plans that it is impossible not to have some sort of crossover. They do not want your idea, nor will they steal it. Remember, they are professionals and would not be in business long if they disclosed confidential information.

Sample Executive Summary

Following is the executive summary section of the business plan prepared for a bank manager. The complete business plan can be found in Appendix A.

Executive Summary

Joe's Trucking Systems, Inc. (JOE'S) is a full-service, 24-hours-a-day, seven-days-a-week, open-deck trucking company. It provides full truck load (FTL) and less than truck load (LTL) transportation services to industrial companies across North America. Sue Switch owns 51 percent of the company; Joe Sample owns 49 percent of the company.

Our vision is to be a steady moneymaker with an annual net profit of 5 percent. We do not want to be the largest company—just consistently profitable.

Forecasted revenues for the year ended September 30, 20XX, are $1,671,000 with a net income of $147,503. Based upon the forecasted financial statements prepared by Everyday Accounting, the company requires a $100,000 line of credit.

When he worked at To and Fro Transport, Joe Sample increased the financial performance of the highway division. The last three months' average revenue per running mile (empty and loaded) were:

- June average: $1.46 per mile
- July average: $1.52 per mile
- August average: $1.72 per mile

JOE'S was recently awarded four new contracts totaling more than $800,000 (for details see Upcoming Contracts in the Marketing and Sales Strategy section).

JOE'S sales assumptions are based upon past sales history of To and Fro Transport and newly awarded contracts. There are 22 accounts that did a total of $1,110,917 of business with To and Fro Transport in the last 12 months.

In a recent survey, 13 of the top 22 accounts (763 total accounts) expect to increase the amount of business with JOE'S in the next 12 months. Of the remaining accounts, all intend to continue doing business with JOE'S. The exact amount of sales that can be expected varies based upon sales and need. (For a detailed list of accounts and volumes, see "Assumptions.")

JOE'S has a purchase agreement with To and Fro Transport. The agreement includes the purchase of the TO AND FRO customer and contact list (763 customers), marketing rights, a non-competition agreement for $10,000 cash, and the assumption of $15,000 of debt (lease operator insurance hold-back).

PART 3

Writing a Business Plan in 30 Days

13

Writing a Business Plan in 30 Days

As we've discussed, writing a business plan is an important task because it reflects the ability of the owner to run the business successfully.

Make no mistake, writing a business plan can be a time-consuming task. You are planning your business for the next three years, and you want to give it the attention it deserves. My personal experience in writing business plans is that it can take me between 50 and 300 hours to finish. The more familiar I am with the industry and market, the faster I can get the plan finished. If you are writing a business plan for the first time, have never been in business before, or are new to the industry, plan to spend more time writing your business plan.

TRAP

Running a business and writing a business plan at the same time is a challenge because the business will likely need your attention. The smaller the business, the greater the potential to be distracted or pulled away from the task of writing your business plan.

TIP

Writing a business plan for a market that does not fit your business is a waste of time. Therefore, starting with your industry and market analysis early in the planning process could save you a lot of time and effort. When writing your plan, be sure to write the sections in the order set out in Part 2.

Minimize Your Distractions

You can easily minimize distractions by getting away from the business to write your plan. If you are unable to get away from the business, choose a quiet period of the day to work on your business plan.

Make your writing time enjoyable. I like to get a fresh cup of coffee from my Starbucks Barista, turn on my favorite music, and focus on nothing else but my word processor. I sometimes close the door because some days the family forgets that I do not want to be interrupted.

Then I make a commitment to myself to write for 60 minutes without a break. Usually I write for 60 minutes, then take a short break for 5 to 15 minutes. If things are going really well, I can write for three to four hours at a stretch! When that happens, I reward myself by taking a much longer break.

Read, Think, Write, Edit

Read, think, write, edit is a simple four-step process I have found helps me to work through gathering information, processing it by determining the meaning, and applying the information within the context of writing my business plan. (See Fig. 13.1.)

Read

Start by reading the chapter of this book that correlates to the specific section of the business plan you are writing. For example, if you are writing the industry analysis, read Chapter 3 to familiarize yourself with the purpose and structure of this part of the plan and to help you visualize the end result.

Next, begin to research and gather information to read. I recommend starting with browsing the World Wide Web. Try using Google or Yahoo to identify authority Web sites that you will be able to use as a resource to learn more

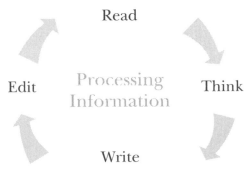

Figure 13.1 Processing Information

about the business or industry. Look for industry, magazine, or trade association Web sites that track, support, and comment on your specific industry.

TIP

I have started using a desktop tool to search the Web for me. I use Devon Agent to search the Web and create a text report based on the keywords I enter. It allows me to scan the text quickly (without advertising interruptions) and drill down to the most important information.

Once you are happy with the resources you have gathered, sit down to read. Print the pages and highlight relevant text, create a mind map (my favorite technique), or copy relevant text into one document for reference purposes. Remember to watch for new topics and mark them for additional research.

Think

Thinking is the most important stage of composing a business plan. In the process of writing your business plan, you could end up reviewing and thinking through more than 400 different pieces of information. Needless to say, that can be overwhelming. The key to preventing yourself from becoming overwhelmed is to get the information out of your mind and down on paper.

This is why a mind map can be such a powerful tool. It allows you to record information and organize it the way it makes sense to you. To make a mind map, you arrange words into a picture. Start with your key concept in the center and then place related words or concepts around it. Link the words and ideas using lines and/or arrows. As other related words or concepts come to mind, write those down as well. They can sprout off another idea or create a completely new branch of the map.

Be flexible, follow your intuition, and let your mind feed off the ideas you write down. Sometimes you will get a really long and detailed branch, and other times you might have a number of branches without a lot of detail. What is important is that you understand the meaning of the mind map.

Write

Do not try to create a perfect essay: You will have time to edit and make it better later. Right now it is important just to get your thoughts down on paper.

Once you have had the opportunity to think about the topic of the business plan you are working on, sit down in front of your computer. Open your word processor and transfer your mind map notes. Create a brief outline about the topic. Then begin adding facts, observations, and relevant details until you feel you have adequately explained the importance, meaning, and impact the topic will have on your business strategy and plan.

TIP

Review the appropriate chapters of this book to keep yourself moving forward, and be sure to stick to the order laid out in Part 2.

Edit

By the time you get ready to do your final edit, most of what you wrote will have sat awhile. That is a good thing because then you will be able to look at it afresh. As I like to say, "Let it sit, then edit."

TRAP

Do not be surprised to find yourself flipping back and forth from section to section, adding content. This is quite normal. Just do not get stuck trying to do the final edit before you have worked on the rest of the plan. For example, you could be adding new information to your marketing strategy based upon your findings in the industry and competition analysis. Or perhaps you made a change in your marketing strategy which will affect your advertising budget. When you need to make these kinds of updates, just mark them down briefly and go back to working on the section you were working on. Don't let yourself get too distracted. You will be able to edit the whole plan once each section is written.

Should you find yourself confused at any point along the way, go back and reread the appropriate chapter, read the other sections of your business plan, or do additional research or reading before continuing.

TIP

Take a critical eye to your business plan. Make sure that you are 100 percent comfortable with what you have committed to paper. Your reputation is on the line. Do not tweak your revenue numbers or artificially reduce your expenses to show a profit. What is most important is accurate disclosure. If your business shows a loss the first year, explain why, when, and how profits will improve. Otherwise you need to revisit, review, and revise.

How to Write a Business Plan in 30 Days

You can write a business plan in 30 days. It requires a focused effort and a plan, but, if you're willing to spend at least two to four hours a day working on it, it can be done.

The following time line is based on 30 days, but whether you choose to work on it for 30 consecutive days, every other day, weekdays only, or one day a week you can still follow this plan. Working on your plan every second day would have your business plan complete in two months (give or take a day). If you choose the weekdays only approach, it will take a little more than six weeks to complete. For one day a week, it would take about seven months to complete.

TIP

It is more important to do a good job on your business plan than to try to rush it. This is not something to do at the last minute to try and make payroll or pay the IRS. Plan ahead and take the time to really put your best effort into your business plan: It will pay dividends for years.

The 30-Day Time Line

Remember to dedicate two to four hours of productive, focused time for each day you commit to working on your plan.

Day 1: Gather Information

Before you start writing, gather the information you are going to need and put it into a file marked "Reference." For an established business get copies of all your brochures, sales letters, correspondence, and product brochures from suppliers. If you have a Web site, print a copy of each page for your file. For a new business visit the Web sites of your competition and print the ones you like, get copies of competitors' brochures, and visit your suppliers or manufacturers' Web sites.

Days 2 and 3: Business Situation Analysis

Days 2 and 3 are dedicated to learning more about your industry, market, competition, and the financial condition of your industry. Start by finding trade magazine Web sites, industry associations, and the local chamber of commerce. You might also pay a visit to the local economic development organization as well.

TIP

Many trade magazines do an annual report on the industry and are often excellent sources for industry size, economic trends, and information on any regulatory issues that are affecting or that could affect the industry.

The local chamber of commerce will be much more focused on local market trends, as will the economic development office. In many cases the economic development authorities look to a larger geographic area (state, county, etc.), and their outlook will reflect that focus. All the information from these sources is a great starting point you can use to augment your personal experience and can be used as authoritative sources as third-party quotes to support your business plan.

If you are really under a time crunch, I recommend purchasing the information you need from BizMiner.com. It sells a variety of reports including financial analyses, marketing research, industry data, state market index, area demographics, business risk index, and franchise research.

- *Financial profiles:* These profiles analyze a base of more than 18 million U.S. firms to develop three-year average sales data for the industry segment, and they present balance sheet and financial ratio benchmarks projected from average sales. The profile shows average balance sheet norms (dollar figures), as well as detailed asset, liability, and income statement breakdowns in percentages. Financial ratios are presented as both average and median measures. Balance sheet data are developed for average firms in over 30,000 business segments, including industry small business and start-up versions. Profiles can be accessed at www.bizminer.com.

- *Marketing research profiles:* These benchmark average and "survivor" firms for employment, sales, growth, and sales per employee, as well as a variety of market vitality measures. Profiles covering more than 1 million industry and area segments can be accessed at www.bizminer.com.

Using BizMiner.com you can get your industry analysis, market analysis, and financial analysis which will provide you with a lot of the data you might need. The Web site is fairly user-friendly, and, depending on the number of reports (which range between $69 to $99 each), you could easily spend $200 + but it will save you a lot of time trying to locate this information on your own. If cost is a concern, go to your local library and visit the reference desk; tell the librarian what you are trying to accomplish, and he or she can point you to resources in the library.

Days 4 and 5: Business Description

Chapter 6 goes into great detail on writing your business description. I recommend reading the entire chapter and including all the recommended content in your business plan. However, if you are really running short on time, focus on defining your vision, business goals, operations, and legal structure.

Days 6 and 7: Products and Services Description

It is very important to do products and services section right, because if you get your product or services wrong, it could spell business failure or result in getting your financing request turned down. You have to demonstrate your knowledge of the market and customers needs.

TIP

No short cuts. Follow all the instructions in Chapter 5.

Days 8 to 11: Industry Analysis

I have allotted four days for writing the industry analysis part of your business plan. That should give you some sense of the importance the industry analysis can have on your business plan and business success.

TRAP

There is a tendency to gloss over this section because you think you have this knowledge in your head based upon your personal experience. Beware: You could have tunnel vision.

Think of this section as an opportunity to learn more about your industry. No matter how long you have worked in an industry, there is always something to be learned by researching and studying it. In fact, the longer you work in an industry, the more tunnel vision you can suffer from without knowing it. This is all the more reason to make sure not to skimp on Chapter 3. Read the entire chapter and follow the instructions.

Look for new ideas and trends in your industry. What do your trade association or trade magazines have to say about the industry? Review a year or two of past issues of the trade magazines, look for trends and common themes in the headlines.

Days 12 to 15: Market Analysis and Competition Analysis

You will need another four days to complete the section on market and competition analysis. Like the industry analysis, this is an opportunity to refine your plans and improve your business by investing 100 percent into writing this section. Read Chapter 4 and follow all instructions.

The acid test for every business plan is the market share calculation. Regardless of what you think you can do, the reality check is when you realize exactly how much market share it will take in order for you to be profitable. For example, when checking the market share for a client, we discovered that the client would have to sell 150 percent of its market to be profitable. We were able to widen the target market and get it down to a much more realistic 1.5 percent.

Market share is a viability barometer because the higher your market share, the more time, effort, and resources (money) you will need to invest. As a start-up in a competitive industry, it is unrealistic to expect to gain a 20 percent market share to be profitable. If you find yourself with this type of market share, either your expenses are too high, you do not understand the market, or you lack business experience. Review and rework all your assumptions until your market share gets into a manageable and realistic range.

TIP

Writing your business plan is a great way to get an education fast. Plus you can make mistakes on paper instead of with money or in customer relationships.

Days 16 to 17: Marketing Strategy

The marketing strategy section is where you tie up everything you learned in Days 1–3 into a nice neat bow called "marketing strategy." Read Chapter 7.

If you have been following this process, you will have a rough draft of the business description, industry analysis, products and services, and market and competition analysis. Read your rough drafts and highlight the parts that stand out to you as important or the areas where you feel you learned something.

TIP

Make notes of the marketing tools (as described in Appendix C) that you plan to use as you read and review your work.

Days 18 and 19: Operations and Management

Read Chapter 8 to write your operations and management section. If you have direct experience in the business, this could be the easiest section of the business plan to write. However, once again make sure you reflect your management style and how you plan to operate the business. This is where you will have the greatest opportunity to really express your expertise, knowledge, and skills.

Seasoned investors and bankers pay special attention to this section because they are trying to determine if you will be able to do what you say. Leave no doubt in their minds. If you have had past business successes, this is the place to tell your story.

Days 20 and 21: Implementation Plan

Chapter 10 details how to write your implementation plan. This is very important for a business that is starting from scratch. Show how you plan to spend money on facilities, equipment, and marketing and sales.

TIP

Create a time line of the events and tactics you plan to employ or plot them into a calendar format.

Days 22 and 23: Contingency and Emergency Planning

Since 2001 I have recommended including a section in a business plan for contingency and emergency planning. If you are in an area that is prone to storms, hurricanes, and tornadoes you should have a separate disaster, emergency response, and business resumption plan.

Industrial businesses, manufacturers, and repair or service shops should have an emergency, first-aid plan in case of minor or major accidents. It is just good business and will mitigate your damages and costs.

Speak to your insurance agent about getting a "business overhead" insurance policy in case you are afflicted with a long-term illness. The funds can be used to replace you, pay bills, or allow you time to do an orderly shutdown of the business.

Read Chapter 11 and follow the instructions.

Days 24 to 27: Financial Plan

Your financial plan (pro forma statements) should reflect everything that happens in your business. You can download Excel worksheets from my Web site at www.sbishere.com to help you organize all your income and expense projections.

Read and implement the instructions in Chapter 9.

Day 28: Executive Summary

The executive summary is left until last because it is the first page your readers will see and should provide them with a brief overview of your whole business plan. Read Chapter 12 and follow the instructions.

Make sure to check my Web site as I will be providing a service to critique, edit, and support online.

Days 29 and 30: Final Review, Edit, and Rewrite

Find business people you trust and respect, and ask them to read your business plan and mark their comments and observations. It will give you fresh feedback and an opportunity to further refine and improve your business plan.

Check the business plan for grammatical and typographical errors. Use the spell check program in your word processor. I suggest waiting until you get feedback from others who have read your plan before making your final changes and edits, to save yourself time.

TIP

When seeking financing from a bank or investor, make sure that you get an accountant to review your pro forma financial projections for accuracy and completeness.

14

Common Mistakes in Writing a Business Plan

In this chapter I reveal the common pitfalls associated with writing a business plan, and I provide some tips to make sure you get the most from your investment of time and energy.

Writing a Business Plan to Get Funding

The first time many entrepreneurs have to come to grips with the concept of putting together a business plan is after a bank manager or investor asks for a business plan. Stress levels start to rise and the feeling of being overwhelmed begins. Relax! If you approach it as a process, use this book as your guide, and are willing to learn as you go, it will all come together in the end.

Getting Free Money

So you have heard about small business grants and some of you may have even bought a book on the subject. As for free money to start a business—I have not found any legitimate sources in the United States, and there are only a few government grant programs in Canada. Back on June 14, 2005, I issued a "Grant Challenge" on my blog, and so far no one who reads it (10,000+ a month) has commented or reported business grants.

TIP

There is no free money for someone wanting to start a business! There are loan programs but no free money programs.

TRAP

I have spoken to many people needing "free money" because they had none. Having no money is a good reason to stop and not bother to write a business plan. If you have no money to invest and do not have a positive "net worth," get a job; do not try to start a business. It takes money to make money. The only exception to this would be if you are starting a service business, and even then most service businesses need $3,000–$5,000 to get started.

Getting a Grant

If you are looking for a grant to start a business and did not read the free money tip above, please read it and then come back. I can only share what I have learned from consulting with entrepreneurs. Most of the people who call me looking for grant money to start a business have attended an expensive seminar, purchased an expensive "grant guide," or hired a firm to write a grant proposal to help them get free money. I can tell you that none of the people I spoke with have been successful finding money this way. Many have actually spent hundreds of dollars buying the services of a grant writer or paying for mailing lists, seminars, or books.

TRAP

The people promoting small business grant programs are making money from an unsuspecting public. Be careful of these programs. If I have not been able to find these free money programs, they do not exist. If you find one, I would sure like to hear from you because no one I have spoken to has actually gotten a dime to start a business using these free money tactics and strategies. They have just spent a lot of money going nowhere.

Getting a Business Loan to Start a Business

Starting a business is a legitimate reason to write a business plan. If you take seriously the process of writing a business plan to start a business and do not give short shrift to the process, you will be rewarded with in-depth knowledge of your business and reasonably accurate financial projections, and you will substantially increase your odds of succeeding. Generally, financial institutions (including Small Business Administration loans) for a business start-up will require you to invest 25 percent of your own capital or have equity you can use as collateral to get the start-up capital.

Getting a Business Loan to Grow an Existing Business

If you already have an existing business, have done some financing with your bank, and are looking for additional funds to expand your business or consolidate debt, it's likely that you already have a business plan. In limited cases some banks and financial institutions accept a "loan proposal" in lieu of a full business plan. When a loan is completed in this manner, it is usually because of a strong banking relationship, very successful business, or a well-qualified business owner (high net worth with perfect credit).

TIP

If you fit the description above, call your banker and ask if he or she will accept a loan proposal with past financial statements in lieu of a full business plan. You might be pleasantly surprised and save yourself a lot of time, effort, and energy.

Getting a Business Loan to Buy a Franchise or Business

Writing a business plan for the purpose of buying a franchise is a good idea because, even though the franchise may have a sample plan or template to help you get financing (some have preferred loan packages they can offer), it is always a good idea to do your own due diligence to protect yourself—especially with older franchises. Older, more established franchises tend to be quite saturated, and any markets that are available are often marginal markets with limited potential. New franchise concepts may not be thoroughly tested and proven. Writing a business plan to enable you to buy a franchise serves an insurance policy—any decisions you make are well informed and carefully thought out. If you are buying an existing business, you will need a business plan whether you go to the bank or get the seller to finance your purchase. Just as with a franchise, a business plan will protect your interests and make sure that you are thinking for yourself, informed and, most important, know you have a plan to succeed.

Writing a Business Plan to Get Your Business Organized

Depending what you are using as a guide to write a business plan, the plan can be a great tool for getting your business started, or it could be setting you up for failure. Using templates or sample business plans to help you start a business is like writing your own legal agreements. You can do it, but all it will do is get you in more trouble than if you had done nothing at all. Instead, follow the steps in this book to examine every aspect of your business, organize yourself, and write a specific and effective business plan.

The Dangers of Using a Template and Just Changing the Names

Sample business plans and templates are simply too general. Just as with a generic legal agreement that lacks specifics, using a business plan template or sample plan without checking its details prevents you from adequately identifying risks and liabilities, and you run the risk of getting the business and its directors in trouble.

TRAP

Unless something is spelled out, disclosed, or excluded, it will be considered to have been included because of the general and broad terms of the business plan. Seek the advice of legal counsel before making major business decisions.

Writing a Business Plan because Your Banker Asked for It

If you have not already heard your banker ask you for a business plan, you soon will.

TIP

You can do a lot to impress a banker by taking your completed business plan to your first meeting.

I guarantee that your banker will be impressed because most people come into the bank with their hat in their hands asking for a business loan. If you do not have a business plan, the banker has no choice but to do the "20 Questions" routine and then, if they are still interested, ask you to come back when you have your business plan to get the process started. If you want to look and be treated professionally and seriously, bring your business plan with you from the beginning.

Writing a Business Plan because You've Been Told You Need One

If you have friends and family telling you to write a business plan, you are lucky because it means you have people around you who care. It may also mean that they are not 100 percent sold on your business idea and their telling you that you need a business plan is their way of telling you indirectly that they are not sold. If you cannot sell the people who are closest to you on your business idea, perhaps it has flaws or is more risky than you can see right now.

Write a business plan to reduce your risk. This is another way of saying that you want to increase your odds of success. Writing a business plan by following the guidelines in this book should reduce your risk. I say "should" because a business plan is only as good as the due diligence exercised examining the assumptions you have made in your plan. In other words, taking the time to obtain independent, third-party verification of your beliefs, data, or facts is necessary.

TIP

You should strive to eliminate all assumptions in your business plan by replacing these assumptions with facts obtained through research, fieldwork, or real world testing.

What to Do If You Have No Business Experience

If you are starting or buying a business that you have no experience in, you are either a gambler at heart or you have not thought the decision all the way through. Perhaps you find yourself unemployed and think that now is the time to make a career change by starting or buying your own business. Good for you, but be careful!

TRAP

While you may be an experienced manager, that is not the same as being a business owner. There are many things an owner must deal with that a manager doesn't. A business plan will help you make sure you think through your decision and put together a realistic plan.

If you are a young person and you just feel the drive to be self-employed, you are joining the ranks of many of your classmates and peers. The ranks of the entrepreneur are being filled with young people (born after 1985) and older baby boomers (age 55+), who are both starting or buying a business for the first time. Learning to write a business plan can be an excellent tool to provide both groups with perspective and insight into the physics of owning a business.

If you plan to start a business that you do not have direct experience or knowledge of, I suggest the following course of action:

- Look for a business partner who does have the experience.
- Recruit a general manager or operations manager with direct industry experience.
- Before you start your business, get a job with your future competitor. Take the time to learn from an expert. It will give you the opportunity to learn about the business directly.

TIP

Hire a business coach with direct experience in your business or with the proven ability to plan, launch, and develop a business from scratch. Have him or her review your business plan and make suggestions. A business coach will teach and educate you as well as provide coaching and support. Feel free to contact me and I will do my best to help you out.

- Direct your energies and efforts toward a venture that more directly suits your skills, experience, and interests. In the long run you'll be much better off, happier, and more successful.
- You could also buy an existing business. What if I told you that it was cheaper, less risky, and that you make more money buying a business versus starting one from scratch? You would want to know more, right? Check out my other book *Tips and Traps When Buying a Business*.

Beware of the B.S. Factor

To stay organized, you will need to reread your business plan and compare your financial projections to your actual results.

TRAP

It is vital that you make changes to your business plan based upon what you learn from your actual results. Otherwise you will join the ranks of those bankrupt firms that had a business plan but never reviewed it, or, worse, never made any changes after reviewing it.

Business owners who do not adjust their plans to the reality of their businesses fall into the worst trap of them all—believing their own B.S. Not a good trait for a profitable and successful entrepreneur.

Writing a Business Plan without Financial Statements

Not doing financial projections is like playing darts blindfolded. If you do mange to hit anything, it is pure dumb luck. Without financial projections you have no benchmark against which to measure the performance of the business.

TIP

Even if you are funding the business yourself, you should still prepare financial statements. After all, you worked hard for your money. Why not protect it?

Making Assumptions and Decisions without All the Facts

Entrepreneurs are known to be independent, strong-minded, and aggressive. They learn to rely on their knowledge, experience, and intuition. Good thing they do because if they did not believe in an idea strongly, many of the products and services we enjoy today would not exist.

TRAP

Making decisions without enough information is often a reflection of the lack of experience of the business owner. When writing a business plan, the same thing can easily happen. Dig for more information, and, if you are stuck, find a friend with more business experience then you and ask that friend for feedback. What would this person do if he or she were in your shoes?

TIP

If there is anything about your business plan that you do not understand or cannot prove with independent, third-party data, proceed with caution. Do not skip, gloss over, or avoid dealing with the issue. Seek to understand the nature of the issue.

It might require reading your business plan over or rereading this book or at least the appropriate section. Just because information is hard to come by does not mean it is not available or that you should ignore it.

TIP

Remember, I am only an e-mail away and, if you need help, just visit my Web site (www.sbishere.com), find the contact section, and send me an e-mail. I answer all inquiries.

Ignoring Risk = Gambling

What creates risk? In my experience it is a lack of balance in the business plan that creates unwarranted and unmanageable risk. So the next question is, what creates imbalance? Lack of experience, because without direct experience or access to someone with experience, making a quality decision can quickly be reduced to a guess. For a business owner who lacks experience in the business, what does he or she have to fall back on? Information.

TIP

Replace your lack of experience with information in the form of your business plan. A business plan will allow you to test your ideas on paper without the risk of spending money, wasting time, or incurring debt. You can research different business ideas online and create different scenarios in your financial projections to see the impact that a drop in sales or increase in costs could have. This information will help you in making decisions about the changes in your business that need to be made.

In every business there are many decisions that need to be made, so if you lack the experience, seek information! Speak with more experienced business owners, conduct research online, and ask questions.

Trying to Go It Alone

Trying to fly solo is fine as long as you have experience. The reason student pilots must first prove themselves with an instructor in the next seat is that, if they get overwhelmed or confused, there is someone there to bail them out.

TRAP

Why do we as entrepreneurs think we can go it alone? Perhaps it is not a life and death situation, but a business that crashes is still a sad event because it is unnecessary. Don't be afraid to ask for help.

Ask a friend for help, or ask someone with more experience than yourself or with a successful track record. If you lack experience, you could take on a partner with experience or recruit and hire experienced personnel. Then the business will not struggle to perform at an acceptable level.

TRAP

There is nothing more frustrating for a customer than dealing with an employee who just does not have experience. Do not get caught in the trap of trying to reinvent the wheel. Hiring inexperienced staff and then training them is very expensive, not to mention the cost of lost opportunities or lost customers.

Not Enough Detail in the Business Plan

Be specific and avoid making generalities and using broad brushstrokes. If your business plan contains generalities or phrases that try to minimize a problem or business issue, you need to rethink your approach.

TIP

You are always much safer with more detail than less because you are less likely to miss an important piece of information and make a poor decision or assumption. After all, the whole point of writing a business plan is to reduce risk.

Not Customizing Your Business Plan for the Reader

Your executive summary should be modified for each person you plan to give it to. Keep in mind that a business plan is written to communicate the viability of an idea so that the person writing the plan can obtain financing or investment capital. Keep in mind who will read it and what they expect to learn from it. Remember, there are basically two audiences:

- *Internal audience:* People such as yourself and your key employees, who will be a part of your firm. Since you will be using the plan on an ongoing basis, make sure that the format and structure are something you are comfortable working with.

- *External audience:* These are people outside the organization who will want to see some or all of the documents that make up your plan before they decide if they want to invest in, contract with, or otherwise have a relationship with you. These include such people as your banker, venture capitalists, credit rating firms, and vendors.

TIP

Remember, you do not always have to provide a full copy of your plan. Sometimes an excerpt, summary, or just financial statements and projections will suffice. When you provide people with a full copy of your plan, get them to sign a confidentiality and nondisclosure agreement. If you are providing them with proprietary information, a secrecy agreement or noncompetition agreement might be appropriate. Use good judgment and exercise caution. Speak to an attorney.

Not Writing a Business Plan or Not Finishing It

A business plan is a valuable document. In fact it is a sales document. It sells the reader—a banker, investor, or venture capital company—on your business idea. Plus, writing a business plan will help you understand your business and ways to improve it.

If a business plan is worth starting, it is worth finishing because from that point forward all you have to do is review it and edit it on an annual basis. It gets easier as the years pass. Furthermore, the discipline of reviewing your business plan will allow you to make adjustments and improvements within the context of actual versus planned results.

TIP

Don't let your business plan fall by the wayside. It deserves to be finished!

Inflating Revenue or the Sales Forecast

You find yourself looking at your financial projections, and you see a lot of numbers in red that are showing a loss. It seems so simple to prevent showing a loss by increasing the revenues until it starts to show a small profit.

TRAP

Simply entering new numbers into a spreadsheet does not make the problem go away. The problem is still there; it is simply masked by an inflated sales forecast.

You need to mirror your actions in real life when building your business plan. Think of it this way. If you found yourself looking at an income statement that showed you were losing money, what would you do? You would investigate to see if you could identify the reason for spending more than you make. You would look for ways to increase sales, too.

TIP

Any time you decide to increase your sales forecast, ask yourself, "How am I going to actually increase sales? What is my strategy? What is the probability that the strategy will work? If my strategy fails what is my plan B?"

Not Starting a Business Plan
Because It's Too Much Work

As Rodney Dangerfield used to say, "I don't get no respect!" Business plans suffer from the same image problem. Just as business has changed in the last 100 years, the process of planning and writing a business plan has also evolved.

I ran across a Web site that published an article by a CPA that said that you do not need a business plan. He goes on to say that what you need instead is a planning process. Well that is exactly what this book is about, a process to help you build a plan for your business and get the financing and funding you need.

I promise that if you read this book and apply the process on putting your plan to paper, you will learn a lot about your business, yourself, and your customers. If you want to learn the nuts and bolts of running a business, writing a business plan will speed your development process.

15

Working with Professional Advisers

The purpose of this chapter is to show you how to get the most from a team of advisers. Professional advisers protect your interests and help you achieve your goals.

To win in the game of football, you need a good offense and a good defense. No one would go into a game of football without a defense because you cannot win if you play only the offensive half of the game. As ridiculous as this sounds many businesses are so focused on the offensive part of their game (sales) that they ignore protecting what they have with a proper defense.

TIP

In business your defensive strategy is made up of bookkeeping and legal and management controls. Your defensive team members include management, bookkeeper, accountant, attorney, and you. Your business plan is a defensive tool that adds balance to your overall offensive and defensive strategy.

It takes both an offensive team (sales, marketing, advertising, etc.) and a defensive team (administration, accounting, legal, etc.) to win the game of business. No one builds a business alone; you should not try to grow a business alone. You need a team of advisers to help you take a close look at the business to make sure you know what it is you are getting yourself into.

History of Business Advisers

The history of business advisers is obviously very long. For the purposes of this chapter, we will deal in the modern era of business advisers. Traditional business advisers are broken down into the following groups:

- *Family:* According to a 2002 study by the National Federation of Independent Businesses (NFIB), the business owner's number 1 adviser is family—by a large margin. Nearly 70 percent of business owners who responded listed "family." Does a family member have the background and experience to be able to competently guide a business owner in planning, decision-making, and implementation?

- *Accountants and lawyers:* these professionals are primarily focused on compliance issues and business owners need a much wider scope of advice. They need help with marketing, sales, customer service, hiring and training an effective workforce, leadership skills, and so on. Accountants simply are not trained in these areas. It is the same with lawyers.

- *Bankers, financial experts:* While business owners will have a close relationship with their banker, the advice a banker can offer is limited in scope.

- *Business consultants and experts:* A consultant can tell you what you "should" do, whereas a coach can deal with the personal effectiveness side of the equation. Business owners are people too and like others tend to stay within their own comfort zone, habits, and experience.

The "Coaching" Side of Business Coaching

The following groups of professionals have all contributed in some way to business coaching practices:

- *The mental health field:* Professionals in this field study the cause-and-effect side of disorders. Many principles are also be used to improve the lives of healthy people. Practices such as neurolinguistic programming (NLP) began to go mainstream even by those outside the mental health field.

- *The "self-help" movement:* The founders of this movement, having studied and formulated theories and practices of personal effectiveness referred to above, helped many people understand their emotions and their ability to effect changes in their lives through books, seminars, and the like.

TRAP

The challenge is that after a self-help seminar, it is easy to fall back into the warm and friendly comfort zone. The large majority of people do not finish reading the books they buy, listen to tapes all the way through, or perform the suggested tasks and exercises.

- *Coaching:* Coaching first arrived as a redirection of the psychological field. Many practitioners who wanted to focus on the future rather than the past adopted this great term. The systematic and recurring contact that coaching provided simply helped people more effectively than seminars, books, and tapes could. Since *habits* define the quality of our lives, the change from old habits to new, more effective habits is achieved through a long-term approach.

TIP

When done properly in a trusting relationship, coaching can and does have a tremendous impact on clients' lives.

- *Executive coaching:* Because the coaching model worked so well for personal effectiveness, it helped harried executives deal with stress, emotions, coworkers, superiors, subordinates, and leadership development. Since these challenges are personal in nature and large companies already have the business resources, it has been, and will continue to be, effective by bringing positive change to both thought and behavioral habits.

Business Coaching

Since personal effectiveness training and coaching worked for people "in business" (see executive coaching above), today's business coaches believe that it should also work for today's business owners.

Many teach that business advice, experience, and knowledge are unnecessary. Why would they say that? Because they feel that business owners are people, and obviously personal effectiveness will help them improve to a certain level.

Unfortunately, most small business owners don't have vice presidents of marketing, sales, customer service, and finance to give them the business portion of their growth! Nor do they have the resources to hire them.

TRAP

Similar to the consultants who focused on the business side and ignored the personal effectiveness side of the equation, business coaches today who focus solely on personal effectiveness while ignoring the business side struggle mightily to deliver real long-term results.

You and Your Team

Your team should be made up of a CPA (financial review), attorney (legal agreements, incorporation, contract review. etc.) and a business coach (to fill the gaps). Be sure to define their roles and responsibilities and tell them what your expectations are of them. Negotiate a fixed fee for their services.

Understand that the purpose of your attorney and CPA is to protect your interests. In a sense, part of their job description is to explain the risks and potential pitfalls. They are looking for holes in your ideas to identify liabilities that you should not be exposing yourself to. Their job is to help you identify potential problems.

TIP

Remember, you are the decision maker.

As important as your advisers are, do not let them set your agenda, negotiate for you, or make decisions for you. Only you can do that, but you do want to ask them for specific advice.

Advisers Provide Perspective

You will want your advisers to work with you to help you find potential errors, omissions, or problems with your strategies and ideas. Their greatest value is that they do not have the same vested interest that you have; they are not running the business themselves but are helping you. By working with them, you get an independent third-party perspective. They have no emotional ties in the transaction and are free to speak from an unemotional perspective.

TRAP

Often owners get emotionally attached to an idea. When this happens to you, I recommend that you spend time working with your advisers. Ask them specific questions and ask for their opinions. Ultimately you will be making the decision, but their perspective could help balance your desire to make a deal with the information and perspective you had not previously enjoyed.

Working with an Accountant and an Attorney

All accountants have a specialty. Some only do tax returns, others specialize in tax planning and financial planning, while still others are experienced in dealing with corporations. If you can find a few with experience in your industry, that experience could be invaluable to you.

Your attorney's job is to help you prepare legal agreements, review contracts, and help you incorporate if you're planning to do so. You should look for an attorney who is willing to offer you advice and to educate you about your legal obligations and fiduciary responsibilities. Especially if you are new to owning a business, there are many specific things you will want to look at including tax remittances, legal obligations to employees, suppliers, and investors or partners.

Informal Advisers

You will also want to have at least one close and trusted friend who is willing to look you in the eye and tell you the truth or that you have lost perspective. You want someone in your corner who is looking out for your best interests and can provide a truly independent perspective.

Some business owners even go so far as to form an informal board of advisers. These advisers might range from other business owners to friends, family members, or other people whom they respect and who can contribute information and feedback from their depth of experience. As a result, you end up being much better prepared to deal with a particular situation. Plus, when you have to make a presentation in front of a group of people whom you trust and like, it really makes you think and it ensures that you're prepared. If you cannot convince your fans why you want to implement a certain strategy, why you think you need to take this approach, or why you want to make certain compromises to your business plan, you have a problem. If you cannot convince them or articulate your reasons with enough passion to sway them, you should probably not be pursuing the idea.

Your team of informal and professional advisers will help protect your interests and help you achieve your goals. That kind of support is always money well spent.

PART 4

Special Considerations for Specific Businesses

16

Business Planning for Inventors

Inventing a product and bringing it to market is an arduous task and can easily become a consuming passion. As you get deeper and deeper into the project, emotional detachment disappears. You become so committed financially and emotionally that your ability to make effective decisions becomes impaired.

The good news is that investing time, effort, and energy into writing a business plan will provide you with the structure and process that will enable you to make decisions and develop your product from the idea stage to a profitable business.

TIP

Developing your idea into a working prototype is the easiest part of bringing a new product or invention to market. The greatest challenge is how to create a profitable business around the product. This is where a business plan comes into play.

The purpose of this chapter is to provide you with specific insights and information on how to approach writing a business plan to get the money and resources to build a business around your invention.

Writing your business plan will definitely be an evolutionary process. Think of your business plan as a living document that evolves and changes to provide the support and information you need to grow your business.

Just as your invention developed, evolved, and changed over time, so will your plan.

As you discover new product features and market potential and meet with your professional advisers, your business plan will evolve. That is the way it should be. Your financial needs could change substantially based upon what you discover in building your prototype or doing a market test, and you will want those changes reflected in your business plan. If you have a written business plan with financial projections, you will easily be able to edit your plan and see immediately what impact these changes will have on your business and finance needs.

Managing the Details

It is a lack of information that is the major hurdle when it comes to writing a business plan. The inventor has the toughest assignment of all business owners when it comes to writing a business plan because there are more variables to deal with. Issues can arise that could completely change your direction.

As the inventor you have a lot of information in your head, information about the product—how it will be used and the need that it will fill. To transform your product from an idea into a profitable business will require that you translate your thoughts onto paper. It is very important to describe your idea and create technical drawings early on in the development process. Then, be willing to apply logic and business principles to bring your product into the real world using your business plan as the tool to help you get there.

In many ways building a business around an invention is very similar to starting a business from scratch, except for the significant investment that typically needs to be made in research and development (R&D).

The major issues that you will want to pay special attention to when writing a business plan are product development, business development, and market research. You will also need to pay special attention to protecting your intellectual property.

Product Development: Building a Prototype

Building a working prototype is a milestone that brings your idea to life. It forces you to work through the manufacturing issues and what you learn will help you tremendously in refining your business plan. Further, once you have the actual product built, you have a wonderful opportunity to put the product into the hands of your potential customers to get their feedback.

TIP

Wait until you have your patent before showing your product to the public. As soon as you put the product out in the public, your nondisclosure agreements could become null and void.

TIP

Consumer testing is a tremendous opportunity to get feedback from actual users, which will allow you to refine and possibly modify your product offering before you launch.

Business Development

Now is the time to start adding more structure to your business by addressing the legal, market, and financial aspects of developing a business around your invention.

Legal Protection

You will need an attorney to create some basic agreements, including a nondisclosure agreement, contracts, and in some cases noncompetition agreements to protect your ideas. A nondisclosure agreement prevents the signing parties from discussing, disclosing, or disseminating your ideas and concepts for a specific period of time. A noncompetition agreement prevents one party from going into the same business for a specific period of time, thereby preventing that party from competing with you. Your attorney may have other agreements that she or he will want to set up based on your individual situation.

TRAP

Do not ever use templates or other agreements that you buy in a stationery store because they are too general and may actually get you into more trouble than if you had no agreement at all. Seek a professional business coach, accountant, or attorney before taking action or making major business decisions.

Market Testing

Once you have tested the product with customers, it is time to conduct test marketing and selling your product in a real-world situation. This is done to gauge the effectiveness of your marketing, advertising, and sales strategies before you do a full product launch.

It is also another chance to have your market teach you how to promote and sell your product.

Financing Research and Development

One of the challenges of bringing a product to market is financing the earliest stages of product development. Most often this is accomplished by the inventor borrowing money from the bank, secured by personal assets. This is by far the cheapest option because taking money from investors will usually require giving them a controlling interest in your company. Handing over control of the company plus the majority of all future profits is the most expensive form of financing.

TRAP

Borrowing money from family can be a good option, but it can also come with strings attached. Further, if relatives ask to be repaid at a time when you do not have the money to spare, it can create hard feelings and unnecessary stress. Proceed with caution.

One of the ways that I have seen biotechnology companies raise funds while in the research and development stage is to license the marketing rights for their product. Essentially, a vendor pays you a sum of money for the marketing rights once the product has received regulatory approval from the FDA (Food and Drug Administration). Then you use that money to continue developing your product. The same opportunity sometimes exists when licensing the distribution rights. Just remember that you need to seek professional assistance before making any major decisions, and you need to consider all your decisions within the context of your business plan.

Market Research

Knowing your competition and whether your market is large enough to support a business around your invention is the first acid test for determining the viability and potential for your invention.

Competition

Examining competitive products is a must for a new product entering a market. By conducting a thorough analysis of competitive products, you can learn about your market and identify how your product differs from what is already out there or refine it to make sure that it is superior.

Market Size

The idea for your invention likely came to you because you recognized a need or better way of doing something. In designing your product, you would have considered the needs of the customer and how the product will be used.

The size of the market that will use your product directly affects the viability and profitability of your product. Therefore determining the market size is a crucial acid test.

As I mentioned in a previous chapter, one of my clients retained me to help them write a business plan for their new software product. They had made certain assumptions about the needs of the market which they had pretty well defined. However, when I went to research the size of the market, I was shocked to discover that in order to meet their revenue assumptions, they would have to sell to 150 percent of the market. In other words, everyone in the market would need to buy their product 1.5 times, a totally impossible and unrealistic goal. The market they were targeting was too small. So what did we do? First, we revisited their definition of the market and the needs of that the market. Then I asked them, "What other markets have similar problems?" Their answer identified a market that was substantially larger.

To meet the needs of this market, my clients had to make some adjustments in the design of the software product and in their marketing approach. But what's important is that we caught the error early enough so that they could make adjustments before the product was finished and they had spent money on marketing and promotion. Ultimately, their market share needed to be only 1.5 percent, which was a realistic estimate for the first year and one hundred times smaller than their first assumption.

The point to take away from this story is that had my clients not started the process of writing a business plan, they would have spent almost all their money developing a product for a market that could not possibly sustain the business. This is something you must find out sooner than later.

TIP

You can easily find market size and market data at bizminer.com for U.S. markets (prices start at $59) and for Canadian markets at the Industry Canada Web site. Just go to http://strategis.ic.gc.ca and search for "Performance Plus."

Advice for Inventors

Slow and steady is the best advice for any inventor. There are so many people wanting to sell you something to help you get to market. Take the time to develop a business plan even if you only plan to license the manufacturing or marketing rights to your product, because it will help you make a quality business decision based on business logic, not emotion.

Protect your Intellectual Property

Protecting your idea with legal agreements and patent protection is the first step to maintaining control. Your idea will become worthless if you share it indiscriminately and do not protect it. No matter how much you need money or need to take advantage of getting into the market first, in most cases you should to wait until you get a patent before moving forward.

In an age of duplication, peer-to-peer sharing of MP3 files, the growth of China's manufacturing capacity, and outsourcing to India, you really need to protect your idea with a patent or copyright. Any time that you lose waiting for a patent will be made up because you have patent protection.

Beware of Fraud

You might be surprised at how many so-called businesses there are out there trying to lighten the inventor's wallet. If it is too good to be true, it is too good to be true.

There are scams that offer everything from patent protection to bringing your product to market, and amazingly they seem to be able to do it for the exact sum of money you say you have available. Beware of these offers, and check them out carefully before proceeding.

TIP

Part of educating yourself should mean a visit to the National Inventor Fraud Center (http://www.inventorfraud.com/index.htm), which will provide U.S. inventors with a great overview of things to look out for, as well as some helpful tips. The site is maintained by a patent attorney.

TIP

If you are an inventor, consider getting a good attorney or lawyer to help you with patent and copyright issues.

Making Money from Your Invention

There are really two reasons to invent a product: to make money and to help people by solving a common problem. Since you are reading a business book, I assume that you're working on your invention for profit. There are a variety of strategies and tools you can use to make money from your invention.

Licensing

A *license* is a document that provides certain rights to the licensee. As a licensor (i.e., the owner), think of licensing your idea as renting it out, because there are no ownership rights inferred or transferred. Licensees are granted specific rights approved by the owner.

For example, these rights could include manufacturing rights (to build your product), marketing rights (to sell your product), or distribution rights (either wholesale or distribution by a third party). These rights can include specific obligations or conditions that need to be fulfilled to maintain, extend, or earn the license.

Fees paid for a license can include lump sums, shares in a company, and/or royalties. Whatever you can negotiate and is legal can be set up to compensate you for your time and the value of your invention.

Buying a Business

One way to keep control of the entire value chain is to buy a business in the industry and use it to manufacture, market, and distribute your product yourself. Buying a business can be an especially attractive option for an inventor. For example, a software developer might buy a business that has existing relationships with other businesses in order to gain access to the market or to sell the software product alongside complementary products.

TRAP

This option is often overlooked even by experienced entrepreneurs, because they are so confident in their abilities that they often fail to thoroughly investigate all their options.

TIP

One of the best reasons for an inventor to buy an existing business is to be able to tap into existing client relationships and substantially reduce the amount of time it takes to get to market when compared to starting from scratch. In my book, *Tips and Traps When Buying a Business,* I list eight reasons to buy a business versus starting from scratch.

Selling Your Invention Outright

If you do not see yourself as a manager, then another great option would be to sell your invention outright. This would bring in a larger lump sum and could also include ongoing royalties.

To sell your invention outright, you really need to have a good idea of the future value that the person buying the invention could gain as a result. This would require a good business plan and likely some operational experience in order to assign an accurate estimate of the earning potential before coming up with an amount you would be willing to accept.

TIP

Selling is a great option for someone who desires to keep inventing products and is not interested in managing a business. This could also be a good decision if your life goals are to focus on retirement.

17

Business Planning for a Retail Business

The job of marketing is to get your message in front of your best customer. In retail it is all about location, location, location.

Describe Your Retail Location

Unlike a business-to-business (B2B) firm that can reach out to potential customers by hiring salespeople, retail businesses have roots. They have to wait for the customer to come to them. Therefore, location of a retail business is a strategic decision that will correlate directly with the success of your retail business.

In your business plan, be sure to explain how you determined that your location is within or very near the market that you intend to serve. Add how the location will reduce your dependence on advertising and marketing to generate store traffic.

High End = High Rent

High-end retail locations get the highest rental rates because they generally get above-average foot traffic. This is a double-edged sword because the high rents mean that you have to either sell at higher prices or do a higher volume of sales to offset the high rent. You need to be able to justify this decision in your business plan.

TRAP

Be cautious in just assuming that you will be able to increase sales to offset the higher rent costs. Prove it to yourself. Run different financial projections using different amounts for rent to see what the impact will be on your profitability and how much you will have to generate in revenues to be profitable.

Do Your Own Investigation

Generally major malls, power centers, or prime downtown locations will demand higher rent per square foot. A real estate agent or mall management should be able to provide you with a wide variety of statistics. Get these statistics, which could range from the average number of cars during peak hours to average daily or monthly foot traffic. In addition to reviewing these statistics, you should perform your own investigation of the retail location.

Get to Know the Neighbors

Let's assume that you're considering locating at a mall. Speak to other tenants in the mall. Find out how things are going and the track record of mall management.

TIP

Make sure to speak with a wide enough cross section to get a good feel from smaller stores, larger tenants, and especially retailers similar to your planned operation.

When you're speaking to other tenants, ask them how they feel about their location and what they would do differently next time. Their answers to these two questions might uncover some very important considerations you had not previously thought of.

Get to Know the Facility

If your location in the mall happens to have a lot of turnover, you can bet that there is a good reason for it. Visit the mall during peak periods and observe the traffic patterns to see what you can discover.

Think about your retail business and the type of products or services you will sell. Are they typically an impulse purchase? If so, then an inside corner location would be a very good choice. Also, be sure to look at neighboring stores. For example, opening a Dollar Store next door to a bank or major grocery store might work well.

TIP

With a high-traffic retail mall location, you will be required to pay a percentage of your sales toward the "advertising pool" administered by mall management. On the other hand, with a lower-priced location the landlord will leave you to fend for yourself, but the lower-cost facility allows you more control over where to invest your advertising and marketing dollars. If you consider yourself a savvy marketer, then going it on your own could be a good choice. But if you like the idea of someone else making those decisions, a high-traffic mall where you pay a percentage of your sales might be right for you.

How to Deal with a Less-Than-Ideal Location

If your location is hidden away at the end of a dead end or cul-de-sac or in another less-than-ideal location, you will need to figure out if you can offset that disadvantage with marketing, advertising, and promotion. One of the advantages of this kind of location is that you will pay less for it and should therefore have a lower breakeven point and more money to allocate to advertising and promotion.

TIP

Pay special attention to your marketing, advertising, and customer service system. In a lower-traffic location advertising and marketing are the backbone of your business, and your banker or investor needs to believe in your ability to make them work. Whatever your choice, a high-end mall with proven traffic statistics or a location that provides more autonomy, explain your decision with supporting statistics, strategies, and tactics.

Document Customer Shopping Patterns and Preferences

Try to determine the patterns and preferences of your potential customers. Do they shop around or buy on impulse? Do they prefer value or convenience? For example, customers might seek out a photographer based on reputation, because they want a portrait to commemorate a special occasion, or they might notice a high-volume, low-price studio in a convenient location and stop in to get a quick picture of the kids.

TIP

Make sure your marketing analysis and strategy reflect the needs, wants, shopping patterns, and preferences of your target market. Knowing this information is not only important to running your business successfully, but it is also something your banker and investor will need to understand.

Drawing Traffic by Locating Close to Other Tenants

A popular strategy in retail is to locate close to a major chain store. As the major chain draws customers to its location, a store located close by can benefit as the chain's customers drop in on their way in or out.

I remember a friend of mine who opened a bulk food and produce store next to a major grocery chain. It was a stroke of genius because his superior (low-margin) produce drew customers in from the grocery store. He made his profit on the bulk food sales that people would pick up while coming in for the produce.

It worked very well for him until the big grocery store chain took action to shore up its wilting produce sales and decided to cut prices and open up their own bulk food section. Unfortunately, my friend ultimately had to close his doors because people were not willing to shop in a second store when they could get everything in one place.

TRAP

Be careful of the assumptions you make based upon drawing traffic from a bigger, brand-name neighbor. It could work, but it could also backfire.

Staff Recruiting and Training

One challenge of operating a retail business is that recruiting younger workers is becoming increasingly difficult because of their small numbers, unwillingness to take entry-level jobs, and a growing preference among college students for self-employment.

Because of this challenge, your personnel plan needs to include a solid recruiting and training system. One of the more recent trends is to recruit semi-retired baby boomers that need to supplement their income or simply like to keep busy. They make good employees because they're generally responsible and have a life full of experience to draw upon. Part-time baby boomers will in time become the labor force for a fast-food and retail industry desperately seeking quality employees.

Buying the Right Inventory

Obviously you will need inventory to sell. An important part of your marketing strategy needs to revolve around product selection. Having the right products at the right time can make all the difference between a great month and a poor one. Make sure that you include your purchasing policies, knowledge of consumer needs, and their purchasing patterns in your business plan.

TRAP

Don't squander the opportunity to make money by purchasing the wrong mix of products. Do your homework before choosing what items to stock.

TIP

Working with your suppliers can help you a lot in making good buying decisions. They should have a good idea of what is selling. The best suppliers will work with you, and most will offer some sort of booking program that allows you to buy at deep discounts and generous payment terms for ordering well in advance. Some may even offer return programs.

The Retail Marketing Secret

Regardless of where you decide to locate, every retail store can easily create its own private marketplace by setting up a loyalty marketing system in which you record the contact information and personal preferences of each of your customers. With a small investment and a little work you can build relationships with your customers and market to them in a manner you deem appropriate.

TRAP

The longer you are in business, the more you will tend to think you understand your market. Be sure that you aren't just operating on assumptions.

Create Your Own Private Marketplace

Register and keep track of every sale you ever make, and then use this list to target customers for special treatment and offers. To do this, you will need to set up a database and a strategy to reward loyalty.

To create a database, begin with customer names, and then segment and tag the list by any defining criterion that makes sense to you. It can include obvious categorization schemes including types of products, season, size, or color preferences. Plan to keep in touch with these customers on an infrequent basis. Do not make it a regular routine unless you have something like a newsletter, where the value of the information is to use it in a timely fashion.

Do not overdo it. The last thing you want is for your customers to feel that they are being "marketed" to. You want them to feel appreciated and reward them occasionally with an unexpected surprise. This surprise can include everything from a personal note to a printed postcard to a small gift or coupon they can redeem. Imagine if over the course of a couple of years you communicated with them at a time when they were not buying or needing your product or service. You would have your own private marketplace, a marketplace that your competitors couldn't tap into unless they had your mailing list (and you're not giving that to them, are you?).

What Type of Retail Business Do You Want?

The more specifically you define what type of retail business you want and the more your goals are congruent with your customers needs, the easier it will be to stay in alignment with the marketplace. This will help you maintain a sustainable competitive advantage.

TIP

Clarify your goals and define your vision and mission.

On a regular basis, hold informal customer focus groups and ask them questions like:

- Why did you choose to do business with me?
- What can I do to improve?
- How have your needs changed in the past year?
- What do you wish I would do or sell that I currently do not offer? Where do you buy it now? How much do you pay? What do you like about the product or business?

Ask lots of questions and listen for your customers' opinions and anything that they express strong feelings about. Their answers will reveal buying tendencies and opinions that can help shape your inventory purchasing strategy.

18

Business Planning for a Manufacturing Business

Writing a business plan for a manufacturing business involves paying special attention to the required resources, equipment, and qualified technical staff. This chapter highlights additional considerations that manufacturers need to include in their business plans. It covers information beyond that found in the standard 10 sections of a business plan.

Manufacturing a finished product requires a different business plan from that of a company that manufactures components for another firm which then assembles the final product.

The biggest difference is in the attention to detail needed to develop accurate pro forma financial statements and in writing the plan.

Specific Operational Information to Include

In your business plan, you will want to include information about utilities, fixtures and equipment, raw materials, transportation costs, and inventory management. Your plan should take into account real estate—specifically buildings and renovations for the period the business plan covers.

Role of Quality Management Systems

Quality management systems should be mentioned in the management section of the business plan. Include a copy of your International Standards

Organization (ISO) certificate from your authorized ISO registrar, if you have one. If you do not yet have an independently certified quality management system it is something you should seriously consider making an investment in. A quality management system takes time and money to create and implement, so make sure to take that into account.

TIP

Find an ISO certified consultant to assist you in the process of developing your system and preparing for certification. Attaining ISO certification can provide a significant competive advantage. In some industries such certification is required just to be able to compete on the same level.

Document Your Input Costs and Considerations

Changes in your input costs need to be built into your financial assumptions. This includes pricing of raw materials, utilities (energy, gas, water, waste management), and transportation costs.

TIP

Do not forget to include the costs of financing your inventory to maintaining a supply of raw materials plus the related costs to carrying and maintaining your inventory.

Equipment Depreciation

Manufacturers have a significant investment in equipment, fixtures, and buildings. Depreciation for each asset needs to be tracked and included in your financial projections.

TIP

Provide a complete list of all your equipment including serial numbers, age, condition, and life expectancy. Also include any capital expenditures that you will need to make to replace aging equipment or fixtures.

Facility Design and Operations Layout

The efficiency of a manufacturing facility is in direct proportion to the design of production and work flow. Include specifics about your facility and operations design. You should provide answers to the following questions:

- What are the major pieces of equipment that will be required to produce the anticipated volume?

- Based on the sales volume you anticipate, how much space will you need?

- What is the maximum output per unit of time in the design of the facility? Are there areas where improvements could be made? What would the financial impact be of these improvements? How will they make the operation more productive?

- Where will you place the equipment? What is your floor plan layout? How do you expect to make use of the space?

- What are the power requirements? Will you need to hire a contractor to make modifications to the power supply? If so, how much will those upgrades cost?

- Where will you store your raw materials? Do you need rail access to offload your raw materials?

- What type of materials handling equipment will you need?

- What are the zoning requirements or restrictions for your type of business?

TIP

Research and find out the local fire, safety, and building zoning requirements for your type of facility.

- If your equipment is heavy, can the floor support the equipment or will you need to make modifications to anchor the equipment?

- Do you plan to lease or own the building? If you plan to own the building, are there any liens on the property? If you plan to lease, will there be an opportunity to expand or will you have to move if you decide to expand?

TIP

If you have to move, you should negotiate a shorter-term lease so that you do not limit your options in the future.

If you are currently in operation, be sure to make a list of all your equipment, its age, its specifications, and the expected annual maintenance costs.

Include Information about Labor, Production, and Process Considerations

Are there specific operational techniques that you can employ to gain a competitive advantage? Make sure that you have adequate space, and draw up a detailed layout of the space. Consider these questions:

- What are the major steps in the production work flow?
- How will work in progress flow from the start to the end of the process?
- What are the packaging requirements? Will you need a separate area for packaging? Will you need extra storage space for packaging materials?
- Do you need skilled labor? What is the status of the local labor market?

TIP

To find this information, you can check with your local chamber of commerce or economic development authority.

- What are the going pay rates, expectations of employee benefits, and availability of experienced trade or engineering professionals in your area?
- What are the raw materials that will be required? Are they available in the immediate trading area or will extra transportation and handling be required?
- What is the cost of raw materials per unit?
- How stable or volatile are the prices of raw materials?
- What is the labor cost per unit?
- What are the anticipated levels of output (units per labor hour) of the design of your operation?
- Have you planned for growth and expansion? If so, how detailed are your plans?
- What are the keys to efficient production in your process?
- What is your contingency plan? How will you respond to an accident, economic downturn, or labor disruption? What is your contingency plan in case of a natural disaster?

- How do you plan to use technology to gain a competitive advantage? What have been the major technological advances in your industry in recent years? How have you leveraged technology and what was the result?

- How do you plan your production and anticipate responding to fluctuations in demand?

- How dependent on local, skilled labor is your production process?

- How are the local educational institutions in training workers for your business?

- What type of in-house training do you plan on implementing?

- What is the percentage of the total production cost dependent on labor, raw materials, or energy?

- How will you monitor and control production costs?

Include Information about Your Health and Safety Programs

As an employer you have a responsibility and duty to monitor, investigate accidents, administer and maintain Occupational Safety and Health Administration (OSHA) required safety programs, conduct audits, and follow up with corrective actions.

TRAP

If you do not have health and safety policies already in place, you will need to develop, monitor, and improve safety performance, including all aspects of environmental program management. In your business plan assign the responsibility to act as a liaison with federal, state, and local regulatory agencies to someone in your organization. Make sure to include an overview of your first-aid and OSHA safety and health program and policies.

The following health and safety questions need to be addressed and answered in your business plan:

- Is there an industry health and safety association or training initiative?

- Will you be handling hazardous waste? If so, how does it need to be handled, and what are the costs associated with disposing of it?

- What will be required for you to comply with environmental, health, and safety regulations?

- Will you need to get environmental approvals before moving into the building or beginning operations?

- What are your plans to initiate a safety education and training program?

- Who is on your safety committee? Will they create or be responsible for maintaining your employee safety handbook?

- How do you plan to manage your Material Safety Data Sheets (MSDS) responsibilities?

- Who will have the supervisory responsibilities for health and safety?

- What is your hazardous material spill response plan? Provide an overview.

Include Your Plans for Training and Education Programs

As a manufacturer you will often be dealing with a significant gap between the current skills of the workers and the skills they need to acquire if the company is to survive and grow. It makes no sense to open new facilities or expand existing ones if you cannot recruit skilled labor capable of staffing, servicing, or working on your production lines.

In your business plan, be sure to include an overview of your indoctrination and training program. Include how you plan to implement your training and education programs. Will you outsource custom training programs or do your own in-house training? Or are there specific industry or government training programs?

19

Business Planning for Wholesale Distributors

Wholesale distributors are intermediaries who buy, store, and import goods in large quantities from manufacturers for resale in smaller quantities to retailers, who in turn sell to the general public. Their customers often include industrial, professional, and institutional suppliers to a specific industry or market.

In general, wholesale distributors sell to jobbers who resell to the public or to retail businesses. A good example of this is the automotive aftermarket, which has an extra level in its distribution system. Goods move from manufacturer to wholesaler to jobber, who then sells to either the end user or a repair garage. In some cases large automotive retailers and repair shops may also buy directly from manufacturers.

While wholesale activity happens in many industries, from money markets to banking, loans and finance, telecommunications, used coins, and commodities, for the purpose of this chapter wholesale will refer to the resale of hard goods.

Industry Analysis

Industry knowledge is vital for anyone writing a business plan for a wholesale business, whether the business plan is for internal or external use.

Most wholesale markets are quite mature, and the competition is fierce. Many wholesale markets (auto parts, food service, etc.) have experienced significant consolidation through a combination of mergers, acquisitions, and restructuring of markets. A thorough industry analysis provides the perspective for a strong marketing strategy.

Whether you are buying an existing distributor's business, looking to establish yourself as a new distributor, creating a new distribution network for your own line of products, or writing a business plan for your existing wholesale business, the following list of considerations will help you jump-start your investigation:

- *Distribution channels:* Investigate and describe the number and type of distribution channels. Provide real-world examples of profit margins each of the resellers achieve.

- *Products:* Do your vendors' products lend themselves to multiple distribution channels? How do other similar manufacturers distribute their products? How could you improve on their model?

- *Viability:* How many levels are in the distribution channel? Is there enough "margin room" to allow each level in the distribution chain to make a decent profit? If not, where can a distribution level be eliminated, and what would the impact be on the business and industry?

- *Formal or informal:* Will contracts be required to buy the product from the distributor or will it be more informal? How important is it to limit the distribution of the product? How important is it to have the rights on an exclusive product line? Is there a way to be more selective in distributing products or should they be available to a wide market?

- *Distribution control:* Who controls and makes decisions on who can distribute the products? How much of a factor do logistics and handling play in the distribution of the product?

- *Distribution support:* Will resellers share in co-op advertising funds? How will warranty be handled? What are the costs involved with storing inventory to keep the pipeline full? Can electronic order processing be used to reduce costs?

Financial Plan

Make sure that your business plan includes a full set of pro forma financial statements including ratio analysis. It is of particular importance to compare your sales per employee figures with industry standards.

TRAP

In my experience it is not a good idea to ballpark your profit margins because profit margins between product lines can vary greatly. To increase the accuracy of your projections, you will need to do additional work building your sales forecast and sales and general administration budget. I highly recommend that you build separate spreadsheets for each product line, because it will make a substantial difference in the accuracy of your financial statements.

Include summaries of your extra work in the appendix of your business plan.

Marketing Strategy

In larger distribution companies it is common to provide branding and advertising programs to resellers. This provides you with the opportunity to gain a long-term commitment from resellers and add value by extending your brand into the resellers' marketplace.

TIP

Make sure to include any strategies you plan to use to provide support, training, and incentives to resellers.

TIP

If your distribution area encompasses a wide geographic region, explain in your plan your sales and territory management strategy for finding new customers and servicing existing customers. This strategy should include your policy on the hiring, training, and management of your sales staff.

Competition

Because most wholesale markets are well established and mature, a well-researched competition analysis will be pivotal in helping to form a marketing strategy out of your marketing analysis. In this section of your business plan, be sure to include a review of your major competitors' entire operations including systems, use of technology, marketing and sales strategies, human resource management, their financial health, and their reputations.

Show the reader of your business plan how you plan to use this information to gain market share.

Customer Surveys

In my experience one of the best ways to uncover customer attitudes, perceptions, and needs is to conduct an in-person survey. It will not only provide you with insight into how your competition operates, but it will also reveal the customers' perception of your competition's strengths and weaknesses.

TIP

Your survey should use an open-ended question format (questions that cannot be answered with a simple yes or no) so that your subjects are required to explain their answers.

Technology

By making use of the Internet, computer networks, and reduced software development costs, there is a great opportunity for any distributor to substantially increase his or her productivity.

For example, think about the electronic system you will use: How can an electronic ordering system that uses the Internet to allow resellers to check inventory levels, place orders, and schedule delivery be used to gain a competitive advantage? How will you use bar-code technology to track inventory and process orders? Be sure to include all this information in your business plan, and, if you are using this type of system, provide a diagram of the system and how it works.

Purchasing and Inventory Management

Using an electronic order desk system (connected via the Internet) and bar-code technology not only makes a self-service wholesale operation affordable, but it can also substantially increase a wholesaler's productivity on the warehouse floor and in managing inventory to maximize turnover.

TIP

Include a section in your business plan on how you plan to leverage technology to increase productivity, profits, and growth potential.

Without an online order desk, you will need a traditional order desk, which means that staff will need to be recruited and trained to take and process customer orders manually. While this system has been used for decades, it does not allow your business to cope with peaks in demand and seasonal fluctuations as easily as an online system. If you cannot answer the phone quickly enough, you could lose orders to your competition.

TIP

If you are planning to process orders manually, it will be pertinent to provide an overview of the systems you have for processing orders and a detailed explanation of your plans for customer service in your business plan.

Delivery and Pick Up

If the majority of your customers are located in an urban area, one way of gaining a competitive advantage is to provide a delivery service. If your customers order often throughout the day, pooling their orders in exchange for providing free delivery a couple of times a day will provide even a manual order desk system with efficiencies that would allow you to better cope with surge in customer demand and seasonal fluctuations. This will require working closely with the customer but could provide your business with a competitive advantage. Spell out how you plan to incorporate delivery and pick up into your overall service offering.

Product Lines

Selecting exclusive product lines allows you time to build a market for your goods and build loyalty to your product line that cannot easily be upset by the competition. This is especially true in mature markets: The right product line combined with exclusivity equals a protected market in which you can build your market share over an extended period of time.

Exclusive products + quality products = Market share

If you have exclusive product lines, make sure to highlight those in your business plan.

Vendor Support and Customer Service

Incentive programs are a great way to build loyalty in a competitive market. In some cases you may be able to negotiate extra discounts from your suppliers to help fund the program. It is common practice in the food distribution business to pay a premium for the best shelf space or an end-of-aisle display in a grocery store.

Another tactic is to provide training and technical support for products that are more complex or involve setup (equipment, etc.). By providing product training and knowledge to a reseller's employees, you create confidence in the product and in the resellers. This can be an excellent method to use to pull your product through the distribution time line.

TIP

 Warranties and free samples can also help to boost your sales. Resellers always want a quality product with minimal problems, so providing a service to handle any warranty issues can give you a leg up on the competition, while getting your suppliers to provide you with free samples will put an important tool in the hands of your sales and territory managers.

For established and loyal customers another common tactic is to provide them with co-op marketing dollars based upon their volume of purchases. This saves your customers money on advertising and promotion and is an incentive for them to keep feeding you their orders instead of your competition. In some markets co-op marketing is not innovative but something your customers will tend to take for granted.

Be sure to explain in your business plan how you will use customer service and support as a marketing tool.

20

Business Planning for a Service Business

What is a service business? Almost every business is a service business, but for the purpose of this chapter we'll consider a service business to be one that does not sell a product but instead delivers a service.

Creating a Positive Customer Experience

A service cannot be inventoried, and it must be delivered in real time between two people, the deliverer (seller) and the receiver (buyer).

TRAP

The one great difference between writing a business plan for a service business and a plan for a product-based business is that in the case of a service business you live or die based on the impression you leave. When you buy a product, even if the service is lacking, you still have the product, but in a service business the service is all you've got. When you're writing your business plan, pay special attention to the areas that will affect the customer experience, particularly how your human resources will be trained.

Before You Write Your Business Plan, Define the Customers' Needs

Read Chapter 5 and then use the following questions to define the customers' needs and wants:

- Who is buying this service now? What are their buying habits? What are current buyers paying for comparable services?

- What factors are most important to buyers when selecting your service? Price, quality, delivery time, and so on?

- What and where are the current gaps in this service?

Identify Competitors

When you're writing your business plan, ask yourself the following questions about your competition:

- Who are the leaders within the industry, and why are they successful?

- How many competitors will I be competing against?

- How do my competitors reach the market?

- Are my competitors making any changes? What are their weaknesses?

- How are my competitors' fees, operations, and marketing structured?

- What do potential or existing customers like about my competitors' services?

- What are current buyers paying for comparable services?

Marketplace

Ask yourself the following questions about the marketplace:

- What makes my service unique, relative to others in the marketplace?

- What is required to succeed in this market?

- Can the market sustain another player?

- Is the industry growing?

- What are the current trends within the industry?

- What types of marketing strategies are prevalent within the industry?

- Are there regulations that affect the industry?

- Is there customer loyalty within the industry?

- Does the industry tend to be sensitive to economic fluctuations?

- Are there technological changes happening or required?
- What are the financial characteristics of the market?

Choose and Define Your Ideal Customer

What, who, and where is your best market? Make sure you have a clearly identifiable target. Describe your ideal customers by defining their characteristics, including age range, percentage of male and female, income, size of family, market segment, or by the specific need your service fulfills for them. What are their attitudes and beliefs as they relate to your business or services? Do they have specific buying habits and trends? Is there anything important to understand about their lifestyle? Is there a change in seasonal demand? What is the growth potential by market segment? What is the value of a customer's first order, year's worth of orders, and lifetime value?

Create a Service Blueprint

Once you have defined your ideal customer, define the experience or the end result your service will create. Create an outline of the entire service delivery process and identify the key points in the process that contribute the most to creating a positive customer experience. Then break down the important milestones in the service delivery process.

TIP

When there are multiple people involved in delivering the service, creating a service blueprint of the delivery process will allow you to train your staff, measure effectiveness, and make improvements. Include a description or overview of your service delivery process in the operations section of your business plan.

Be sure to identify all the people involved in the service delivery process and their roles in creating or adding value. Identify your weaknesses in the process and what you will need to do to offset those weaknesses. Decide how you will market and leverage your strengths. What will your customer need to know or experience for that strength to be a truly overt benefit?

Watch for New Revenue Opportunities

It is not unusual to observe unmet needs in the marketplace when working on your business plan, especially when you are defining your ideal customer and creating a customer service blueprint.

TIP

One of the ways a service business can add value and thereby open new revenue opportunities is to package other services together or bundle products with the service. This could include anything from partnering with another business to providing a service to your customers that includes a product when they buy your service. For example, you could include a CD or DVD or another product that fits with the customers' needs.

Describe the Operation of Your Service Business

Describe the service you provide in sufficient detail so that the reader can understand your service. One paragraph is best, but your description should be no more than two to three paragraphs. Address the following questions in your description:

- How do you deliver the service? Who is responsible for delivery of the service? Include any special training, qualifications, or experience your staff will have.

- What steps are involved at each stage performing the service? Create a service blueprint and include a flowchart to provide the reader with an understanding of the process.

- What unique competitive advantage does your service provide? How will you differentiate yourself from the competition?

- What is the key factor in succeeding in this business? What one part of your service, if it was removed, could kill the business?

- What in-house services, assembly, or support is directly or indirectly involved with delivering the service?

- What components of the service are subcontracted? What portion of the total cost of the service does subcontracting or in-house manufacturing provide?

- How many service representatives will be required? What guarantees, warranties, or maintenance agreements accompany the service?

- What is the cost per hour or per employee to deliver the service?

- What is the breakeven level of services for the company?

- What systems are in place for controlling and measuring quality and customer satisfaction?

- What percentage of the total cost of delivering your service is attributed to variable or fixed costs?

21

Business Planning for Consultants and Professionals

Consultants and professional service firms have specific challenges unique to their industry that need to be addressed in a business plan. These issues include seasonal work, marketing, and what happens to the firm if the principal gets "hit by a truck."

Seasonal Fluctuations in Sales Volume

Getting a large bulge of your work in a two-to-three-month period creates a number of significant problems, including difficulties with cash flow and having adequate staff to meet the demand. A good example of a seasonal business is an accounting firm. Most accounting firms focus on year-end tax returns and do the majority of their work in a two-to-three-month period. This can be a real barrier to starting a new firm because, until tax season, there is not a lot of revenue potential. The same thing is true of any seasonal business.

Having said that, keep in mind that there is no right or wrong time to start your business. For example, starting up an accounting firm during tax season could be feasible if you had a lot of contacts interested in getting their tax returns completed. On the other hand, starting during the off-season could also work, because it would provide you with enough time to build your network, relationships, and client list for the upcoming tax season. It all depends on your personal preference. Personally, I think it would be better to start in the off-season.

Obtain Financing to Bridge the Gap

A business plan for a consulting or professional services firm will most likely center on obtaining a line of credit to bridge the off-season lull. The good news is that the consulting and professional services firms that I have seen are quite profitable.

TIP

The best solution for a seasonal business is a line of credit because you can draw on the line of credit when you need to. Preparing a detailed cash flow projection that shows how revenue fluctuates while expenses remain the same will demonstrate the need for the line of credit.

A start-up will not have a business track record but will still be able to show detailed pro forma (cash flow) financial projections. Regardless, getting a line of credit for your start-up will be based on your credit score and the availability of collateral you can pledge to guarantee the line of credit.

For an established firm your historical data (number of clients and transaction volume) will provide a solid track record. However, your bank will still require a cash flow projection in addition to historical data.

Sales and Marketing Plan

In my experience one of the greatest challenges for consulting firms is the marketing and sales side of the business. What often happens is that you get a consulting project that consumes most of your available time while prospecting for new business and developing customer relationships get put on the back burner.

To compensate for this reality and weakness in the business model, build your marketing plan to include at least 10 different marketing strategies. These represent 10 different ways that you will generate qualified leads, which will keep the sales funnel full.

Financial Projections and Cash Flow Analysis

Calculating your breakeven point, hourly rate, and gross margins are crucial to making sure your consulting business does not fall into the trap of having too much work that is not profitable, which would limit your ability to outsource or expand.

TRAP

In my experience, the biggest mistake consultants make is not charging enough per billing hour.

Most consulting businesses charge an hourly rate. Coming up with the right selling price for your service business is essential if you want to be profitable. Figuring out how much to charge per hour is simple. All you have to do is answer a few questions and do some basic math:

1. *Personal money:* How much money do you want in your pocket after taxes (per month)?

2. *Income taxes:* How much income tax will you have to pay? To calculate this, all you have to do is find the mean tax rate for your income bracket. If you have an accountant, he or she can supply this information. If not, a quick phone call to your local IRS or Revenue Canada office will supply you with this percentage of income tax.

3. *Overhead:* How much is your monthly overhead? What are the basic expenses (rent, phone, taxes, etc.)?

4. *Total billable hours:* What are your total billable hours per month? In other words, what percent of your total working hours will you be able to bill each month? Total working hours per month are 160, but few people can achieve 100 percent billable hours. You have to allocate time for record keeping, bookkeeping, phone calls, and marketing and sales.

5. *Profit:* This is your working capital or reserve fund. How much profit do you want or need? I suggest for most small consulting or service businesses that a three-month reserve is a good goal.

6. *Billing Rate:* Now with two simple calculations (see Figure 21.1) you will arrive at the rate you need to charge per hour to be able to pay your overhead and be profitable.

If you follow the example in Figure 21.1, you will arrive at a profitable billable rate per hour.

Note: This example produces $12,000 before-tax profit. If you change any of the assumptions, you change the end result. For example, if your billable hours were only 50 percent instead of 80 percent, you would have to charge $138.39 per hour to pay your overhead and bank $1,000 per month.

Before beginning to use the billing rate you arrived at, first you have to answer some important questions: How competitive is this rate? Will people pay this rate? What are your competitors charging per hour?

1. After-tax income goal (ATIG)	$4,000	This is the amount you want left over in your pocket after all the bills and taxes are paid.
2. Determine income tax factor (ITF)—the amount of income tax payable, i.e., mean percentage of income tax	30% $5,714.28	*Determine ITF :* 1.00—mean tax rate *Calculation:* 1.00 − 0.30 = 0.70 *Formula:* ATIG divided by tax factor *Calculation:* $4,000/0.70 = $5,714.28 *Answer:* $5,714.28
3. Add monthly overhead	$1,000 $6,714.28	Determine monthly overhead *Formula:* Answer from Step 2 plus overhead *Calculation:* $5,714.28 + $1,000 = $6,714.28 *Answer:* $6,714.28
4. Percent of billable hours (PBHM) per month	80% $8,057.13	Determine % billable hours *Formula:* 1.00 plus PBHM = 1.XX *Calculation 1:* 1.00 + (1.00 − PBHM) 0.20 = 1.20 *Calculation 2:* 1.20 × $6,714.28 = $8,057.13 *Answer:* $8,057.13
5. Desired profit (DP)	$1,000 $9,057.13	Determine DP *Formula:* Answer from Step 4 plus profit *Calculation:* $8,057.13 + $1,000 = $9,057.13 *Answer:* $9,057.13
6. Hourly billing rate	$70.75 per hour	*Formula:* 160 hours × PBMH *Calculation 1:* 160 hours × 80% = 128 Hours *Calculation 2:* $9,057.13 divided by 128 hours *Answer:* $70.75 per hour

Figure 21.1   Consultants' Sample Calculation

TIP

Read Chapter 7, "Marketing and Sales Strategy," for specific recommendations to help you determine a viable market price strategy.

22

Business Planning for Large and Public Companies

A business plan for a public company will most likely be an internal document, as there are strict guidelines on the filing of the company's prospectus and annual report. However, the need for a full business plan is the same as for any other business.

The major difference in writing a business plan for a public company is not the content, but who puts which section of the business plan together and how it all gets pulled together to form a cohesive plan for the entire company.

Team Approach to Building Your Business Plan

If you are reading this section, you are either a CEO, CFO, executive, or a manager who has responsibility for writing a business plan.

TRAP

As the CEO, you may think you can write the entire business plan yourself, and you probably can. But should you? Probably not, as the task of researching, finding market intelligence, and pulling the information together can often be better assembled by other members of your staff.

This chapter provides you with suggestions on how to utilize the expertise of your senior executives and managers to produce the business plan.

Bottom-Up Approach

Start working with your junior managers and department heads requesting a report that spells out their current situation, goals, and needs. Then edit and insert each report into the appropriate section of your business plan.

TIP

When writing your business plan for a large or public company, using a bottom-up approach will allow you to tap into the experience, knowledge, and passion of your department and division managers.

The advantage of using a bottom-up approach is that you will receive unique insights because you are able to "see" the business through the eyes of your managers and executives.

Depending on the size of your company and your management model, the bottom-up approach could also bring a breath of fresh air into your planning, as well as provide you with the opportunity to get closer to those serving the customer on a daily basis.

Role of the CEO and Senior Executives in the Business Planning Process

As CEO, your first responsibility is to pull the planning team together, set the vision, and create some boundaries on the direction of the business plan. In my experience the more general you are in your vision, the more general the business plan will end up, so it is important to be specific. The boundaries you set should limit your team's direction without inhibiting members' creativity and emotional buy-in to the process.

After the vision and boundaries have been set and agreed upon, it is time to assign researching and writing responsibilities to various team members. I recommend:

- *CEO:* Acquisitions, mergers, CSA/Sarbanes-Oxley (see below for an explanation of this).
- *CFO and CEO:* The financial plan.
- *Vice president:* The marketing strategy.
- *Executives, manager of departments or divisions:* This group should focus on the parts of the business they are closest to, including the industry analysis, operations plan, market analysis, and products and services.

Sarbanes-Oxley (SOX)

The Sarbanes-Oxley Act (Public Company Accounting Reform and Investor Protection Act of 2002) is often called SOX or Sarbox. It was signed into law on July 30, 2002, by President Bush in the wake of a series of corporate financial scandals, including those affecting Enron, Arthur Andersen, and WorldCom.

Whether you are a U.S. CEO or a Canadian CEO with operations in the United States, there are requirements for you to become SOX-certified. There are 10 issues you should begin to take interest in:

1. Proper recording and control of complex, extraordinary, and non-routine transactions.
2. Adequate extension of controls following a merger or acquisition.
3. Formal preparation and processes for financial disclosure and reporting.
4. Strong control of the IT systems.
5. Need for executive-driven internal control management program, enterprise-wide.
6. Management program to formally control risk throughout the enterprise.
7. Full board and audit committee cooperation; understanding of risk and control.
8. Hands-on control of the financial closing process.
9. Defined, documented, and consistent accounting policies and procedures.
10. Ability to audit and control outsourced business processes.

TIP

Because of the complexity and seriousness of compliance with SOX, it is essential to hire a firm to assist you with the process of certification, audit, and compliance.

The expectation is that you will personally certify the completeness and accuracy of the material facts in your filings. Plus, you also are expected to declare that your financial statements and information "fairly represent" the financial condition of your company.

Industry Analysis

The purpose of the industry analysis is to examine the external factors that affect your business but are beyond your control. As CEO it will be helpful for you to share your thoughts with the person working on the industry analysis. This task should be delegated to someone who is well connected and can obtain access to influencers and observers who have a wide view of your industry and whose perspective you trust.

You might be the best person to do this research, but, depending on your industry, another member of the team might be able to utilize his or her connections and back channels to gain insight into industry developments and information. These connections could become especially significant when it comes time conduct the competitive analysis.

TRAP

Don't assume that the CEO is the best person to handle the industry analysis. Someone else might be able to better employ his or her position and contacts with suppliers, friends, and subcontractors as natural connections to gain insight into the direction and development priorities of your competitors.

Market Analysis

Conducting a marketing audit to gather information about your customers and build customer profiles will help to frame the direction of your market analysis.

TIP

Hiring a research firm to conduct a focus group is an excellent way to research customer needs, confirm marketing priorities, and test ideas in a closed and confidential environment. Plus, focus groups are a great way to gain information on the customers' perception of your competition, and in some cases they provide new information about competitors.

TIP

If you are looking to confirm the market potential of a specific idea, then a confidential telemarketing survey will be able to help quantify the potential market opportunities.

Marketing Strategy

Formulating your marketing strategy becomes less complex when you have completed the industry and market analysis. Pay special attention to operational level promotions and advertising to get the message as close as possible to the customer.

Operations Plan

The operation plan could be the single largest section of your business plan. If each department or division prepared its own operation plan, condensing this into a cogent summary will not only help you coordinate, consolidate, and develop your operations plan, but it will also provide you with the operational budgets to help form the financial plan.

Products and Services

The end of the twentieth century will be remembered as the Information Age. The beginning of the twenty-first century will be known for the expression of people's creativity, ingenuity, and innovation.

New products and services will be created by those who, in pursuit of a solution to their own problems, discover new opportunities. The next great innovation is right under your nose waiting to be discovered. Be sure to include any innovative ideas you have in your business plan.

Create an Innovation System

To recognize innovations and opportunities, you need a system to recognize the milestones of creativity that will fuel the next innovation.

Ask this question: Based on a specific trend, what product or service will be needed or desired by each social group? Identify the basic needs and desires for each of the social groups you identified.

1. Make a list of trends taken from magazines, books, Web sites, newspapers, analyst reports, from what you know of the industry and anywhere you can observe them. Then consolidate that list.

2. Next transfer them to 3 × 5 cards.

3. Then position them on a whiteboard or wall with a time line at the bottom.

4. Then identify the key milestones that would need to be in place before that trend can become a reality.

(Continued)

(Continued)

5. Looking at each of those milestones, review each one and identify those milestones that have technology that already exists or has research dollars allocated to it.

6. Finally, identify those milestones that do not currently have research activity or funding. Look closely at those milestones because that becomes the opportunity—the place where you want to focus your efforts to research and look for opportunities to innovate.

Courtesy of Phil McKinney, from the Killer Innovations Podcast, used with permission.

Business Description and Executive Summary

The business description and executive summary should be written last because they hinge on all the work from the other sections of the business plan.

TIP

When your business direction and development make a significant shift, it is important to document these changes in the executive summary.

In the business description explain the current situation, including the problems that the business is currently coping with, and explain what it will mean for the business once the change is complete. Finally, describe the new business focus and opportunities that the business will pursue.

23

Business Planning for Small-Medium Businesses (SMB)

A small-medium business (SMB) is an employer with as few as five and as many as 1,000 employees.

You Might Be a Small Business, but Growth Is a Priority

In the last eight years, entrepreneurial activity in the United States has grown from 7,200,770 businesses to 20,038,163 (according to the 2000 census). A 2005 study by Frank N. Magid Associates found that 76 percent of small businesses stated that they wanted to grow their businesses significantly. In Canada the number of self-employed persons has doubled since 1976 to 2,412,700 (Statistics Canada, January 2004.) The trend is clear: self-employment and small business is well entrenched in North America and growing strong.

Growth Potential = Growth in Human Resources

The opportunity for growth in the small business sector is significant. The challenge for achieving growth regardless of size is human resources. Without the right people in the right seats, it is difficult to grow a business because so many young people are seeking self-employment.

The Herman Group has uncovered an early trend indicating that Generation Y (also known as the Echo Boomers or the Millennials, born between 1977 and 2002) seem to have a "strong orientation toward entrepreneurship. They feel confident that they can achieve great results—at least earn a satisfactory living—by going into business for themselves. This population cohort is showing itself to be self-aware, astute, creative, and comfortable taking the risks involved with businesses." To read more on this subject, check out Chapter 3, "Industry Analysis."

TIP

Add a "personnel plan" to your operations and management plan.

In your personnel plan, you will want to include details for recruiting and hiring. Topics should include:

- A three-year staffing estimate and budgets based upon the growth reflected in your business plan.
- Demographics and makeup of your workforce. Identify the average age of your workers and trends in your industry.
- The length of time that employees stay with the company before moving on.
- Recruiting, benefits, and retention plan that sets out a framework for meeting the firm's staffing needs.

Industry Analysis

Document the number of businesses in your industry by age, size, and location. Try to determine the growth rate of firms similar to your own and identify the criteria that most contributes to the growth of your industry. Is it access to technology? Access to training facilities, post-secondary education for supplying a skilled and trained labor force, or is it about achieving critical mass in sales volume?

TIP

The one area of planning that produces the greatest benefit for established small and medium-sized businesses is studying the competition.

Understanding the competitive environment will help you identify gaps in the market that are not currently being serviced that you can address when you're writing your marketing strategy. The key is to identify how your business needs to change to capitalize on industry trends and opportunities.

Marketing Strategy

Formulate a strong marketing plan that builds upon your strengths and capitalizes on the opportunities you identified in the industry analysis. Formulate your marketing strategy to leverage new opportunities and new markets. This is an ideal time to completely review your brand, market position, and marketing tools and strategies. Ensure that your customer profile is accurate and clearly identifies the customers' needs and how your marketing strategy will tap into those needs.

Operations Plan

Your operations plan needs to focus not only on effectiveness but also on capacity. Pay special attention to your building, equipment, and human resources. Identify the key performance indicators that will be used as a guide to trigger your growth and expansion plan.

If your plan calls for a major renovation or a new building, make sure to include consulting fees for working with an architect or contractor. Also include building plans, floor plans, plant layout, and renderings of any new construction along with cost estimates.

Financial Plan

Reread Chapter 9 and pay special attention to working capital and long-term capital. Be cautious in using working capital to fund long-term investments like buildings and equipment because that strategy could severely limit your firm's ability to purchase inventory during peak or growth periods.

TRAP

Using cash to satisfy your long-term obligations creates an imbalance in capital structure and knocks your ratios out of whack. This will inhibit your ability to obtain bank financing if the bank feels uncomfortable with your approach to managing the business and its financial situation.

Exit Strategy, Sarbanes-Oxley (SOX)

If your exit plan includes selling to a public company, you will need to be aware of the impact of the federal Sarbanes-Oxley Act and get yourself and your chief financial officer SOX-certified.

Read Chapter 22, "Business Planning for Large and Public Companies," to learn more about Sarbanes-Oxley.

24

Business Planning for Small-Small Businesses

A small-small business is a business with fewer than four employees and often will have no employees other than the owner. These small-small businesses are also called *micro-businesses* or *"solo entrepreneurs."* They see themselves as professionals who prefer to go it alone. They identify with a life and business without boundaries and employees.

The Big Business Trend? Keeping It Small

Of the 20,038,163 U.S. businesses (source: 2000 census), I calculate that there are about 8 million small-small businesses. For whatever reason, the owners have made a conscious decision to keep it small. The primary purpose of these small-small businesses is to provide income for the owner.

We used to call these solo entrepreneurs freelancers, sole proprietors, and free agents. You will find them operating service-based businesses that include consulting, financial planning, Web development, business coaching, arts, and even independent software developers (also known as micro ISV).

TIP

Many small-small business owners work from home, although that is not their only defining characteristic.

Small-small business owners have a strong conviction in their abilities and a thirst for personal freedom, flexibility, and control of their lifestyle. Combined with a strong drive, these entrepreneurs have the expertise, vision, and passion to live the dream. Characterized by a dedication to lifelong learning, these business owners believe in themselves and are committed to going it alone.

Build a Diversified Marketing and Sales Plan

Creating a business plan with a diversified marketing and sales plan may seem counterintuitive to the solo entrepreneur. Talented people attract opportunities, and solo entrepreneurs are no different. As the owner of a small-small business, you have a lot of flexibility, but without diversifying your source(s) of income, your business is vulnerable to major economic shifts and adjustments.

For many small businesses, prior to September 11 their growth could be likened to drinking from a fire hose, while post-September 11, they had to make do with a trickle from a garden hose. Most small businesses could not absorb the financial shock when revenue dropped by as much as 90 percent. Therefore, the key to long-term stability of the small-small business is to generate revenue from multiple sources.

TIP

To be insulated from eventual economic swings, you have to diversify your marketing and sales activities. Read Appendix C and choose at least 10 different marketing strategies. Then plan how you will implement and use those strategies to build your inventory of prospects.

Create a Development Plan to Increase Your Interpersonal Skills

In the small-small business environment the ability to communicate effectively contributes not only to your ability to generate sales but it also sets reasonable expectations in the minds of your customers and clients. If you have never taken a sales training program, make sure to include the cost of a good sales training program in your business plan. Think of it as your insurance policy to make sure that you are able to convert the new prospects generated from your marketing activities into paying customers.

Avoid the Trap of "Breakevenitis"— Create a Profit Plan

I said earlier that having a diversified marketing and sales plan is important, and it is. But a good marketing plan promoting services that only break even is a losing proposition.

TRAP

The biggest mistake small-small business owners make is not charging enough for their services. They think they have accomplished something significant if they are able to maintain their lifestyle. That is good, but if you are only breaking even, you will have nothing for a rainy day.

Without a solid profit plan you will have no surplus, no net profit. Your net profit is the money you use to reinvest in your business or wage your next marketing and sales campaign.

TIP

If you are not currently making a net profit, you will have to build downtime into your billing rates.

Your Customers Fund Your Downtime

Your customers should be paying for your next marketing campaign, and, if you build your profit plan right, they will. Marketing and sales are a cost of doing business and are part of the cost of every product or service.

The single most expensive item in your marketing plan is your downtime. Downtime is anything you do in the business that cannot be directly billed back to a client. It is this simple: if you do not include your downtime as a cost factor to set your billing rate, you most likely own a business that some-day will not be able to afford to stay in business.

Have I got your attention?

Your downtime is the time you spend networking, building relationships, and making sales presentations. It is also time spent writing proposals, responding to an RFP (request for proposal), and bookkeeping.

TIP

This is not an ethical or moral dilemma. If you cannot afford to include your downtime in the amount you charge for your services, then you are subsidizing your customers. Plus you are fooling yourself because, if a major economic hiccup occurs (trust me, they are happening more often these days), you will not have a surplus to fall back on. Or worse, after successfully completing a major project, you will not be able to afford the marketing and sales activities to find your next customer or contract.

Calculate a Profitable Rate and Build a Profit Plan

Calculating your breakeven hourly rate and gross margins is crucial to making sure you do not fall into the trap of "breakevenitis."

Start by making a decision to charge for your services by the hour rather than by the job or project. This way, if the project scope changes or expands, then all you have to do is apply your hourly rate.

Figuring out how much to charge per hour is simple. All you have to do is answer a few questions:

1. How much money do you want in your pocket after taxes (per month)?

2. How much income tax will you have to pay? All you have to do is find out the mean tax rates for your income bracket. If you have an accountant, he or she can supply this information. If not, a quick phone call to your local IRS or Revenue Canada office will supply you with the percentage of income that goes to your taxes.

3. How much is your monthly overhead? What are the basic expenses (rent, phone, marketing and sales costs, taxes, etc.)?

4. Determine your total billable hours per month. In other words, what percent of your total working hours can be billed each month? Total working hours per month are 160, but few people can achieve 100 percent billable hours. You have to allocate time for record keeping, bookkeeping, phone calls, and time you will spend doing marketing and sales.

5. Profit is your working capital or reserve fund. How much profit do you want or need? I suggest for most small consultants or service businesses that building a three-month reserve is a good goal to start with.

6. Now with two simple calculations you will arrive at the billing rate—the amount you need to charge per hour to be able to pay your overhead and be profitable.

1. After-tax income goal (ATIG)	$4,000	This is the amount you want left over in your pocket after all the bills and taxes are paid.
2. Determine income tax factor (ITF), the amount of income tax payable, i.e., mean percentage of income tax	30% $5,714.28	*Determine ITF:* 1.00—mean tax rate *Calculation:* 1.00 − 0.30 = 0.70 *Formula:* ATIG divided by tax factor *Calculation:* $4,000/0.70 = $5,714.28 *Answer:* $5,714.28
3. Add monthly overhead	$1,000 $6,714.28	Determine monthly overhead *Formula:* Answer from Step 2 plus overhead *Calculation:* $5,714.28 + $1,000 = $6,714.28 *Answer:* $6,714.28
4. Percent of billable hours (PBHM) per month	80% $8,057.13	Determine % billable hours *Formula:* 1.00 plus PBHM = 1.XX *Calculation 1:* 1.00 + (1.00 − PBHM) 0.20 = 1.20 *Calculation 2:* 1.20 × $6,714.28 = $8,057.13 *Answer:* $8,057.13
5. Desired profit (DP)	$1,000 $9,057.13	Determine DP *Formula:* Answer from Step 4 plus profit *Calculation:* $8,057.13 + $1,000 = $9,057.13 *Answer:* $9,057.13
6. Hourly billing rate	$70.75 per hour	*Formula:* 160 hours × PBMH *Calculation 1:* 160 hours × 80% = 128 Hours *Calculation 2:* $9,057.13 divided by 128 hours *Answer:* $70.75 per hour

Figure 24.1 Sample Calculation for a Small-Small Business

If you follow Figure 24.1 line-by-line, item-by-item using this example, you will at the end have a profitable billable rate per hour.

Note: this example produces $12,000 of before-tax profit. If you change any of the assumptions, you change the end result. For example, if your billable hours were only 50 percent instead of 80 percent, you would have to charge $138.39 per hour to pay your overhead and bank $1,000 per month.

Before you use this billing rate, you must first determine how competitive it is. Will people pay this rate? What are your competitors charging per hour?

Read Chapter 7 for specific recommendations to help you determine a viable market price strategy.

Keep an Eye on Economic and Business Trends

When there is a major market adjustment (e.g., recession, terrorist attack, natural disaster) the likelihood that your projects will be shelved or proposals set aside is great. Small-small businesses are most vulnerable to economic downturns and events.

TRAP

Maintaining a keen eye on the news and listening for the Federal Reserve Board Chairman to inject optimism into the business and investment community is like checking the paper daily to watch stock prices; it is agonizing. Few have the strength and discipline to time the market accurately, so why would you try to do the same thing with your business or marketing strategy?

If you follow the profit plan strategy outlined in this chapter, you can rest knowing that at least you have some cushion to weather a storm.

Taking Outsourced Work from Larger Companies—Get a Good Contract

Subcontracting is becoming a popular option for large businesses. These contracts can be good for your business because they provide regular work and cash flow. However, unless you have a contract to protect you, a change in company policy can find you on the outside looking in.

TRAP

Be sure to include a section in your contract that deals with termination of the contract. Make sure that it includes a specific time period that acts as a buffer if the contract is cancelled. It should also include a penalty if the contract is cancelled suddenly without notice or cause.

U.S. Entrepreneurship Outlook

According to a report from The Global Entrepreneurship Center at Florida International University, about 31 million people are business principals in the United States, with 13.7 million involved in 7.4 million start-ups; 7.6 million owner-managers of 4.5 million new firms (less than 3.5 years old); and 15 million as owner-managers of 8.6 million existing firms.

The report goes on to state that entrepreneurial activity continues at a high level in the United States, compared to all other advanced economies. The U.S. context continues to be unique in several ways:

- Potential for substantial informal financial support.

- Presence of a substantial research and development sector.

- A system of regulations and procedures that is not excessively burdensome for business creation and termination.

- A society that accepts entrepreneurship as an appropriate and respectable career option.

Manage Cash Flow by Managing the Sales Process

Everything in your small-small business is very tightly integrated. Therefore, the only real way to manage cash flow is to manage your sales activity aggressively by making sure that you have enough qualified prospects in the mill to keep the cash flowing at a level that meets the goals of your business plan.

If you have been in business before or have taken sales training, you have heard a lot of ideas, philosophies, and concepts presented as essential to a successful sales career. Some of them include communication skills, closing strategies, presentation tools, pre-qualifying your prospect, networking, asking for referrals, and after-sales follow-up. Every one of these strategies is important, but there is one that trumps all of them: your sales activity.

Even if you master all the strategies mentioned above, if you fail to maintain adequate sales activity levels, you will not earn what you need. Following is a formula you can use to calculate the level of sales activity you will need to achieve your goals.

Calculate Required Sales Activity

Before you start this section, make sure that you have worked on your profit plan and have solid numbers that you have confidence in and believe you can achieve. If you haven't, keep working the profit plan until you are comfortable with it.

The most successful salespeople track their progress daily and know exactly how much and what type of activity they need in order to meet their goals. They know their ratios. Do you know your ratios? Answer these questions:

- How many leads do you need to end up with one qualified prospect?
- How many qualified prospects do you need to get one new customer?

Below is a worksheet to assist you in calculating what your activity should be. Get a blank sheet of paper and answer the questions and follow the instructions. Have fun!

Steps for Calculating Required Activity Goals

1. What is my monthly income goal?
2. What will be my average commission or sale?
3. Divide your monthly income goal (Q1) by your average commission or sale (from Q2). The result = number of sales required.
4. What do I expect my close ratio to be? 10 percent, 30 percent, 50 percent, or more?
5. Take the number of sales (Q3) and divide it by your expected close ratio (Q4). This will give you the number of presentations you will need to make.
6. What will be my close ratio in getting appointments?
7. Take the answer to (Q5) and divide it by your expected conversion ratio (Q6). This will give you the number of qualified prospects required.
8. What will be my conversion ratio from a cold lead to a qualified prospect?
9. Take the answer to (Q7) and divide it by your expected conversion ratio (Q8) and multiply the result by 100. This will tell you how many raw leads you will need to start with each month unless your ratios change.

Now that you have finished the math and have your numbers, it is time to focus on how to:

- Increase the total number of raw leads.
- Create a tracking system.
- Increase your closing skills to improve your ratios.

Depending on your sales skills and sales goals, you may need to get help. Ask another small-small business owner or sales consultant to look at your numbers and provide you with some feedback. Sit down and create a plan, plus be prepared to track your results.

TRAP

If you are not prepared to track your performance, get out of business. Do something else because, if you do not track your performance and results, you will likely not attain your goals.

Tracking your results is very important because tracking will help you grow and improve your skills, and best of all, you will make more money because you will be able to spot fluctuations in sales and make appropriate changes to offset changes in sales levels. Good luck!

Long Hours When Successful

After maintaining a high level of networking and sales activity, you are finally starting to see a return on your marketing and sales efforts, but now you may find yourself very busy and wondering, "Where did my life go?" You may also find yourself wondering how you will get all the work done, and it's important to address this in your business plan. There are options:

- *Get Your Own "Apprentice":* You do not have to be Donald Trump or have a prime time TV show to find good people. You can hire a protégé, someone you feel has long-term potential and whom you are willing to train to eventually take over your business.

- *Leverage Your Experience:* Hire and train others to do what you do, and then you make money or an override on what they sell. If things go really well, they can assume over 80 percent of your clientele, and you enjoy retirement while you maintain a small but select clientele.

- *Transform the Business:* Another proven tactic is to reinvest your profits into real estate or the building in which your business is housed. You build assets and wealth in your real estate holdings.

Getting a Business Loan for a Small-Small Business

Most small-small businesses should not need a lot of start-up capital, especially if they are service businesses. You might need to purchase some office equipment, computers, and furniture. If you are moving into an office, you will need some money for renovations unless you can get the landlord to pay those costs.

A service-based business should be cash flow positive immediately if not within the first few months. However, if you decide to get financing, here are some things you need to know:

- *You still need a business plan:* Your banker will likely ask you for a business plan because it is needed to protect the bank's interests and demonstrates your entrepreneurial skills.

- *Personal credit:* In a small-small business your personal credit-worthiness is a reflection of your character. Past repayment of debt is an indication of how you will act toward new debt.

- *Collateral:* Banks do not take risks; they will always want some form of security. In many cases they may want some form of real estate or other asset to guarantee the payment in addition to your personal guarantee.

TIP

I always recommend that you start with the bank that holds your personal account because it will be familiar with your track record and credit history. If you have borrowed and repaid loans previously, the bank will already be familiar with you and your assets. It might grant the loan without a full business plan and accept a simple proposal instead. Ask your banker what is needed.

25

Business Planning for a Web-Based Business

The Internet has made starting a small business easier and spawned many new Web-based businesses. While business basics still apply, there are specific strategies to take into account in writing your business plan.

Vision and Goals

Being clear about what you want to achieve, the type of applications you want to develop, and what size company you want to become will help to keep you focused in a Web-based world of unlimited opportunities. Web-based businesses can target and serve small, specific market niches, unlike traditional bricks-and-mortar businesses. What is your ultimate long-term vision? For example:

- *Build a company:* Are you looking to build a great company with the next innovative application?

- *Solo act:* Are you looking for projects within your own skill set that allow you to handle them yourself?

- *Build and sell:* Perhaps you want to start a company and get it going with a specific product and then sell the company and move on to the next challenge?

Your vision will make a substantial difference in how you develop your business plan and build the company. Since Sarbanes-Oxley (also known as

SarBox) came out, there has been a myth that you can avoid the costly impact of SarBox by selling your business instead of chasing after an IPO. Just one problem: If you ever expect to sell to a public company, you will need to be Sarbanes-Oxley compliant. The reality of selling to a public company can be quite dramatic because it could cost you tens or hundreds of thousands of dollars in transaction costs to become SarBox compliant.

Choose Your Market Wisely

Follow the strategies in Chapter 3 to study your customers' markets as well as your own. This effort will help you know your market, which then allows you to do a deeper market analysis using the information in Chapter 4.

TIP

Your vision will in large part dictate the market you serve and will also shape your product and business development strategies.

For an example of how your business plan would vary depending on your market, compare the following analysis of three markets:

Large Companies

Since the early 2000s, the focus for enterprise information technology (IT) departments was to reduce costs. This is now starting to turn around a little, depending on the industry. For example, banks continue to invest in IT. Manufacturing has been undergoing some heavy investment and, depending on your viewpoint, the opportunity in serving the manufacturing market may have already peaked. However, there is still a lot of IT development and interest in the security segment of the enterprise IT market.

If you were planning to target large companies, your business plan for this market would need to reflect a specialty in a specific industry or type of application. Sales and marketing efforts would dictate the need for an experienced, dedicated sales management team with the appropriate sales budget and time lines included in the business plan.

The days of a company (of any size) paying big bucks to get an application developed hoping for a return on investment are long gone. Your business plan will need to reflect this new reality in making adjustments to your business model. You will need to decide upon your revenue model, for example, by subscription, per seat, outside the company firewall off your own Web server.

Serving Small- and Medium-Sized (SMBs) Companies

Once again the market you choose to enter will dictate a lot of the realities of your business plan. For example, specializing in Web-based applications represents a good opportunity for SMBs. Plus the sizes of projects are generally smaller and, depending on your programming capacity, can be a great fit. Often the process for purchasing tends to be informal, which can make your sales and production teams a lot more productive because of the shorter sales cycles.

SMBs can make really good customers for Web developers because, with the increased productivity and lower development costs, they can actually afford custom applications or Web-based applications.

If you are in a start-up and the development cycle of your application requires a full-time effort, you will need to self-finance the development or get a loan from the bank. The other option is to build a working prototype and then demonstrate the product to potential clients. If they like it, they can pay you a deposit to help offset your development costs so that you can afford to finish the project.

Consumer Market

In the world of open source software, demo, and shareware, the try-before-you-buy model is a proven and reliable way to distribute your product, and consumers expect to be able to try before they buy. Some markets are more open to shareware than others. For example, Apple users are loyal users who love to buy specialized applications at affordable prices with a try-before-you-buy option (shareware, demo). The World Wide Web definitely makes distribution of small, specialized applications doable.

TIP

Some developers develop a product part-time, release the product as freeware/shareware, and then continue to develop the product into a full-fledged application that eventually transitions to a shareware try-before-you-buy software product.

Think You'll Need Venture Capital?

In the early 2000s, if you were going to develop a product for the enterprise IT or SME market, you would develop your plan and then go get the venture capital company (VC) to fund the development. Today, the cost of developing a product is substantially less than it was then.

Venture capital firms now expect to see a working prototype or a truly innovative application before they will entertain funding requests. If you truly feel you have a unique and innovative product, you need to include the following information in your business plan:

- *Protecting your intellectual property:* The best bet is to see a patent attorney as early as you can afford it. Going to a VC with patent in hand will garner respect and serious attention. This will also allow you to choose a VC based on what else it can bring to the table besides money.

- *Management team:* Building a great company takes great people. While it is not always crucial, going to your VC with a complete team is prudent. Whoever you bring with you will at least be someone you know and perhaps have worked with before. VCs are used to helping recruit a vice president of sales or other positions because that is what a good VC should do—help you build your company.

- *Your expectations of the VC:* In your business plan you should make it clear what you expect from the VC other than money. The process of finding a VC is similar to finding a business partner. Look for a partner who has a track record and is familiar with your market or product. The VC's experience and connections can make a big difference helping you build the next great company.

Bootstrap It

The other option is for you to finance your product yourself and bootstrap its formation, development, and prototyping.

TIP

Increasingly, VCs love to invest in entrepreneurs who have a developed product, have tested and proven the market with some initial sales, and have the potential for substantial growth with additional funding.

TIP

The truth is that most innovations are accidents. They are products that have often been developed to help the creator solve some problem or meet a specific need. The best strategy is to create something you need. As a user of your own product, you will have a critical eye to the product and the drive and passion for getting it just right.

Use Wisdom When You Write
Your Business Plan

If you have a truly innovative product, large customers will be willing to buy it if it will give them a competitive advantage.

TRAP

Just remember, if you sell your product to large customers and they gain the competitive advantage, you will miss the opportunity to sell your product to smaller customers.

Being clear about your intentions is a type of wisdom. Apply that wisdom to everything in your business plan and in your business. You do not have to accept the first offer or first employee. You can afford to wait because whatever you feel you lose in the short term is always made up in the long term.

Rapid Development

The mantra in software and Web development today is get it built fast, get it out to the market so you can recoup your investment quickly. In your business plan, show how you can develop the product quickly and how the product can be scaled up to meet market demand later.

Stay Small and Agile

Keeping valuations low is possible because it doesn't cost much to start a business anymore (especially if you keep the scope narrow). Besides the obvious techniques, one way to stay small and agile is to use turnkey services to lower your overhead.

Business Model

Your revenue model needs to be practical and realistic. Corporate customers today want managed services more than they want to lay out big bucks for a solution. Think of it this way: your customers want to taste your product before they buy a whole case.

TIP

Sell your customers small portions of your product or service by having them pay for it by subscription.

From a strategic viewpoint, if you are confident in your product, selling a subscription gets potential customers hooked and familiar with the product. You make a little bit of money over a period of time while the customer becomes dependent on the product. In addition, once customers have experienced the product, they are more likely to pay more than if they had not used it at all.

TIP

Allow adequate time for development and testing. Do not release the product to the public until you are proud of it.

I heard the story of an engineer who studied how long it took people to actually complete a task compared with how long they thought it would take. His findings were shocking. On average he found that people needed to multiply whatever amount of time they thought it would take by a factor of 2.8. That means doubling or tripling your product development time lines. That also means that you will need two to three times more money, too.

Personnel Plan

Recruiting and keeping talent is a big part of any company, and how you choose to manage your human resources will say a lot about you as a manager. As the owner of a technology company, it is your job to recruit talented people who have the needed technical knowledge and experience and who can help implement your vision.

TIP

Explain in your personnel plan how you intend to balance benefits, working conditions, and productivity.

Be sure to describe the corporate culture and how you plan to cultivate a compelling culture that reflects the mission of the company. Suggestions include:

- Set and achieve meaningful goals.
- Educate employees on your approach to project planning and management.
- Encourage and utilize creativity.
- Plan for managing stress in the workplace.
- Support employee education and development.
- Establishment of standards for customer service and managing the customer experience.

TIP

One of the realities of managing a technology company is that you may not always be able to afford to hire all the people you need as paid staff members. Outsourcing is a realistic alternative to filling positions.

TIP

Remember to explain how you will deal with protecting your intellectual property using project contracts and nondisclosure, and noncompetition agreements.

Marketing Strategy

Because of the technical nature of your business, online marketing should be a natural extension of what you do. Create your marketing strategy as described in Chapter 7 with a special focus on:

- *Customer needs:* Include the problem your product or service will solve.
- *Product attributes:* Describe the different attributes of each service or product and how they add value for each segment of your target market.
- *Marketing and sales cycle:* Show how your Web marketing strategy is designed to attract prospects and move them through the sales and marketing cycle.
- *Customer preferences and motivation:* Some information on preferences will come from the industry and market analysis.
- *Internet marketing:* Include your own Web site, search engine marketing, pay-per-click advertising, pay-per-call lead generation, video cast, podcast, Weblog, Really Simple Syndication (RSS) article distribution, e-zine subscriptions and distribution, e-mail marketing, autoresponders, social bookmarking, and online networks.

- *Branding:* Include packaging your company: name of company, unique selling proposition (USP) slogan, consistent and congruent logo, testimonials, features, history, guarantees, awards, press releases/public relations info, brochures, business cards, letterhead, community and sports team sponsorships, uniforms.

PART 5

Getting the Money You Need

26
Applying for a Business Loan

Small business loans can be used for a variety of purposes. For example, a business loan can help you buy a business, start a new business, and expand your business. You will deal directly with the bank's loan officers. Make no mistake however, major small business loans are reviewed by loan committees. Typically, loan officers are not part of a loan committee.

Increasingly all loans are reviewed via software developed by the bank. The software analyzes data entered by your loan officer and in some cases actually approves or declines the loan. Larger financial institutions will compare your financial ratios with those of their other customers in the same business as you and make comparisons to industry averages as well.

Understanding your role and the role of the loan officer and the loan committee will help guide you through the approval process. It is a team game, and, as they say, there is no "I" in "team."

Preparing to Apply for a Small Business Loan

Remember, from a banker's perspective past financial performance, including loan repayment history, is very predictive of future financial performance. Before approving your loan request, the loan officer's job is to document this kind information; this is referred to as the "due diligence" process.

Loan officers will then calculate the critical financial performance ratios for the time period your financing or business plan covers. Then they compare your ratios to those of similar companies in your industry.

TIP

I highly recommend that, before you start to talk to your commercial loan officer or apply for a small business loan, you do some preparation by bringing your bookkeeping up to date and by reviewing your financial statements with your accountant. Ask your accountant to review your projected financial statements and the implications borrowing money will have on the financial health of your business.

After the Loan Application

After your application has been submitted, your loan officer begins building a business case for your loan request. This will contain information about your business and financial condition. It will also contain information about the ownership of your business, banking activity, previous borrowing experience, and information from third-party credit reporting agencies.

Your loan request may also contain anecdotal information about your customers, competitors, or suppliers, if they happen to have a relationship with the same commercial finance organization.

Unseen Decision Makers

Major small business loan decisions are made by a group of people who remain unseen by the borrower. Commercial loan officers have the authority to approve loans up to a certain level. Some can approve small loans of $50,000 to $100,000; however, most loans over $250,000 are normally approved by a committee. Some loans of over $1 million may require the approval of the board of directors, depending on the lending institution.

The Loan Committee

Most lending institutions have a relatively formal committee and decision-making process for handling commercial loans. Depending on the type of financial institution, your loan may have to be submitted to a loan committee for approval. Loan committees can have a wide range of authority. Most have little or no authority for granting loans; however, the function of those committees is to weed out loan requests before the requests are seen by senior management. Some loan committees have authority to grant small business loans up to the legal limit of the bank.

Other banks and lending organizations provide a fairly wide scope of authority for loan officers to approve or disapprove most of the loans they handle. In those types of institutions the committees review the loans after they've been made.

Depending on the size and structure of the bank, the annual report may indicate which directors serve on which loan committees. You may also ask your loan officer for the names and identities of the committee members who sit on the loan committee that will be processing your loan request so you can introduce yourself and your business. Building rapport with the decision makers does not guarantee that your loan will be approved, but anything that can help put a human face on the loan is a good thing.

The Loan Officer's Role

Your loan officer knows you and your business the best. He or she will also have a good feel for what type of loan may or may not be approved as well as the types of loans available and the terms under which loans may be granted.

Some loan officers' personal styles are more like advocates who aggressively package, defend, and represent your loan request to the committee. Pay attention to any feedback and suggestions your loan officer provides regarding structure, information, collateral, and guarantees that will be required. Remember, your loan officer knows the rules and the organization's policies and procedures.

Plan Ahead

TRAP

Do not make a last-minute request for financing. Waiting until the last minute to request financing can hurt your chances for approval, especially if you don't have all the right information needed. You need to allow the bank or lending institution plenty of time to go through its own procedures. There can be a lot paperwork, analysis of your financial statements, credit checks, preparation of legal agreements, and so forth.

It's important to have good financial management and control of your business. One of the ways you can show this is by taking the time to make a proper presentation by writing a business plan. It is most common to present your loan request with a business plan detailing your vision, situation, and finance needs. In rare cases you may be able to present an executive summary with copies of your last three years' financial statements—this happens very rarely, depending on the loan officers' experience and bank policy.

Work with the System

Many entrepreneurs and businesspeople have the perception that banks and commercial lenders do not like to lend money to a small business. Nothing could be further from the truth. They are in business to make loans—profitable loans.

TIP

Don't fight banks or commercial lenders: think of them as partners. Talk to your loan officer to learn as much as you can about the approval process. Talk to other entrepreneurs and small business owners who may have dealt with the organization previously. They may have insights about how the organization works and functions.

Think of your relationship with the loan officer this way:

Commercial lender: The lending institution is really an information gathering system. You have to provide assurance to the bank or lending institution that you have the capacity to repay the loan as planned.

Borrower: Think of your role as the information provider. Provide the institution with quality information. It will help the people there make a decision about your loan request and help you get the money want, at the terms you want.

Eliminate the tug-of-war and work closely with your loan officer—you will be pleased with the results.

Supporting Documents Needed for a New Commercial Business Loan

Your bank will expect to see a complete business plan plus financial projections including income statement, balance sheet, cash flow projections, and your résumé or bio. It will also want to see your personal net worth statement (include a separate list of assets and liabilities if there are a lot of items), a copy of your personal identification and social insurance number, a copy of either your certificate of incorporation or DBA (doing business as trade-name) registration, and list of personal bank accounts and credit references. A list of company bank accounts and credit references (if any) should also be included.

In addition, if you are applying for a new business loan for a business you have been operating, they will want to see a complete set of company financial statements for past years (bring the last three years if you have them) and current year to date financial statements. Any financial statements should also include a copy of your accounts payables and receivables.

The Loan Application Process for a Commercial Business Loan

Expect that most loan officers will want to get to know you and learn more about your business before getting down to details. They will most likely ask you about your business, what the money will be used for, and whether it is a new business or an established, on-going entity.

Depending on your loan officer's level of experience, he or she may begin to go through the business plan with you sitting right there. Be prepared to answer questions and perhaps make clarifications.

TIP

The executive summary of your business plan should include how much money you are looking for, projected revenues, profits, and the type of loan you are requesting.

If the loan officer is inexperienced or new to business loans, she or he may ask for some time to look over the business plan. This is not unusual. In cases like this feel free to ask how long it will be until you could meet again and ask for clarification about the loan decision process.

TIP

Be patient and work with the loan officer. If you need a quick decision, tell the officer that up front and explain your reasons. Just because you are anxious and want to know right away is not a good enough reason. If you push too hard, the officer will be wondering why you need to move so quickly and what might be missing or what you may not have disclosed.

Patience is a virtue. Feel free to ask good questions, but always keep it professional.

Small Business Administration Loans

To get a small business loan from the Small Business Administration (SBA), it will help a great deal if you understand the procedures it uses.

An SBA loan is a guaranteed loan but the actual funds come from SBA participants (lenders). They make the decisions on whether to apply to the SBA for a guaranty on their loan. Therefore, the key to getting a business loan is to be adequately prepared before applying and to work with the lender during the processing.

Prepare your business plan according to the guidelines in this book and make sure to state that you want an SBA-guaranteed loan.

TIP

Once your business plan is ready, take all available financial and other business information to a financial institution. I highly recommend that you start with the bank that has your checking account. If your bank does not have experience with SBA loans, shop around for a bank or credit union that does have the experience of making loans using the SBA's guaranty loan programs.

TIP

The SBA no longer has any direct loan funds, so the historical requirement that an applicant needs to be turned down by the banks before being able to apply to SBA for a direct loan is no longer applicable.

Alternative Financing Options

Banks are not the only alternative for financing your business. You can also get the funds you need from private investors, franchise financing, factoring, or making an equity play.

Private Investors

Selling equity in your business, as a way to get money to fund your company, is very expensive because you are giving up a percentage of your business forever. Getting a loan is cheaper because you retain full ownership and control and only pay the interest costs.

When finalizing your business plan, customize it to include a description of the amount of money you need from an investor and how you plan to repay the loan. Disclose whether or not you are prepared to provide investors with equity in your firm and what percentage of shares they would receive in exchange for the funds provided to you.

TIP

Remember, borrowing money is always cheaper.

If you are a new entity, new to business, or need money to continue product development and research, then private investors are the way to go. They will take the risk when other lenders will not assume risk.

Line of Credit

A line of credit is a flexible lending instrument secured by assets. As an example, you are approved for a ceiling of say $100,000. It allows you to run up a $100,000 "overdraft" in your operating or corporate checking account. Then, when you make your bank deposit, the deposit is applied to reduce the line of credit.

This provides a great deal of flexibility and can be a valuable buffer for paying your accounts payable before your receivables come in.

Most often, a line of credit is granted based upon sales volume and your accounts receivables (AR). Each month you report your sales and AR (there may be other reporting required as well). Based upon the amount of sales and AR, the bank calculates a percentage of your AR to determine the amount of your line of credit.

Typically, you will be provided with somewhere between 20 and 30 percent of your total AR but I have seen it much higher, depending on the borrower. The older the aging of your AR, the less the bank will lend. For example, amounts over 60 days will not likely be included in the calculation.

A line of credit can be secured with other assets as well, but using your AR is the most common. You will also likely be required to sign a personal note or guarantee. This would allow the bank to liquidate your personal assets if your business failed and the line of credit is not repaid.

TIP

A personal guarantee should state a specific amount (the amount of the line of credit), but it is often required that you sign an unlimited personal guarantee. That way you cannot go elsewhere to borrow money since you have no more "room" to assign a personal guarantee to another person or institution. You will likely also be required to sign a letter that restricts your borrowing money elsewhere without approval. Ask lots of questions when talking to your banker, read everything before you sign it, and make sure that you have a good relationship. It can make a world of difference!

How Do Factoring Services Work?

A factor service discounts invoices or accounts receivables. It pays you before your normal payment terms and before the customer pays. In fact it often pays within a few days to a week after your application has been approved.

Factoring is an alternative to a line of credit at a bank, and it can be an effective method of raising cash in a hurry. There are different ways of managing the process, depending on the factoring company. In my experience factoring services will review your business and invoices and may even do an audit. Once approved, you invoice your customers as usual, but they will provide you with instructions on how to do the invoicing.

It is common practice to send out a letter to your customers advising them that you are using this service and that they should pay your invoice to the factoring company.

Depending on your arrangement, you can choose which invoices to factor. If you decide to use this method, you will probably want to get a stamp made so you can indicate which invoices to pay to the factoring company.

If your business is growing quickly or if you are starved for cash and the banks will not lend you the cash, factoring is a way of getting the cash that is sitting in your accounts receivables into your hands. The cash can be helpful if you need to buy inventory or buy raw materials to build more goods for your growing business. However, if you are using these funds to pay other bills, you may be in too much financial trouble for factoring to solve your problems.

TIP

If you have signed a loan agreement at a bank, it probably states that you need permission to use other forms of financing, such as a factoring service. So read your loan agreement, personal guarantee, or caveat that you are being asked to sign before taking any action. Most likely you will be asked to sign an agreement that states something to the effect that you will not do anything that would dilute the cash within the business. Giving yourself a bonus above the amount you included for yourself in the business plan or paying dividends would reduce the equity within the business, and this would contravene your agreement with the bank. The bank's options are to demand immediate repayment, and, if you are unable to repay the loan within the time specified, the final option is to foreclose.

Franchise Financing

As franchising has matured, so too have the different offerings and franchise opportunities. Many of the new franchise concepts do not yet have a successful track record of placing people in new units. This makes it difficult for a would-be franchise operator to obtain financing because there is not much difference in the risk between a start-up and some franchises, and the banks know it.

Make an Equity Play

In cases like these it is best to seek financing by offering investors equity. This can be accomplished by getting a manager or a partner with direct experience to invest in the operation. Sure, you give up a portion of equity and future profits, but unless you are willing to pledge personal assets and a personal guarantee, you will not get the financing you need.

Trends indicate that prospective franchise owners are looking for investments of less than $250,000. They all want something that is easy to run and has fewer than 10 employees.

TIP

Check out the franchise first. When doing your research in selecting your franchise, there is one simple thing you can do to make sure that you get the financing you need. Make sure that the franchisor is listed in the U.S. Small Business Administration registry. Not all are.

To be on the list a franchisor has to submit a uniform franchise offering circular and pay a fee to the SBA. The SBA then conducts a complete review to make sure that the franchisor adheres to the SBA standard operating procedures, one of the important steps to approval. Without the SBA approval, even if you are a strong borrower, the SBA will deny the loan guarantee. This means that the bank has to assume all the risk or else get you to assume more risk by bringing in a partner who is solid financially. That way if things go south, they have two owners invested in making the business a success.

Get the Franchisor to Help with Financing

If the franchise has been around for awhile, it should be able to help you obtain financing. In some cases it may have an exclusive relationship with a specific bank. This speeds the process and reduces fees because the franchisor may pay those costs. At a minimum it should be able to suggest lenders who know the system and track record and understand the business.

TIP

One way of getting more information is to ask the franchisor if it has any former bankers as franchisees or owners. If so, ask to be referred to them. When you call, query them for specific information that they felt was important for their bank to know. If they were former employees, they likely provided the bank with a thorough explanation of how the franchise system works and explained the concept. That way when you walk in, the bank is familiar with the concept and can use the past performance of other franchisees to assess the risk.

Industry Experience May Be a Requirement

Since 9/11 some franchisors have added additional restrictions, such as requiring specific industry experience to qualify people to open a franchise.

In my experience franchisors prefer people who have general business and management experience.

Get the Franchisor to Finance the Real Estate

One of the trends we can expect to see more of as interest rates rise is the use of sale/leasebacks. The franchisor literally buys the property and then leases it back to the operator. This can be an important strategy for franchisors because they can put the excess equity to work expanding the franchise by building new units.

27

Getting Funding from Investors, Family, and Friends

Involving others to invest in your business is a popular way of raising the required capital to finance a business. However, money from friends, family, and investors come with strings attached, so be careful.

Get a Loan or Sell Equity

Sooner or later you will be faced with a decision: Should I take a business loan or sell equity in my business? It seems an easy enough question to answer, but your decision should depend on a number of factors.

If you can qualify for a business loan, it is always cheaper because you keep your equity and just repay the loan with interest. Whereas, when you sell equity in your business as a way to raise funds, you are giving up a percentage of your business forever.

Many years ago when I was in start-up mode, I took money from a couple of businesspeople and gave them 49 percent of the company. On the way to the bank, I wondered if I was making a mistake. But I deposited the money anyway. It was a secure feeling having the extra cash in the account.

However, I should have listened to myself because within the first 30 days I had closed deals that created $40,000 in profit or four to six months of operating expenses. As it turned out, I did not need the capital and had more than enough cash without the financing. But I gave up 49 percent of my company for that initial investment, and it became the most expensive financing ever.

TIP

If you are a new entity, new to business, or need money to continue product development and research, then selling equity is the way to go because the people who buy the equity will take a chance where other lenders will not assume risk.

Finding Money

TIP

Look for potential investors like salespeople would look for a customer. Preparation is the key.

A friend of mine (a strategic planner) once decided to take up bow hunting as a hobby. He studied everything, and I mean everything. He took shooting lessons, studied deer migration patterns, talked to old hunters, and purchased topical maps of the hunting area. He went a year in advance to visit the location of the hunt and took pictures of the vegetation. Next year he returned to the exact knoll he had identified the year previous, all camouflaged to blend into the background. He waited. Then a few deer arrived, and he killed a deer with one arrow. From a planning perspective the lengths he went to might seem extreme, but he did accomplish his goal. Take time to plan how you want to finance your business.

Make a List of Investors

Once you have your plan prepared, make a list of all the investors you know. Don't know any? Think of businesspeople you know or affluent people in your community.

Another thought: if the people on your list are unable to help you, ask them for names of other people who might be able to. You might ask them the following:

- Can you provide a direct lead (name, phone number) for an investor who fits my profile?
- Can you name someone else who might know an ideal investor?
- Can you introduce me personally to another center of influence—someone who knows a lot of people? (Such a person might be able to help you find someone to finance your venture.)

The key is to dig. It has been said that you can meet anyone in the world if you ask the right seven people to help you.

Should I Ask for More Money Than I Need to Create a Cushion?

If you think that you might need more money later and think you'd better to get it now because you may not be able to get it later, then you have a problem with your perception about borrowing money for a business.

Business finance is about achieving balance. The best way to achieve that balance is to do the job right the first time. That means taking the time to prepare a business plan and financial plan that make sense. When they make sense to you, they will make sense to everyone else reading it.

Make sure you ask for every nickel you need and not one penny less. Make sure it will be enough because no one will entertain your coming back to ask for more money when you have yet to repay the money you borrowed the first time.

TRAP

Do not fall into the ego trap of feeling that getting the money you need to start the business is some sort of a sign or confirmation that you are on the right track. You might be on a track but just not the right track to be profitable. Make sure your business plan is worthy of the investment. Family members are the ones most likely lend you money just because they know you, not because your business idea is solid. Double-check your work and be honest with yourself.

Asking for an inappropriate amount of money (too much or too little) is one way for an investor to begin to question your idea. You have to be able to justify your request for financing.

Investors know a business needs adequate financing. They just want to be sure your business idea will work and that you have done enough research and planning to make it a success. These are the questions they are asking themselves:

- Can you actually deliver on the commitments made in the business plan?
- Do you have the experience to manage this business?
- Are you able to assemble and lead a team?

- How financially committed to this business are you? From a financial viewpoint, do you really need this business to succeed? Or will you quit, bolt, or freeze up when the going gets tough?

- Do you have a good grasp on the industry, market, and trends affecting this business?

- Do you have a track record of running a successful business?

Be Professional in Your Business Dealings

Even if your mother writes you a check to help you start your business, do a good job of explaining the details to her. Make sure you have proper documentation of the loan. Treat the situation the way you would if you were dealing with your bank.

TIP

Have a loan contract drawn up with the specifics of the loan, including the amount, interest rate, and payments. Make sure to provide some security or collateral. It will show that you are serious, and it will be a good reminder when the going gets tough and you need to make some hard choices.

Choosing an Investor

One of the best reasons to obtain financing from private investors is to be able to tap into their business experience. They will naturally be interested in the business, and an experienced entrepreneur can bring a lot of value to the table, which can become more valuable than the money itself.

Having this seasoned veteran businessperson on your team will help create balance in your decision making because you are able to consult with and learn from this person.

Owning a business can be a humbling experience. It will test your resolve in ways that you cannot even imagine right now. If you are too proud to seek good counsel on important decisions, you should not be in business because you are not willing to be coached, to be taught.

TRAP

Nobody knows everything, but I thought I did. Deep down I knew I did not know enough and needed help, but I let my pride get in the way. Something I could have learned by seeking advice took me years and a lot of money to learn. Do not make the same mistake.

Take some time to think about what type of investor you would like. If you could create the ideal investor, what knowledge, experience, and traits would this person have? What would your expectations be of this investor? What boundaries would you set? What type of support do you really need?

PART 6

Appendixes

Appendix A
Business Plan

The company represented in this plan is Canadian. The distances are in miles; the money amounts are in Canadian dollars.

Executive Summary

Joe's Trucking Systems, Inc. (JOE'S) is a full-service, 24-hours-a-day, seven-days-a-week, open-deck trucking company. It provides full truck load (FTL) and less than truck load (LTL) transportation services to industrial companies across North America. Sue Switch owns 51 percent of the company; Joe Sample own 49 percent of the company.

Our vision is to be a steady money maker with an annual net profit of 5 percent. We do not want to be the largest company—just consistently profitable.

Forecasted revenues for the year ended September 30, 2006, are $1,671,000 with a net income of $147,503. Based upon the forecasted financial statements prepared by Everyday Accounting, the company requires a $100,000 line of credit.

When he worked at To and Fro Transport, Joe Sample increased the financial performance of the highway division. The last three months' average revenues per running mile (empty and loaded) were:

- June average: $1.46 per mile Canadian
- July average: $1.52 per mile Canadian
- August average: $1.72 per mile Canadian

JOE'S was recently awarded four new contracts totaling more than $800,000 (for details see Upcoming Contracts in the Marketing and Sales Strategy section).

315

JOE'S sales assumptions are based upon past sales history of To and Fro Transport and newly awarded contracts. There are 22 accounts that did a total of $1,110,917 of business with To and Fro Transport in the last 12 months.

In a recent survey, 13 of the top 22 accounts (763 total accounts) expect to increase the amount of business with JOE'S in the next 12 months. Of the remaining accounts, all intend to continue doing business with JOE'S. The exact amount of sales that can be expected varies based upon sales and need. (For a detailed list of accounts and volumes, see "Assumptions and Potential Risks.")

JOE'S has a purchase agreement with To and Fro Transport. The agreement includes the purchase of the TO AND FRO customer and contact list (763 customers), marketing rights, a non-competition agreement for $10,000 cash, and the assumption of $15,000 of debt (lease operator insurance hold-back).

Business Description

JOE'S is a full-service, 24-hours-a-day, seven-days-a-week, open-deck trucking company. It provides FTL and LTL transportation services to industrial companies across North America.

Vision   Our company vision is to be a steady money maker with an annual net profit of 5 percent. We do not want to be the largest—just consistently profitable.

Mission Statement   Joe's Trucking Systems, Inc., is a reliable and trusted business partner that works with customers to achieve on-time delivery, throughout North America.

Ethics Statement   Joe's Trucking Systems, Inc., is dedicated to open, honest communications with all customers, suppliers, and staff members. Whenever necessary, we take the time to educate and explain to our customers the reasons behind our systems, processes, and decisions.

Goals—First 30 Days

- To make a smooth transition from To and Fro Transport to JOE'S.
- To confirm that all major customers will continue doing business with JOE'S.

Goal—First 60 to 90 Days

- To increase our western Canadian sales volume and reduce the use of brokers for reload opportunities.

Goals—First Year

- To increase revenue through the addition of two new lease operators.
- To focus on the development of sales, dispatch, and administrative systems in order to increase efficiency. We will accomplish this through the use of computer software and technology to improve productivity in sales/dispatch and administration (accounting, fuel tax tracking, etc.).

Legal   JOE'S is an operating and marketing company and is owned 51 percent by Sue Switch and 49 percent by Joe Sample.

Sue & Joe Transport is the holding company that owns and leases equipment (four trucks, four trailers, and pilot car) to JOE'S. The majority shareholder is Joe Sample. The benefits of this strategy include reducing potential legal liability in the United States and lowering insurance costs. It will also provide additional tax planning options to the owners.

Services

JOE'S has a fleet of seven units and relationships with hundreds of carriers throughout North America. JOE'S provides clients with excellent equipment coverage. The transportation services business evolves and changes to suit client needs. The sales mix is best defined through understanding the types of commodities and destinations JOE'S expects to serve. The services mix is:

- 50 percent of our loads are related to industrial construction.
- 25 percent are lumber or related products.
- 25 percent are miscellaneous.
- 65 percent of our loads are transborder.
- 35 percent are to Western Canada (in November a series of large industrial construction contracts will begin).
- The majority of our loads are requested by Canadian companies, with freight to move either to the United States or from the United States to Canada.

Services

- Dimensional and overweight shipments.
- Permit and escort setup.
- Job site pickup and delivery.
- Centralized dispatch.
- Expedited (hotshot) service.
- $250,000 cargo insurance.

Equipment   All equipment is air ride:

- *Flatbeds and step deck trailers:* 48 ft and 53 ft. Aluminum and steel combo and all steel trailers.
- *Double-drop trailers:* similar to flatbeds except they have a drop deck closer to the ground. Drop decks are used for oversized, overweight, wide, and heavy equipment loads. 48 ft and 53 ft with well dimensions from 25 ft to 45 ft, and these can go to a 10-axle combo set up to 110,000 lb.

Expansion Costs   The cost to add a new lease operator is $4,500 to cover unit start-up costs and the first two months of unit operating expenses. These include:

- Two months of U.S. fuel (pay cash via fuel cards).
- $250 for decals.

- $100 for drug and alcohol testing.
- $800 for cash advances (petty cash for drivers for toll roads and incidental expenses).

The lease operator expansion costs are then recovered through a 5 percent holdback on each lease operator's gross monthly revenue.

Average monthly revenue per unit is $16,000 per month or approximately 10,000 miles. When our fleet average per unit is consistently at or about $20,000 per month, purchase of a new unit or the addition of a lease operator should be considered in order meet increased customer demand, maintain service levels, and prevent driver burnout or lost production.

Service Costs   Revenue and costs are calculated by the mile. Our numbers are:

- Breakeven is $1.04 Canadian per mile.
- Selling price minimum is $1.65 CDN per mile and up. *Note:* some jobs in western Canada are sold at $2–$2.50 CDN per mile. Canadian freight generally runs at a 20 percent higher margin than transborder trips (United States–Canada) and is easier to dispatch and manage because it is easier to get return trips.

Revenue per Running Mile Experience   The last three months' average revenues per running mile (including empty and loaded miles) were:

- June 2000 average: $1.46 per mile.
- July 2000 average: $1.52 per mile
- August 2000 average: $1.72 per mile

Service/Customer Life Cycle   Typically a good client will have a life cycle of 12 months, where a strong relationship and high degree of trust exists. It is typical for clients to conduct a thorough review and competitive tender every 12 months to verify that they are getting a fair price.

Expansion and Redesign   After three years it is expected that continued growth will be dependent upon building a fleet of company-owned vehicles to service the western Canadian market. Also, the integration of satellite, computer, and telephone technology will make the communications and management of the fleet far more effective and efficient.

Changes in Costs and Profit   Other than fuel costs, the company does not anticipate any major changes in costs. Today's tractors are much more fuel-efficient and durable than they used to be. The company will maintain tight sales tracking systems and cost controls on a unit-by-unit basis. Profits are also expected to remain stable. As fuel costs rise, the company will add a fuel surcharge to existing rates.

Customer Profile   The majority of JOE'S customers are mainly industrial or manufacturing companies, such as:

- Industrial construction.
- Fabrication.
- Lumber companies.
- Produce (potatoes, onions, or watermelons).
- Manufacturing.
- Oil fields.

Industry Analysis

Government Regulations The trucking industry is a highly regulated industry. Some of the areas of regulation include:

- *Motor Vehicle Safety Act:* http://www.tc.gc.ca/actsregs/mvsa/tocmvs.htm.
- *Uniform Cargo JOE's Shipment Standard:* For highway transport vehicles, http://www.ab.org/ccmta/ccmta.html.
- *Federal Register online via GPO access:* The *Federal Register* is the official daily publication for rules, proposed rules, and notices of federal agencies and organizations, http://www.access.gpo.gov/su_docs/aces/aces140.html.
- *Running authorities:* Individual extra regulations per province.
- *National Safety Code:* Covers hours of service regulations, commercial driver's license explanations, pre- and posttrip inspections, brake problems to look for and CVSA inspections, weights and dimensions, tires, differences between Canadian and U.S. regulations, etc.
- *U.S. Department of Transport (DOT) Compliance:* JOE'S is compliant with all aspects of U.S. DOT.
- *Transportation of Dangerous Goods (TDG):* Covers the transportation of dangerous goods. It covers TDG training requirements; classification and identification of dangerous goods; shipper, carrier, and consignee responsibilities; incident reporting; emergency response planning; and other crucial topics.

The Trucking Industry Two main segments characterize the Canadian trucking industry:

- For-hire companies, which transport the freight of others for compensation. For-hire fleets are three times more likely to use owner-operators than are private fleets.
- Private firms transport their own products. In dollar terms, private trucking accounts for nearly one-half the industry. These companies are typically involved in private trucking as they have a need to control service. Private firms tend to use smaller units and trailers. Private trucking dominates the urban goods movement, accounting for approximately 85 percent of truck movements in this market.

At distances of 500 kilometers (310 miles), private trucking accounts for approximately 25 percent of trucking movements. In 1998 Canadian-based, long-distance for-hire carriers experienced an increase of almost 5 percent from 1997.[1]

Transborder traffic has grown by 9 percent per annum over the past five years.[2]

On distances above approximately 500 to 1,000 kilometers (310 to 620 miles), for-hire trucking accounts for approximately 90 percent of all trips. For-hire trucking accounts for 78 percent of interprovincial trips, and 59 percent of longer distance intraprovincial trips.[3]

The for-hire trucking industry in Canada had $13 billion in revenues in 1993 (for-hire carriers and couriers). The industry is a $37 billion (including the value of private fleets) a year industry (1995)—an increase of $6 billion over 1993 estimates. Private trucking accounts for $19 billion of the total. 90 percent of private fleets consist of 10 vehicles or fewer, with most of these fleets consisting of 1 or 2 vehicles. However, there are many private fleets with up to several hundred vehicles. The same data indicate that overall private fleets outnumber for-hire fleets by a factor of 2 or 3 to 1.

Economic Impact of the For-Hire Canadian Trucking Industry   Trucks handle over half of all Canada's trade as measured by the value of the commodities. In 1994 two-thirds or $218 billion of all truck shipments were carried across the Canada–United States border. No wonder there are close to 10 million truck trips a year back and forth across the border.

The trucking industry (for-hire carriers and couriers) accounts for one out of every three dollars spent on commercial, for-hire transportation in Canada (this includes both freight and passenger transportation).

Another estimate, considering private trucking as well as for-hire trucking, suggests that trucking accounts for 47 percent of all commercial passenger and freight transportation in the country.

For-hire trucks account for 29 percent of the transport component of Canada's gross domestic product.

A 2001 estimate puts the total level of taxation of the trucking industry at 13.5 percent of revenues. A rough extrapolation from this indicates that highway tractors generate between $30,000 and $40,000 in taxes every year, and this does not take into account the taxes paid by the people driving those trucks.

Every job created in the for-hire trucking industry creates 0.7 jobs somewhere else; every dollar of output adds $0.69 in sales to some other industry; and every dollar of Gross Domestic Product (GDP) produced by the trucking industry creates an additional $0.73 in GDP for other industries.

Over the last three decades (1970–2000), the total economy has grown at an average annual rate of 3.8 percent. For-hire trucking has grown at an average annual rate of 4.2 percent; faster than airlines, shipping companies, railways, bus operations, and urban transit.

Barriers to Entry and Growth   The three primary barriers to entry and growth in this industry are:

- *Capital cost:* Obviously the high capital cost of trucks and trailers makes entry and growth a challenge.

- *Human resources:* The demand and growth for trucking services has outstripped the ability of the industry to attract new people to enter the field. The driver population is at least two years older than the age of the average worker. The under-25 age group is attracted to the trades, secondary education and technology jobs.

- *Customer perception:* To be a credible trucking company that can consistently meet the needs of the average industrial customer, you need to have approximately six or more trucks. That is the number needed to be able to cope with the dynamic nature of the trucking industry and changing customer needs.

Impact of Innovation and Technology   Probably one of the most important technology issues for the trucking industry is the impact of the Internet. In the last two to three years a number of companies have launched load-matching services online. These services take one of four forms:

1. *Software:* This approach requires the purchase and installation of special software designed for the trucking industry.

2. *Online load matching:* For a small monthly fee you can search for and find a load or post truck availability.

3. *Complete solution:* This service looks after all billing, credit approval, and collection.

4. *Auctions:* Online auctions provide an opportunity to list equipment and shipments available and allow shippers and trucking companies to bid competitively for loads. These services are relatively new. Shippers place loads they need moved and trucking companies use the auction to bid for the load. Because the load is placed in a competitive auction, the practice tends to drive down the rates and sometimes the load descriptions can be misleading and the trucking company ends up having to take the load regardless.

Using the Internet to match equipment with loads is here to stay. The Internet will reduce costs by helping to eliminate empty miles.

Another trend is trucking companies that have special sections in their Web sites that are password-protected and allow customers to log in and request a quote, track a shipment, and even get an invoice.

Market Analysis

The nature of the trucking industry is to serve local businesses that need to move products and manufactured goods. Typically, the majority of a trucking company's loads are generated by a local business. Therefore the economic outlook for Edmonton and the surrounding area is an important success indicator for JOE'S.

Positive Economic Trends   According to the Conference Board of Canada, Edmonton has the most diverse economy of any area in Canada. Major projects in northern Alberta are now valued at $43 billion. Statistics that support economic growth include:

- In 1996, exports of manufactured products reached more than $12 billion—39.6 percent of Alberta's total exports.[4]

- Manufacturing shipments in the Edmonton region—Alberta's leading manufacturing area—are valued at more than $14 billion a year. [5]

- $8.3 billion of manufactured commodities were imported by the United States. Exports to the United States were $1.0 billion higher in 1998 than in 1997.[6]

- Alberta's manufacturing industry grew in 1998 by 12.8 percent, while Canadian overall industry grew by 6.5 percent.[7]

- Valued at $38.7 billion in 1998, manufacturing in Alberta now out-paces revenues from the agriculture, construction, and business services sectors.[8]

- Exports of manufactured goods more than doubled between 1993 and 1998.[9]

- In 1998, Alberta surpassed British Columbia for the first time in industrial manufacturing shipments. Manufacturing accounts for about 10 percent of Alberta's economy.[10]

- There were 2,190 manufacturing companies registered in the Edmonton region in June 1999, a 6 percent increase from June 1998. Much of the manufacturing activity in the Edmonton capital region is concentrated in the areas of agrifood products, chemicals, metal fabrication, oil refining, and machinery.[11]

- Manufactured products are the fastest growing category of export in Alberta. In 1996, exports of manufactured products reached more than $12 billion—39.6 percent of Alberta's total exports.[12]

- Manufactured products are forecasted to represent more than 45 percent of Alberta's total exports by 2001. Currently, two-thirds of all manufacturing

shipments are value-added resource-based (food-processing, refined petroleum, and forest) products.[13]

**For-Hire Trucking (Commodity Origin and Destination)—Second Half
of 1999**   Canada-based, long-distance, for-hire carriers carried more than
269 million tons of freight in 1999, an increase of 15 percent over 1998. (See
Fig. A.1.)

Regional Transborder Market Splits   On a regional basis, private trucking accounts for 9 to 16 percent of long-distance transborder trips. Use of
private trucking is greatest in the Atlantic Provinces and British Columbia.
(See Fig. A.2.)

Commodity Types   Commodities hauled by private trucks are similar to
those hauled by the for-hire sector. (See Fig. A.3.)
    Figure A.3 shows the type of commodities that JOE'S hauls include LTL,
machinery, other manufactured goods, metals and products, wood and
wood products, and food.

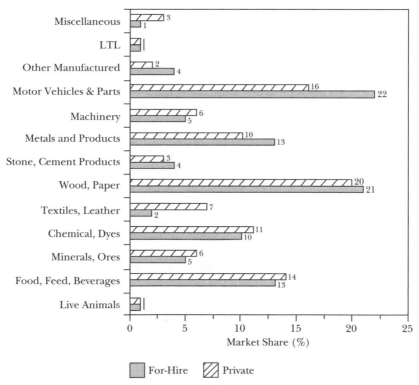

Figure A.1   Transborder Commodity Types

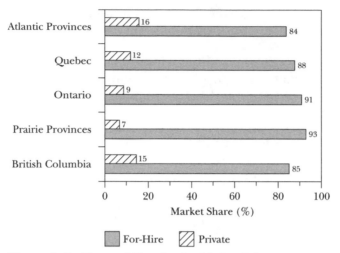

Figure A.2   Regional Transborder Market Splits

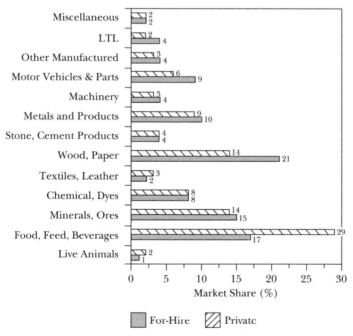

Figure A.3   Intraprovincial Commodities

Northern Alberta Major Projects, 2000[14]

Industry	Value ($Millions)
Oil, gas, and oilsands	26,220.0
Pipelines	5,233.9
Chemicals and petrochemicals	2,806.0
Infrastructure	2,452.4
Power	1,640.0
Forestry and related	1,420.0
Commercial/retail	940.4
Agriculture and related	626.2
Institutional	578.2
Tourism/recreation	380.4
Other industrial	322.0
Residential	283.9
Mining	257.5
Manufacturing	84.5
Total projects	43,245.4

Note: Major projects are defined as projects valued at $2 million or greater that are currently under construction or are proposed to start construction within two years.

Individual Projects in Edmonton Service Area Worth $1 Billion or More[15]

Company	Value ($billions)	Location	Project Description
Syncrude Canada Ltd.	$3.0	Muskeg River	Oilsands Mining/ Extraction plant
Alliance Pipeline Ltd. Partnership	$2.4	Muskeg River	Natural gas pipeline to Shell Co-gen Facility
Syncrude Canada Ltd.	$2.3	Cold Lake	Heavy oil pilot plant
Suncor Energy Inc.	$2.2	Cold Lake	Heavy oil commercial facility

(*Continued*)

Company	Value ($billions)	Location	Project Description
Albian Sands . Energy Inc	$1.8	near Elk Point	New facility
Mobil Oil Ltd.	$1.7	Cold Lake and Beartrap, Charlotte and Pelican Lakes	In situ bitumen Canada production
Shell Canada/ Western Oil Sands/ Chevron Canada Resources	$1.7	Primrose/ Wolf Lake	In situ bitumen production
Syncrude Canada Ltd.	$1.5	Empress to Fort Saskatchewan	Straddle plant and pipeline
Mobil Oil Canada Ltd.	$1.4	Surmont	SAGD bitumen commercial project, phase 1
Koch Exploration/ UTSEnergy	$1.3	Surmont	SAGD bitumen commercial project, phase 2
Petrovera Resources Ltd.	$1.2	Lloydminster	Upgrader expansion/ debottleneck
NOVA Chemicals/ UnionCarbide Canada	$1.1	Joffre	Polyethylene plant (PE2)
Alberta Infrastructure	$1.0	Cold Lake area	Highway 28 upgrading
Syncrude Canada Ltd.	$1.0	Cold Lake	Heavy oil plant expansion
Nova Gas Transmission Ltd.	$1.0	Fort McMurray toHardisty	Wild Rose pipeline, phase 2

Trucking Market Trends in Canada

Growth of the Canadian trucking industry in Canada tends to follow increases in manufacturing, resource, and economic cycles. Long-distance highway trucking has continued to grow from year to year despite regional economic realities.

1999	Tonnage	Shipments	Revenue Share[16]
Transborder	26%	22%	46%
Domestic	74%	78%	54%

1998	Tonnage	Shipments	Revenue Share[17]
Transborder	24%	20%	42%
Domestic	76%	80%	56%

Market Share   There are $2.7 billion in transportation services by Canadian-based for-hire carriers and couriers across the Canada–U.S. border. Revenues earned on this cross border traffic have been growing at an annual rate of 12.6 percent since 1980—much faster than revenues for domestic business.

To meet its revenue and profit objectives in the first year of operation, JOE'S requires a market share of 0.000618 percent. This is a small and attainable projection. This does not include growth in JOE'S western Canadian marketplace where four new contracts totaling over $800,000 are in place. Further growth in the western Canadian market is anticipated because of these contracts, and the $43 billion in major projects in northern Alberta over the next two years (see Table A.1 for details).

Table A.1   Market Share Analysis

No. of Units: 7

Annual average dollar amount per unit	$192,000.00
Annual volume	$1,671,000.00
Transborder volume, in dollars	$2,700,000,000.00
Market share	0.000618
Canadian industry average per unit	260,000

JOE'S Major Accounts

Customer	$ YTD	Next 12 months
Right Here Products	$39,321.06	Increase
Next Door Logistics	$147,208.46	Varies
Hard Steel	$19,689.28	Increase
We Know the Way Transportation Ltd	$17,151.90	Varies
No One Knows Metals	$44,481.42	Varies
Black White & Gray	$20,534.96	Increase

(*Continued*)

Customer	$ YTD	Next 12 months
Canadian Imitation Products Co.	$53,921.95	Increase
Edmonton Growers	$63,484.54	Varies
Oilfield Tubes	$63,464.17	Increase
Big Tanks & Equip Ltd.	$28,833.72	Increase
ABCD	$125,786.90	Increase
To and Fro Transportation (TO AND FRO)	$34,500.00	Varies
Big Guy Industries	$40,006.17	Increase
Metal Buildings Inc.	$37,154.50	Increase
Heavy Equip. Sales	$17,840.00	Increase
Big Bird Transportation Inc. (Sunpine)	$85,980.34	Varies
Both Sides Intl. Transport Inc.	$11,520.00	Varies
Transportation Company	$9,100.00	Varies
Always On Time Logistics Ltd.	$43,928.00	Varies
Three Small Men Holdings Ltd.	$88,991.99	Increase
The Weather Is Bad Here	$46,675.00	Increase
Oilfield Welding & Overhead Cranes	$105,843.21	Increase
Total business YTD	**$1,145,417.00**	

For-Hire Motor Carriers of Freight, All Carriers—Third and Fourth Quarter 1999   In the second half of 1999, there were approximately 2,500 for-hire trucking companies based in Canada with annual revenues of $1 million or more compared with an estimated 2,350 carriers during the same period in 1998.

Second half of 1999 operating revenues climbed to $9.0 billion ($4.4 billion in the third quarter and $4.6 billion in the fourth quarter). Operating expenses reached $8.3 billion ($4.1 billion in the third quarter and $4.3 billion in the fourth quarter).

Average operating expenses increased by 11 percent over the second half of 1998 to $3.35 million. In particular, for-hire trucking companies reported a 19 percent increase in average owner-operator expenses and spent substantially more on fuel (+12 %) compared with the last six months of 1998. The operating ratio (operating expenses divided by operating revenues) was 0.93, unchanged from the same period in 1997. Any ratio under 1.00 represents an operating profit.[18]

For-Hire Motor Carriers of Freight (Top Carriers)—First Quarter 2000 The top 82 for-hire motor carriers of freight (Canada-based trucking companies earning $25 million or more annually) generated operating revenues of $1.65 billion during the first three months of 2000. Although there were two fewer top carriers in the first quarter compared with the first quarter of 1999, average revenue per carrier increased by 14 percent. Average operating expenses for top carriers also increased by 14 percent over the first quarter of 1999 to $19.1 million. After higher fuel expenditures in the third and fourth quarters of 1999, top carriers in the first quarter paid 34 percent more for fuel than in the first quarter of 1999.

The operating ratio (operating expenses divided by operating revenues) for all top for-hire carriers and the largest subgroup, general freight carriers, was unchanged from the first quarter of 1999 at 0.95 (a ratio of greater than 1.00 represents an operating loss). However, revenues outpaced expenses among carriers hauling bulk liquids, dry bulk materials, forest products, and other specialized freight, resulting in an improvement of 2 points in the specialized freight carrier operating ratio (0.94) over the first quarter of 1999.[19]

Marketing and Sales Strategy

JOE'S will focus its sales and marketing efforts on moving LTL and FTL open-deck freight in two primary geographic areas:

- Western Canada.
- Canada to the United States and the United States to Canada.

The highway transportation industry is a fast-moving business. Load and equipment availability change quickly throughout any given day. The ability to respond quickly to customer requests for price is essential. Therefore, we will utilize the latest database marketing, telemarketing, and Internet tools to communicate with our customers. Other marketing tools to support the sales and marketing efforts will include:

- Telephone, fax, direct marketing, and sales.
- Internet and Web site.
- Driver distributed flyers (select locations).
- Networking and leads from customers.

One of JOE'S best methods for acquiring new leads and potential customers is through a combination of:

- Capital projects announcements.
- Observations of and networking by drivers.
- Dispatcher supervision of local loading: provides an opportunity to get to know operations staff and fosters an atmosphere of a little extra care and attention as well as seeing what customers have in the yard that may need to be transported somewhere.
- Networking with existing customers: listening to which bids they lost and to whom, upcoming work, and industry and competitor news.
- Announcements in newspaper.

Existing Sales Volume JOE'S sales assumptions are based upon past sales history of To and Fro Transport and that all major customers have agreed to continue business with JOE'S. There are 22 major accounts that did a total of $1,110,917 of business with To and Fro Transport in the last 12 months.

In a recent survey, 13 of those accounts expect to do more business with JOE'S in the next 12 months. Of the remaining nine, all intend on continuing doing business with JOE'S. The exact amount of sales that can be expected varies and cannot be confirmed at this time. (For a detailed list of accounts and volumes see "Assumptions and Potential Risks.")

Upcoming Contracts JOE'S has confirmed four new contracts:

- Starting in October 2000, JOE'S has been awarded a $108,000 transportation contract from WE Do It All Industrial (Clear Creek project).
- $74,200 Looking For More, September–November 2000, moving pump jacks.
- $55,000 from Jumble, moving pre-engineered buildings on the way back from another customer in the area.
- May 2001 to May 2004/2005, a $650,000 transportation contract with Anywhere Industrial.

Customer Profile The company's primary target market is industrial companies that have the type of freight that will not fit into a van trailer and that requires an open deck. This type of freight includes:

- LTL
- Machinery
- Metals and fabricated products
- Wood, paper
- Electrical cable tray
- Oil field equipment: pump jacks, vessels, etc.
- Produce: potatoes
- Tubing, pipe
- Vessels
- Pre-engineered buildings
- Mining equipment
- Cranes

Database Marketing and Telemarketing Survey For the first six months the customer service representative will conduct a survey to further qualify and segment our database. As a result we will:

- Know which customers ship to which lane ways (destinations).
- Determine what types of commodities they ship or receive.
- Know the contact name of shipper, project manager, or decision maker.
- Determine how often they ship (number of loads per week or month).

The database will allow us to communicate quickly via fax, e-mail, or telephone, and find more productive reloads.

Pricing   JOE'S pricing strategy will be to maximize profit margins through close monitoring of bids and administrative and operations expenses.

- Average gross revenue per mile: $1.52 per mile Canadian (includes empty miles).
- Minimum selling price: $1.65 per mile Canadian.

A focus on western Canadian freight has three main advantages:

- Generally sells for a higher price per mile.
- Generally paid round trip.
- Runs lower-cost capital equipment.

Depending upon the job, the selling price per mile in western Canada runs between $1.75 to $2.50 Canadian

Competition Analysis

Name	Market Area	Size	Reputation
Three-Way	Canada and U.S.	Same	Respected, good competitor
Cancer	Western Canada	Larger	Respected, good competitor
First Guy	Western Canada	Larger	Unreliable and sloppy
So Many More	Western Canada	Larger	Unreliable and sloppy
First Time	Canada and U.S.	Larger	Unreliable, poor business practices
Next Line	Canada and U.S.	Larger	Cheap, big, poor business practices
Hangon	Canada and U.S.	Larger	Respected, expensive
Big Bird	Canada and U.S	Broker	Excellent competitor
Four Bros.	Canada and U.S	Small	Poor business practices
Needs Help	Western Canada	Small	Poor image and business practices

Competitive Strategy   JOE'S objective is to provide consistent on-time delivery. The company's policy is to always be honest when a delay or mishap occurs, offering both an explanation and a solution whenever possible.

JOE'S experience has proven that being accountable, open, and honest in communications and dealings not only creates trust but also builds relationships. Customers routinely call JOE'S to help them out of a tight spot because they know they will get an honest answer and that JOE'S delivers on its promises.

Management, Operations, and Organization

All major decisions that have the potential to negatively affect the company's ability to maintain a 5 percent net profit must pass a case study and be reviewed by the owners and the company's professional advisers. The goal will be to always maintain a 5 percent net profit.

Administration and Office Manager (Sue Switch)   Responsible for all administration, office management, and financial record keeping and reporting. Her jobs will include:

- Cash flow management: tracks and analyzes financial performance.
- Internal control systems: budgets, purchase orders, credit approval and collection.
- Weekly and monthly ratio reports and analysis reports.
- Accounts receivable collections: maintains average receivables aging 51–52 days.
- Job costing.
- Payroll.
- Accounts payable (A/P) and accounts receivable (A/R).
- Overseeing of shop expenses.
- Handling of bank reconciliations.
- Forecasting of A/P and A/R on a weekly basis with operations manager.
- Individual case studies for major purchases, as needed.

Operations Manager—Dispatch and Sales (Joe Sample)   Management of the day-to-day operations, which include:

- Procuring loads and quoting rates for Canada and U.S. at a minimum of $1.65 per running mile.
- Maintaining on-time pickup and delivery schedules.
- Maintaining daily drivers' logs.
- *Lease operations:* Achieving a minimum $16,000 gross revenue per month per unit and maintaining a positive mood and working environment.
- *Sales:* Maintaining contact with all major accounts (weekly) and actively establishing relationships with new customers (two per week).

- Completing dispatch and billing orders.
- Compiling weekly management reports.
- Being available for work Monday to Friday 8:00 a.m.–5:00 p.m. (starting 7:00 a.m. on Mondays) and being on call 24/7.

Customer Service Representative (Sara Kale)   Reporting to the operations manager, she keeps all office- and dispatch-related procedures running smoothly, including:

- Completion and tracking of all paperwork: preparation of bills of lading for invoicing purposes.
- Maintaining customer database: updating all customer lists and broker contact lists.
- Assisting dispatcher to find loads, when required.
- Maintaining dispatch production sheets.
- Preparing and submitting via fax or the Internet rate quotes once completed by dispatcher.
- Preparing dispatch sheets for all hired units.

Credit Policy   All accounts will be required to complete and sign a credit application. Administration will check credit references and check with Equifax/Creditel. Credit terms are:

- Terms net 30 days.
- Collection follow-up on the 31st day.
- Any accounts at 60 days aging will be reviewed by the dispatcher, and services will be provided at his discretion. At 90 days dispatcher will hold shipment until payment is received.
- The operational goal is to maintain a 51–52 day average aging on A/R. (Cash flow projections based upon 60 days.)

Office Hours   The office will be open 8 a.m. to 5 p.m., with 24/7 after hours service via pager and cell phone.

Owner-Operators   The key to attracting and retaining good owner-operators is to treat them with respect, recognize that they have a small business, and help them build and grow their business.

Equipment Maintenance   JOE'S has an agreement with a customer (Tony's Equipment) to do all major service and repairs.

Maintenance Facilities and Office Space JOE'S is remaining in the To and Fro location. Included in our rental agreement is the use of an office including photocopier, fax machine, and lunch room. Also included is a heated indoor truck parking bay, parts and inventory storage, and the use of the wash and service bay.

Office Equipment For an additional $2,700, JOE'S is purchasing computer equipment and office furniture. (See the Appendix for a complete list.)

Organizational Structure

Joe Sample—Operations Manager, Sales, Dispatch, and Operations

Sara Kale—Customer Service Representative

Sue Switch—Administration and Office Manager

Professional Advisers

Legal: Three Guys & Company
John Smith
Barrister and Solicitor
123 Main Street
Northern AB
HOH OHO
Phone: 555-555-1234
Fax 555-555-1692

Accountant: Everyday Accounting, Chartered Accountants LLP
Accounting Way
Northern AB
A3G 9H6
Phone: 555-555-1578
Fax: 555-666-3918
E-mail: hismail@signuphere.com

Business Consultant: The Company Way
Greg Jones
47 Sweet Street
Northern, AB
K7T 9H6
Phone: 555-725-1232
Fax: 555-982-2492
Services include: marketing, business development support, graphic design, Web site design, and Internet marketing.

Computer Hardware
It's Broke Computers
Mr. Fix It
Northern, AB
Phone: 555-333-1686

Implementation Plan

Marketing Campaign and Announcement   Formal announcement of the start-up and acquisition of To and Fro Transport:

First 30 Days

- *Furniture and fixtures:* As part of the purchase agreement with To and Fro Transport, we will be purchasing computers, desks and chairs, and so forth.
- Fax flyer to all customers.
- Phone campaign to ask former To and Fro Transport customers (763) to confirm their patronage.
- Distribution of business cards and printed flyers via drivers to existing and new customers.
- *Staff training:* Further train Sarah Sunset as customer service representative:
  - Sales and telemarketing.
  - *Software:* use of ACT! 2000 (database), Dispatch 2000.
  - Trucking industry.

60 to 90 Days

- *Part-time/spare driver:* Hired an experienced, semi-retired driver on an as-needed basis to:
  - Provide relief to other drivers.
  - Do in-town work.
  - Pilot car and hotshot.
  - Train new drivers.
  - Increase operations efficiency.

The First Year

- *Dispatch systems and software:* JOE'S plans to use dispatch and truck load management software as well as an online load-matching service.
- *Communication:* In order to offer 24/7 service and keep in touch with our drivers, customers, and suppliers, we will use a combination of:

- E-mail.
- Phone.
- Fax.
- Cellular phones.
- Pagers.

■ *Bookkeeping:* All bookkeeping and accounting will be done with Quick Books Pro 2000 accounting software.

■ *Research and development:* As part of our continuing development, we will have a database of customers and potential customers, with types of loads, lane ways, and destinations.

Assumptions and Potential Risks

Rising Fuel Costs   A typical load of a little over 20 tons could be handled for about 36.1 liters of fuel per thousand ton-kilometer in 1975. Today, a typical load of 30 tons (trucks are larger now) can be handled for about 13.3 liters per thousand ton-kilometers. And this is considering "typical" loads. There are a lot of big trucks that do considerably better than this today. In our cash-flow projections fuel costs are estimated based upon a historical average as 20 percent of revenue. While fuel costs can be expected to rise, we will compensate by adding fuel surcharges to existing rates.

Aging Driver Population   The average age of a truck driver is two to three years older than that of average workers in general. In 2005, a large number of drivers will be either retiring or considering retirement within a few years. The industry has not been successful attracting workers under 25 years of age to consider trucking as an occupation. The biggest factor in driver retention is a fair wage, respect, and making the job easy with the right type of truck and equipment (i.e., chains, straps, etc.) Our driver recruiting strategy will include creating a strategic alliance with a driving school and finding drivers who are willing to apprentice and be trained. The other method will be to keep an eye out for good experienced lease operators.

Private Fleet Growth   Many private carriers believe that their fleet costs are comparable to or lower than those of for-hire carriers, and the visibility they receive from using their own trucks is considered to be a positive factor. Private trucking accounts for 28 percent of truck movements. This market share decreases to 10 percent on longer-distance trans border trips. JOE'S will focus on longer highway trips, where for-hire fleets have 90 percent of the market share.

Sales Assumptions   Our sales assumptions are based upon previous revenue experience with To and Fro Transport. The customers identified below have been contacted and all have agreed to continue business with JOE'S.

JOE'S Major Accounts

Customer	$ YTD	Next 12 months
Right Here Products	$39,321.06	Increase
Next Door Logistics	$147,208.46	Varies
Hard Steel	$19,689.28	Increase
We Know the Way Transportation Ltd	$17,151.90	Varies
No One Knows Metals	$44,481.42	Varies

Black White & Gray	$20,534.96	Increase
Canadian Imitation Products Co.	$53,921.95	Increase
Edmonton Growers	$63,484.54	Varies
Oilfield Tubes	$63,464.17	Increase
Big Tanks & Equip Ltd.	$28,833.72	Increase
ABCD	$125,786.90	Increase
To and Fro Transportation (TO AND FRO)	$34,500.00	Varies
Big Guy Industries	$40,006.17	Increase
Metal Buildings Inc.	$37,154.50	Increase
Heavy Equip. Sales	$17,840.00	Increase
Big Bird Transportation Inc. (Sunpine)	$85,980.34	Varies
Both Sides Intl. Transport Inc.	$11,520.00	Varies
Transportation Company	$9,100.00	Varies
Always On Time Logistics Ltd.	$43,928.00	Varies
Three Small Men Holdings Ltd.	$88,991.99	Increase
The Weather Is Bad Here	$46,675.00	Increase
Oilfield Welding & Overhead Cranes	$105,843.21	Increase
Total business YTD	**$1,145,417.00**	

Financial

Finance Request   For the first year of operation, Joe's Trucking Systems, Inc., will require a $100,000 line of credit based upon the following:

- Schedule of start-up costs.
- Forecasted financial statements—year ended September 30, 20XX.

See attached forecasted financial statements for the year ended September 30, 20XX as prepared by Everyday Accounting.

Schedule of Start-Up Costs

Start-Up Costs

Telephone system	$ 1,250.00
Telephone connection	447.00
Insurance	5,950.00
Prorate/authorities	7,695.90
Fuel (U.S. prepaid)	5,000.00
Driver testing	750.00
Benefits	700.00
Rent	1,300.00
Printing	1,200.00
Office supplies	300.00
Business consultant	3,500.00
Web page, domain namc, etc.	450.00
Decals on units	1,750.00
Parts stock inventory	2,500.00
Total	$32,792.90

Appendix

Equipment List   After October 1, 2000, Sue & Joe Transport will own the following equipment:

- Unit 037—1998 Freight Push FLD 120 tandem axle tractor
- Unit 039—1995 Kentruck T800 tandem axle tractor
- Unit 1000—1995 Peterbiltit 379L tandem axle tractor
- Unit 1100—1998 Kentruck W900L tandem axle tractor

Trailers:

- Unit 2100—1994 Lodekqueen tandem axle 48 ft flatdeck with sliding axle and side kit
- Unit 2000—1997 Doit tandem axle 48 ft flat-deck with side kit
- Unit 3702—1996 Lodequeen tandem axle 48 ft flat-deck with side kit
- Unit 3701—1995 Doit tri-axle 48 ft step-deck
- *Pilot Car:* 1997 Chevrolet S1500

Desks, computers:

- 2 Pentium computers with accessories
- 1 Epson Stylus 400 printer
- 1 fax machine
- 1 desk (stand-alone)
- 1 desk (wrap-around with hutch)
- 2 office chairs
- Software: PC Miler, ACT! 2000 database, Win fax Pro

Miscellaneous: office equipment: white board

General and Administrative Expenses (Operating Budget)

	Month 1	Month 2	Month 3	Month 4	Month 5	Month 6	Month 7	Month 8	Month 9	Month 10	Month 11	Month 12	Total
Office Supplies	$102	$90	$66	$22	$150	$30	$50	$600	$180	$268	$775	$60	
Rent	$5,000	$5,000	$5,000	$5,000	$5,000	$5,000	$5,000	$5,000	$5,000	$5,000	$5,000	$5,000	
Travel	$500	$500	$500	$500	$500	$500	$500	$500	$500	$500	$500	$500	
Training			$300			$1,500			$290				
Mktg. & Promo													
Stationary		$540											
Brochures		$900											
Website	$1,500	$10	$10	$10	$10	$10	$10	$10	$10	$10	$10	$10	
Promotional Items				$400			$500				$600		
Advertising	$785	$785	$785	$785	$785	$785	$785	$785	$785	$785	$785	$785	
Dues & Subscriptions	$89						$89						
Consulting	$1,500	$1,500	$1,500	$1,500	$1,500	$1,500	$1,500	$1,500	$1,500	$1,500	$1,500	$1,500	
Accounting												$2,000	
Payroll	$4,888	$4,888	$4,888	$4,888	$4,888	$4,888	$4,888	$4,888	$4,888	$4,888	$4,888	$4,888	
Payroll Burden/Taxes	$2,478	$1,506	$1,645	$1,460	$1,414	$1,414	$1,645	$1,784	$1,876	$2,015	$2,108	$2,200	
Owners Draw	$5,000	$5,000	$5,000	$5,000	$5,000	$5,000	$5,000	$5,000	$5,000	$5,000	$5,000	$5,000	
Group Benefits	$1,483	$1,483	$1,483	$1,483	$1,483	$1,483	$1,483	$1,483	$1,483	$1,483	$1,483	$1,483	
Interest	800	800	800	800	800	800	800	800	800	800	800	800	
Bank Service Charges	100	100	100	100	100	100	100	100	100	100	100	100	
Licenses & Fees	$500												
Utilities & Telephone	2000	2000	2000	2000	2000	2000	2000	2000	2000	2000	2000	2000	
Other													
Repairs & Maintenance		500	500	500		500		500		500		500	
Insurance	10000												
Total Gen. & Admin	$24,225	$23,103	$22,077	$21,948	$21,630	$23,010	$22,350	$22,450	$22,413	$22,349	$23,549	$24,326	

Sales Forecast Year 1 ABC Example Manufacturing Co.

Conversion Rate 50.00% Average Unit Sale $950

	Month 1	Month 2	Month 3	Month 4	Month 5	Month 6	Month 7	Month 8	Month 9	Month 10	Month 11	Month 12	Total
Leads													
Existing & Past Cust.	15	10	15	15	10	10	15	20	20	25	25	25	205
New Leads	200	100	110	90	90	90	110	120	130	140	150	160	1,490
Total Leads	215	110	125	105	100	100	125	140	150	165	175	185	1,695
Total No. New Cust.	107.5	55	62.5	52.5	50	50	62.5	70	75	82.5	87.5	92.5	$ 847.50
Total Revenue	$102,125	$52,250	$59,375	$49,875	$47,500	$47,500	$59,375	$66,500	$71,250	$78,375	$83,125	$87,875	$805,125

Income Statement for ABC Example Manufacturing Co.
31-Dec-05

	Month 1	Month 2	Month 3	Month 4	Month 5	Month 6	Month 7	Month 8	Month 9	Month 10	Month 11	Month 12	Total
Revenue from Sales	$102,125	$52,250	$59,375	$49,875	$47,500	$47,500	$59,375	$66,500	$71,250	$78,375	$83,125	$87,875	$885,125
Loan Proceeds													
Revenue from Investing		$80,000											
Revenue from Equip Sold													
Total Income	$102,125	$132,250	$59,375	$49,875	$47,500	$47,500	$59,375	$66,500	$71,250	$78,375	$83,125	$87,875	
Expenses													
Cost of Goods Sold	$43,484	$22,248	$25,281	$21,236	$20,225	$20,225	$25,281	$28,315	$30,338	$33,371	$35,394	$37,416	$342,814
General & Admin	$24,225	$23,103	$22,077	$21,948	$21,630	$23,010	$22,350	$22,450	$22,413	$22,348	$23,549	$24,326	$273,430
Total Expenses	$67,709	$45,350	$47,359	$43,185	$41,855	$43,235	$47,632	$50,765	$52,750	$55,721	$58,943	$61,743	$616,244
Net Income	$34,417	$86,900	$12,017	$6,691	$5,645	$4,265	$11,744	$15,735	$18,500	$22,655	$24,183	$26,133	$268,882

Cost of Sales   ABC Example Manufacturing Co.

Raw Material Cost/Unit $150   Labor/Unit $185   Packaging/Unit $10   Inbound Freight $12   Sales Commissions 5.00%

	Month 1	Month 2	Month 3	Month 4	Month 5	Month 6	Month 7	Month 8	Month 9	Month 10	Month 11	Month 12	Total
Raw Materials	$16,125	$8,250	$9,375	$7,875	$7,500	$7,500	$9,375	$10,500	$11,250	$12,375	$13,125	$13,875	$127,125
Labor	$19,888	$10,175	$11,563	$9,713	$9,250	$9,250	$11,563	$12,950	$13,875	$15,263	$16,188	$17,113	$156,788
Packaging	$1,075	$550	$625	$525	$500	$500	$625	$700	$750	$825	$875	$925	$8,475
Inbound Shipping	$1,290	$660	$750	$630	$600	$600	$750	$840	$900	$990	$1,050	$1,110	$10,170
Sales Comm.	$5,106	$2,613	$2,969	$2,494	$2,375	$2,375	$2,969	$3,325	$3,563	$3,919	$4,156	$4,394	$40,256
Total Cost of Sales	$43,484	$22,248	$25,281	$21,236	$20,225	$20,225	$25,281	$28,315	$30,338	$33,371	$35,394	$37,416	$342,814

Statement of Cash Flows - ABC Example Manufacturing Co

Receivables 30 days 40.00%
Receivables 60 days 60.00%

	Month 1	Month 2	Month 3	Month 4	Month 5	Month 6	Month 7	Month 8	Month 9	Month 10	Month 11	Month 12	Total
Beginning Cash Balance	$100,000	-$68,120	$4,881	$19,207	$19,163	$15,133	$4,293	-$11,350	-$25,965	-$34,240	-$41,101	-$45,843	
Cash In (income)													
Accounts Receivables Collection 30 days		$40,850	$20,900	$23,750	$19,950	$19,000	$19,000	$23,750	$26,600	$28,500	$31,350	$33,250	$286,900
Accounts Receivables Collection 60 days			$61,275	$31,350	$35,625	$29,925	$28,500	$28,500	$35,625	$39,900	$42,750	$47,025	$380,475
Loan Proceeds		$80,000											
Cash Sales & Receipts													
Other													
Total Cash Inflows	$100,000	$120,850	$82,175	$55,100	$55,575	$48,925	$47,500	$52,250	$62,225	$68,400	$74,100	$80,275	
Available Cash	$100,000	$52,731	$87,056	$74,307	$74,738	$64,058	$51,793	$40,900	$36,260	$34,160	$33,000	$34,432	
Cash Out													
Raw Materials	$16,125	$8,250	$9,375	$7,875	$7,500	$7,500	$9,375	$10,500	$11,250	$12,375	$13,125	$13,875	$111,000
Production Labor	$19,888	$10,175	$11,563	$9,713	$9,250	$9,250	$11,563	$12,950	$13,875	$15,263	$16,188	$17,113	$136,900
Packaging	$1,075	$550	$625	$525	$500	$500	$625	$700	$750	$825	$875	$925	$7,400
Inbound Shipping	$1,290	$660	$750	$630	$600	$600	$750	$840	$900	$990	$1,050	$1,110	$8,880
Sales Commissions	$5,106	$2,613	$2,969	$2,494	$2,375	$2,375	$2,969	$3,325	$3,563	$3,919	$4,156	$4,394	$35,150
Office Supplies	$102	$90	$66	$22	$150	$30	$50	$600	$180	$268	$775	$60	$2,291
Rent	$5,000	$5,000	$5,000	$5,000	$5,000	$5,000	$5,000	$5,000	$5,000	$5,000	$5,000	$5,000	$55,000
Travel	$500	$500	$500	$500	$500	$500	$500	$500	$500	$500	$500	$500	$5,500
Training	$0	$0	$300	$0	$0	$1,500	$0	$0	$290	$0	$0	$0	$2,090
Mktg. & Promo													
Stationary	$0	$540	$0	$0	$0	$0	$0	$0	$0	$0	$0	$0	$540
Brochures	$0	$900	$0	$0	$0	$0	$0	$0	$0	$0	$0	$0	$900
Website	$1,500	$10	$10	$10	$10	$10	$10	$10	$10	$10	$10	$10	$110
Promotional Items	$0	$0	$0	$400	$0	$0	$500	$0	$0	$0	$600	$0	$1,500
Advertising	$785	$785	$785	$785	$785	$785	$785	$785	$785	$785	$785	$785	$8,635
Dues & Subscriptions													$0
Consulting	$1,500	$1,500	$1,500	$1,500	$1,500	$1,500	$1,500	$1,500	$1,500	$1,500	$1,500	$1,500	$16,500
Accounting	$0	$0	$0	$0	$0	$0	$0	$0	$0	$0	$0	$2,000	$2,000
Payroll	$4,888	$4,888	$4,888	$4,888	$4,888	$4,888	$4,888	$4,888	$4,888	$4,888	$4,888	$4,888	$53,768
Payroll Burden/Taxes	$2,478	$1,506	$1,645	$1,460	$1,414	$1,414	$1,645	$1,784	$1,876	$2,015	$2,108	$2,200	$19,067
Group Benefits	$1,483	$1,483	$1,483	$1,483	$1,483	$1,483	$1,483	$1,483	$1,483	$1,483	$1,483	$1,483	$16,315
Interest	$800	$800	$800	$800	$800	$800	$800	$800	$800	$800	$800	$800	$8,800
Bank Service Charges	$100	$100	$100	$100	$100	$100	$100	$100	$100	$100	$100	$100	$1,100
Licenses & Fees	$500	$0	$0	$0	$0	$0	$0	$0	$0	$0	$0	$0	$0
Utilities & Telephone	$2,000	$2,000	$2,000	$2,000	$2,000	$2,000	$2,000	$2,000	$2,000	$2,000	$2,000	$2,000	$22,000
Other	$0	$0	$0	$0	$0	$0	$0	$0	$0	$0	$0	$0	$0
Repairs & Maintenance	$0	$500	$0	$500	$0	$500	$0	$500	$0	$500	$0	$500	$3,000
Insurance	$10,000	$0	$0	$0	$0	$0	$0	$0	$0	$0	$0	$0	$0
Sub-Total	$75,120	$42,850	$44,359	$40,685	$38,855	$40,735	$44,543	$48,265	$49,750	$53,221	$55,943	$59,243	$518,446
Other Cash Outflows													
Capital Purchases	$5,000												
Building Construction	$65,000												
Decorating	$8,000												
Fixtures & Equipment	$10,000												
Install Fixtures & Equip.													
Remodeling													
Lease Payments													
Loan Principal					$5,000	$5,000	$5,000	$5,000	$5,000	$5,000	$5,000	$5,000	$40,000
Owner's Draw	$5,000	$5,000	$5,000	$5,000	$5,000	$5,000	$5,000	$5,000	$5,000	$5,000	$5,000	$5,000	$50,000
Accounts Payables (60 days)			$18,490	$9,460	$10,750	$9,030	$8,600	$8,600	$10,750	$12,040	$12,900	$14,190	$114,810
Other:													
Sub-Total	$93,000	$5,000	$23,490	$14,460	$20,750	$19,030	$18,600	$18,600	$20,750	$22,040	$22,900	$24,190	$204,810
Total Cash Outflows	$168,120	$47,850	$67,849	$55,145	$59,605	$59,765	$63,143	$66,865	$70,500	$75,261	$78,843	$83,433	$680,406
Ending Cash Balance	-$68,120	$4,881	$19,207	$19,163	$15,133	$4,293	-$11,350	-$25,965	-$34,240	-$41,101	-$45,843	-$49,001	

Balance Sheet to Dec 31 20XX

Assets		**Liabilities**	
Cash	-$49,001	Current Liabilities	
		Accounts Payables	$12,470
Current Assets			
Accounts Receivables	-$667,375	Long-Term Liabilities	
Inventory	$60,675	Owner's Equity	-$603,171
Fixed Assets			
Equipment	$65,000		
Total		Total Liabilities	
Assets	-$590,701	and Owner's Equity	-$590,701

Joe S. Sample
1234-99 Street
Northern, AB
(555) 555-5555
E-mail: joe1@theplanet.net

EDUCATION

1986	Advanced Diploma, Northern Place Composite High School
1989	Diploma in Business Administration, Northern City Community College
1992	Fourth- level CMA, Northern Alberta Institute of Technology

EXPERIENCE

To and Fro Transport
October 1998 to present

Operations manager, controller and highway division manager: dispatch fleet of Canada/U.S. trucks, sales management division.

Sue & Joe Transport
October 1998 to present

Own and manage two tractor trailer units.

Large Industrial Ltd.
April 1993–October 1998

Purchasing/warehouse manager.

Just North of Northern Driving Range
1991–1993

Owner–operator.

Sue B. Switch
9874 Side Street
Northern, AB
(555) 555–5555
E-mail: mymail@theplanet.net

EDUCATION

1988 General Diploma, Business focus
North Composite High School

1988–1990	Business administration, accounting focus, North North Regional College
1991–1993	Bachelor of Education, university transfer, North Regional College
1992	Received Joanne Smith Scholarship
1993–1995	Bachelor of Education, Elementary Route, University of the North

EXPERIENCE

To and Fro Transport
October 1998–Present, part owner

Position: Accounting technician involved in management services, custom financial reporting packages.

Small Apple Transport Ltd.
January 2000–Present

Position: Controller

Get My Share Transportation Ltd.
March 2000–Present

Position: Bookkeeper

Northern 49 Transportation Inc.
April 2000–Present

Position: Controller

On and Off Transport Ltd.
June 1999–May 2000

Position: Controller

Dogs and Cats Ltd.
December 1998–October 1999

Position: Administrator

Notes

1 Statistics Canada—The Daily, June 10, 1999.

2 Profile of Private Trucking in Canada, 1998, a joint report of Industry Canada and the Private Motor Truck Council of Canada. http://strategis.ic.gc.ca/epic/internet/ints-sdc.nsf/en/fd01101e.html.

3 Profile of Private Trucking in Canada, 1998, a joint report of Industry Canada and the Private Motor Truck Council of Canada. http://strategis.ic.gc.ca/epic/internet/ints-sdc.nsf/en/fd01101e.html.

4 Alberta Economic Development.

5 Alberta Economic Development.

6 Alberta International Trade Review 1998; Alberta Economic Development.

7 Alberta Economic Development.

8 Alberta Economic Development.

9 Alberta Economic Development.

10 Alberta Economic Development.

11 Conference Board of Canada (Metropolitan Outlook, Autumn 1999), Canadian Business Register, Alliance of Manufacturers & Exporters Canada.

12 Alliance of Manufacturers & Exporters Canada (Manufacturing in Alberta–1999), Alberta Economic Development.

13 Alliance of Manufacturers & Exporters Canada (Manufacturing in Alberta–1999), Alberta Economic Development.

14 Alberta Economic Development, prepared by Economic Development Edmonton, February 2000.

15 Alberta Economic Development, prepared by Economic Development Edmonton, February 2000.

16 The Daily, May17, 2000.

17 The Daily, June 10, 1999.

18 Statistics Canada—The Daily, June 7, 2000.

19 Statistics Canada—The Daily, June 19, 2000.

Appendix **B**

Business Dictionary

accounts payable Money owed to suppliers.

accounts receivable Money owed by customers.

acid-test ratio The ratio of current assets minus inventories, accruals, and prepaid items to current liabilities. Also called the *quick ratio*.

accountant Person who keeps, audits, and inspects the financial records of individuals or businesses and prepares financial and tax reports.

acquisition of assets A merger or consolidation in which an acquirer purchases the selling firm's assets.

acquisition plan A type of a business plan specifically written to help the buyer make a business decision; can also be used to help obtain financing.

acquisition of stock A merger or consolidation in which an acquirer purchases the acquiree's stock.

articles of incorporation A legal document that establishes a corporation and its structure and purpose.

assets A company's total resources.

attorney A professional person authorized to practice law; conduct lawsuits, or give legal advice.

balance sheet A summary of the assets, liabilities, and owner's equity; sometimes referred to as the *statement of financial condition*.

bankruptcy Transfer of ownership of a firm's assets from the stockholders to the lien holders; occurs when a company is unable to pay its debts.

boilerplate Standard terms and conditions often used by attorneys or accountants. Also called *template*.

book value A company's total assets minus intangible assets and liabilities, such as debt. A company's book value might be more or less than its fair market value.

business plan(s) A comprehensive document that discloses the writer's intention to develop a business. It is usually prepared to assist in gaining financing from a lending institution.

business risk The risk that the cash flow of a business will be impaired because of adverse economic conditions, making it difficult for the company to meet its operating expenses.

business valuation An amount in dollars estimated by a qualified appraiser of the value of a company.

capital expenditures Amount used during a particular period to acquire or improve the long-term assets of the company, such as property, plant, or equipment.

cash discount An incentive offered to purchasers of a company's product for payment within a specified time period, such as 10 days.

cash flow The flow of money that results from the normal business operations through sales of the company's products or services. Cash flow is important to a corporation because it indicates the company's ability to pay dividends.

collateral Assets than can be repossessed if a borrower defaults on a loan.

CPA (certified public accountant) Accountant who has passed a national uniform examination and has met other requirements; CPA certificates are issued and monitored by state boards of accountancy or similar agencies.

debt-equity ratio Indicator of financial leverage. Compares assets provided by creditors to assets provided by shareholders. Determined by dividing long-term debt by shareholder or stockholder equity.

dividend A portion of a company's profit paid to common and preferred shareholders.

due diligence The investigation of a firm's business to determine whether the firm's business and financial situation and its prospects are adequately disclosed by the seller in the prospectus for the offering.

earnings Net income of a company during a specified period of time.

equity Ownership interest in a firm and the residual dollar value assuming the company's liquidation.

fair market value Amount at which an asset would change hands between two parties, both having knowledge of the relevant facts.

financial plan A financial blueprint for the financial future of a company.

fixed asset A property owned long term and used by a company in the production of its income. Tangible fixed assets include real estate, plant, and equipment. Intangible fixed assets include patents, trademarks, and customer recognition.

generally accepted accounting principles (GAAP) A technical accounting term that encompasses the conventions, rules, and procedures necessary to define accepted accounting practice at a particular time.

goodwill The amount paid by a buyer to the seller of a business that exceeds the value of the assets of the business.

gross profit margin Gross profit divided by sales. This is also equal to each sales dollar left over after the cost of goods sold are paid for.

hard assets The equipment, inventory, and building or property of a business.

income statement A financial statement that contains a summary of a business' financial operations for a specific period and shows the net profit or loss for the period by stating the company's revenues and expenses.

industry The category in which a company's primary business activity is conducted.

inventory Raw materials as well as items available for sale or in the process of being made ready for sale.

liability A financial obligation or the cash outlay that must be made at a specific time to satisfy contractual terms of the financial obligation. The amount owed by a firm to its creditors.

line of credit An informal and flexible arrangement between a bank and a customer establishing a maximum loan balance that the bank will permit the borrower to maintain.

marketing The process of communicating with a specific market to offer goods or services for sale.

P&L (profit and loss statement) See *income statement.*

pro forma financial statements Hypothetical financial statements created to reflect a projected or planned set of business transactions or assumptions.

product life cycle The time it takes to bring new or improved products to market.

quick ratio Indicator of a company's financial strength (or weakness). Calculated by taking current assets less inventories, divided by current liabilities. This ratio provides information regarding the firm's liquidity and ability to meet its obligations. Also called *acid-test ratio.*

reorganization A plan to restructure a debtor's business for the purpose of restoring its financial health.

return on investment (ROI) Generally, income as a proportion of net book value.

revenue Cash; the result of the sale of a company's products or services.

risk The deviation of the return on total investment by a company or the degree of uncertainty of return on an asset.

security Piece of paper that proves ownership of investments.

shares Certificates representing ownership in a corporation.

soft assets The intangible, intellectual property, or goodwill of a business.

stockholder Holder of equity shares in a corporation.

stockholders' equity The residual claims that stockholders have against a company's assets, calculated by subtracting total liabilities from total assets.

takeover General term referring to transfer of control of a firm from one group of shareholders to another group of shareholders.

taxable income Gross income less a set of deductions.

101+ Marketing Tools, Tactics, and Strategies

When marketing is executed elegantly, the prospect will be motivated to investigate further and/or acquire the item or service. Accomplishing this objective will involve the use of numerous tools and strategies.

Sample Tools and Strategies

Marketing calendar/plan: A 12-month marketing calendar with projects, tactics, dates, and costs recorded.

Identify customer needs: Conduct focus groups surveys, and person-on-the-street interviews; interview customers; shop your competitors.

Back-end, up sell: Add new, complimentary products and services, create back-end products including CDs, DVDs, product of the month.

Media: Includes television advertising, infomercials, radio advertising, on-hold messages, billboards, and cable channel advertising.

Internet marketing: Your own Web site, search engine marketing, pay-per-click advertising, pay-per-call lead generation, video cast, podcast, Weblog, Really Simple Syndication (RSS) article distribution, e-zine subscriptions and distribution, e-mail marketing, auto responders, social book marking, and online networks.

Branding: Packaging your company; name of company, USP slogan, consistent and congruent logo, testimonials, features, history, guarantees, awards, press releases/public relations, brochures, business cards, letterhead, community and sports team sponsorships, uniforms.

Print advertising: Options include local newspaper, daily newspaper, magazine, trade journal, industry newsletter, strategic alliance newsletter, local school or university newspaper, flyers, catalogs, posters and other newspapers or newsletters, Yellow-Pages and white-pages advertising.

Signage: Building and vehicle signs, window signs, taxi backs, display, wrap advertising, and in-store signs or point-of-sale (POS) advertising.

Host-beneficiary relationships: Piggyback mailings, joint ventures, complementary businesses due to proximity, and complementary businesses due to similar target market.

Promotional items: Include pens, clothing, and other items with your name or logo imprinted on them, calendar, stickers, tags, golf balls, and magnets.

Direct mail: Personalized letters, flyers, postcards, newsletter, Christmas and birthday cards, reminder cards.

Networking: strategic alliances, chamber of commerce, trade associations, tip clubs, barter clubs, sponsorships, and club or association memberships.

Special events: Special closed-door sales, in-home workshops, teleseminars and day-long seminars, industry expert seminars.

Loyalty marketing: Record and track all purchases by customer, reward system, service contracts, birthday cards, special offers, offer lifetime "oil change," holiday cards, special offer on next purchase.

Lead generation: Build target market database, referral system, cold calling and telemarketing, trade shows, gift certificates, frcc trials, referral rewards, contests/sweepstakes, write and publish articles, and send faxes.

Sample Application of Marketing Tools

Brochures: Support for salespeople in the field. Left behind brochures can be a silent salesperson.

Postcard: Great for follow-up or to introduce your company and its products or services to new prospects.

Business card: Standard equipment. Adding information on the back or using a fold over card can set you apart from your competitors.

Newsletter: Excellent tool to educate prospects and add value before the sale.

Logo: A well-designed logo and corporate image can make a new company look like it has been around a long time.

Web site: There are many different Web site design models and uses. They can be e-commerce to sell products online. Disseminate information and educate prospects about products or services. Build an online community and build relationships. Boost your image by creating a high-image Web site. Display photos of past projects: for service or construction businesses Web sites can provide a great opportunity to show past work and testimonials.

Telemarketing campaigns: When combined with other marketing tools, such as direct mail, telemarketing campaigns can substantially increase your conversion ratio.

Direct mail: Can be just a letter or a complete package with brochure, letter, response card, sample, or even a coupon.

Advertising: Certain types of advertising can be very effective if used as a part of an overall marketing campaign. Do not make the error of thinking that an advertising campaign is your marketing campaign. It is simply a tool and part of your overall approach to communicate your marketing message.

Networking: Many service businesses rely heavily on this strategy. In certain industries, networking is marketing.

Press releases: If you have a newsworthy story, a press release can be a powerful way of getting some publicity and market exposure.

Book: Writing a book can provide prestige in a way that no other marketing tool can. It allows you to share your knowledge and educate potential customers on important issues.

E-zine: Similar to a printed newsletter and delivered through e-mail directly to the customers in-box. This strategy allows you to capture the e-mail address of a potential and interested prospect.

Appendix **D**

Getting Help Writing Your Business Plan

For the record, I do not write business plans as a consultant. The reason I don't is important for you to understand. Please continue reading.

In Appendix G, "How the Author Can Help," I tell the story of how I came to the point of writing a book on business planning and why I think you should write your own business plan.

If for some reason you must outsource the writing of your business plan, here are a few tips.

How to Select, Screen, and Hire a Business Plan Writer or Business Plan Professional

I am not a proponent of hiring someone to write a business plan to obtain financing for your business. I used to write business plans for clients and made money doing it. Today, I no longer provide my services as a business plan writer because it is most often not in the business owners' best interest.

Do not delegate your leadership role. It is your business, and, if you cannot explain your business, goals, and strengths, to the person writing your plan, the writer will have to use his or her imagination—and suddenly your business plan becomes a work of fiction.

You know the business best. No matter how much experience the person helping you has in your business or industry, he or she does not have your knowledge, experience, and vision.

When it comes time to sit in front of your banker or investor, you will be peppered with questions. A lot of weight will be given to your ability to answer these questions because it demonstrates your knowledge of the business and ability to manage it to meet the goals outlined in your business plan.

Be able to articulate, explain, and sell your business plan. You can read and study the business plan written by someone else, but you do not have an intimate understanding of the interrelationship between your goals, marketing, and financial statements. There is nothing quite as powerful for absorbing the intricacies of a business plan as writing it personally. If your schedule dictates that you outsource your business plan, make sure you are the project manager and the "senior editor" responsible for the final document that is simply drafted by the business plan writer or professional you hire.

Hiring someone to write your business plan should not be viewed as an opportunity to delegate or download a difficult job. As I have said, you need to see yourself in the multiple roles of project manager, senior editor, and sales manager. A business plan is a highly structured document designed to sell financial institutions or investors on your financing proposal. It is structured to provide them with information in a familiar format so that the information they need to make a decision to loan you the money you need to start or expand your business is accessible.

Consultants versus Contractors

At some point in the life of your business, you will hire a consultant. Start with understanding the difference between a consultant and a contractor. A contractor is hired to get something done that you do not have time for or not enough work for a full-time employee. In my opinion a consultant is someone you hire to share his or her knowledge and expertise with you. In a sense consultants teach you what they have taken years to learn.

If a consultant has 25 years of experience and writes a book sharing that knowledge and expertise, you buy the book and read it. You will leverage that person's knowledge and compress it into the time it takes you to read and *apply* what you've learned.

The same should be true of the business coaches you hire. They should be consultants, not contractors. They should have the ability to teach, coach, and provide leadership. In other words, they should be able to transfer their knowledge and skills to you.

The Selection and Screening Process

Following is a list of questions you can use to screen business plan writers:

- What qualifies them to write a business plan for your business?

- Do they have direct experience in your industry?
- How many business plans have they written?
- What is their background? Do they consider themselves a business plan writer or a professional?
- Ask for the names and phone numbers of their last three customers.
- How long have they been in business? How long have they been writing business plans?

Types of Business Plan Advisers

Business plan professionals are people who have either the training (CPA, etc.)or the practical experience (retired entrepreneur or other professional) to create good pro forma financial projections. Their weakness will likely be in the area of marketing and sales. If that is your strength, you are in good shape. If not, you will need to find a marketing professional to provide support and expertise to round out your plan.

When you Google the phrase "business plan writer," you will get search results that can range from software to people selling their writing services. People who market themselves as "business plan writers" are likely technical writers with a business background. They have strong writing and organizational skills. If they have a weakness, it will likely be in the preparation of financial statements. They can do a good job of helping you get your knowledge, plans, and goals down on paper.

Other Resources

There are other possibilities to consider:

- *Business planning books:* Consider the authors of such books. Are they academics, professionals, or business owners? What qualifies them to write a book on writing a business plan? Is the book practical? Does it provide you with the background and information you need to understand the importance of each section of the plan, or is it filled with generalizations? Compare it to my own guide on how to write a business plan.
- *Business coach:* I think this is the best option because an experienced business plan coach will have the expertise and coaching skills to help you write your business plan. Use the questions above to screen a coach as you would any other business plan professional.

If you follow these guidelines and work hard, you can write a business plan yourself. You will be rewarded with an in-depth knowledge of your business and plan, and you will be able to speak about it with confidence.

How to Get Maximum Value When You Hire a Business Coach

If you decide to hire a coach, follow these guidelines to get the most for your money.

- Be realistic in your expectations. In my opinion, the main reason for hiring a consultant is to gain a new perspective, plus access knowledge and expertise not readily available. Therefore, it is important that the consultant have the ability and willingness to transfer skills and expertise.

- Remember that you own the business. You are the only one who can make a decision, and you are the one who will be left holding the bag at the end of the day. The consultant is not there to make decisions for you, but to provide perspective, information, and observations. The consultant is also there to train you.

- Listen to the coach. Hear out what the consultant has to say—ask questions. Do not be afraid to say you do not understand what is being told to you. Take in the information, ask for guidance on how to apply the information, and make your own decision.

- Provide the coach with feedback. Let him or her know what you like and what could be improved on.

- Ask the coach to agree to identify measurable standards of performance as part of the contract. In other words, how will you be able to measure success? How will you know if you are making progress by hiring a coach?

- Give the consultant permission to speak his or her mind and tell you the truth. You do not need someone to "tickle" your ears. You do not need someone who agrees with everything you say. The consultant should have the confidence and communication skills to challenge you.

If you do all these things and hire someone you trust and respect, you will have a great experience. Most importantly, you and the business will be better off.

Appendix E
Web Resources and Links

Author's blog (Greg Balanko-Dickson)
   http://www.sbishere.com/

Business glossary
   http://www.bized.ac.uk/glossary/bizglos.htm

The Glossarist
   http://www.glossarist.com/glossaries/business/

Performance Plus – Strategis (Canadian site)
   http://strategis.ic.gc.ca/epic/internet/inpp-pp.nsf/en/
   h_pm00000e.html

National Inventor Fraud Center
   http://www.inventorfraud.com/index.htm

What's Your Brand Mantra?
   http://brand.blogs.com/mantra/

Market positioning
   http://www.quintcareers.com/jobseeker_marketing_glossary.html
   http://www.oup.com/uk/booksites/content/0199274894/student/
   glossary/glossary.htm

Product positioning
   http://wps.pearsoned.co.uk/wps/media/objects/1452/1487687/glossary/
   glossary.html

Imagination Prompt
http://www.creativity-portal.com/prompts/imagination.prompt.html

SCORE: Counselors to America's Small Business
http://www.score.org/

Small Business Administration (SBA)
http://www.sba.gov/

SBA Business Plan Workbook
http://www.sba.gov/gopher/Business-Development/Business-Initiatives-Education-Training/Business-Plan/busplan.txt

SBA state profiles
http://www.sba.gov/advo/research/profiles/

U.S. Economic Development Administration
http://www.eda.gov/

U.S. National Labor Relations Board
http://www.nlrb.gov/nlrb/home/default.asp

Minority Business Development Agency
http://www.mbda.gov/

Appendix F

Software That Can Help

With this book and Microsoft Word and Excel you have all the software you need. If you send me an e-mail (gregbd@sbishere.com), I will provide you with access to my financial plan spreadsheet.

Business planning software is a tool for, not a solution to, writing a business plan. The software will help you with the technical part of making spreadsheets work and prompting you with questions. Some even have a wizard format.

Following are the top four software products in no particular order:

Plan Write: http://www.brs-inc.com/compare.html

Plan Magic: http://planmagic.com/products.html

Business Plan Pro: http://www.paloalto.com

Biz Plan Builder by Jian: http://www.jian.com

Appendix G

How the Author Can Help

Between the contents and the index you should be able to find answers for most of your questions. If you would like to ask the author a question, he can be reached at gregbd@sbishere.com

Getting Support While You're Writing Your Business Plan

I no longer write business plans for my clients. However, I offer three different options that can provide you with support while you're reading this book and writing your business plan.

1. You can e-mail me at gregbd@sbishere.com to get answers to your questions at no charge.

2. I conduct affordable tele seminars as time permits. You can visit www.sbishere.com to see when the next one will be held.

3. I also provide private coaching, and you can read more about my coaching services at www.sbishere.com.

Why I Do Not Write Business Plans for Other People

If I were to write a business plan for you, you would get a document that you could use to get the financing you need and you would be happy. So where is the harm? Think of your business as if it were a puzzle.

I put the puzzle together for you and leave. Later the unthinkable happens; the puzzle gets knocked off the table, and I am long gone. You are left to your own devices to put the puzzle back together. The strategy I used to put it together is in my mind, not yours. That is wrong because, when the business struggles or stumbles, everyone is going to look to you, not me.

When you develop your own business plan, you will acquire an understanding of the business that becomes a part of you at a deep, intuitive level. That depth of understanding your business is a gift that becomes an asset that cannot be taken from you.

So when it comes time for you to reinvent, transform, or give it an extreme makeover, you will be up to the task because you did it once before and now you just need to revisit the process outlined in this book and rewrite your business plan. No consultant needed.

Why I Wrote This Book

Ever since I can remember I have always been curious about how things work. Whether it was ripping an engine apart, building a coffee table, or trying to understand the root of business problems, my curious nature has always driven me to research, deconstruct, and find ways to help my customers.

Initially, my career started on the sales side of business. When I started, I was in the marketing and promotion side of business with my own corporate publishing and design firm. As I got to know my clients, it became obvious that marketing and promotion could help only so much when there are more serious business problems.

Eventually my clients and I would end up discussing that to really fix the issues in their business, we would need to take a more holistic approach—a business planning approach. It was during these discussions that I learned some of my most important lessons about business development and planning.

Common Problems Facing Business Owners

While this is not an exhaustive list of problems, they are the most common I have experienced.

Business Complexity

Eventually every business owner bumps his or her head on the ceiling of complexity. As a business grows, so do the intricacies. When my father and grandfather were in business, they did not have to deal with instant access to information (Internet), global competition, or massive economic shifts every three to five years. Without a plan, control, and structure a business will wilt in the heat of the dynamic and global marketplace.

Management

I am not a management guru. I did not go to college despite my father's encouragement. Everything in this book is based upon what I have learned from being on the front lines and helping hundreds of clients in more than 30 different industries.

My philosophy of business management is a systems, communication, and training perspective. I have not found a management problem that could not be resolved through a combination of improving communication, training, and the creation of systems.

Product Mix

One of the other issues I see is a company with the wrong mix of products. It is like putting a square peg into a round hole—it creates a lot of noise but accomplishes nothing. The only reason that this happens is that the owner does not understand the market as well as he or she thinks. The best fix to not having the right mix of products or services is to go back to the drawing board—the customer and understand the customer's needs.

Price

Most companies do not have a market price strategy and end up not understanding the value they offer, and you cannot sell something you do not know you have. The only thing more costly than pricing your product wrong is spending time, money, and resources pursuing a business idea or marketing strategy that fails—and you learn nothing from it. The true cost of that strategy is double or triple what you think because, if you had not wasted those resources, you could have been doing something else that actually made money. So not only did you loose the money and time invested but you also lost out on what you could have been making had you made a better decision.

Human Resource Problems

Every business that exists is a service business. Some sell products, others manufacture products, and still others distribute or resell products. Even those are service-based businesses because in most businesses the service component often becomes more valuable than the product itself.

Services are experienced between two people—your staff and the customer. Staff problems create customers problems. In a perfect world, you could just tell your staff to shape up and they would do whatever needed to be done to address the situation. All would be well with the world. We do not live in a perfect world.

Most human resource problems are to the result of having the wrong person in the wrong seat, and sometimes that person is you, the business owner. When you have a staff member in the wrong seat, it is simple move that person to a new seat within the business or move him or her out.

When the problem is that you are trying to do too much and doing work that is not within your skill set or natural to you, it consumes a tremendous amount of energy. This leads to stress, things not getting done or things being not up to customers' expectations and standards. That is where my coaching services come in. You can read more about them later in this appendix.

Marketing

Just like having the wrong product mix, many marketing challenges are the result of:

- Not understanding the needs of the market.
- Lack of an effective positioning and branding strategy.
- No marketing plan or failure of marketing to achieve a measurable and profitable result.

The process outlined in the market analysis and marketing strategy provides specific information for developing an effective strategy. If you would like some coaching to help you out, just e-mail me at gregbd@sbishere.com

Financial Problems

There are two kinds of businesses with financial problems. A growing business and a shrinking business; each has the same symptoms for different reasons. A growing business may have financial problems because of a lack of consistent cash flow; it has receivables or the ability to pay its bills once it collects what it is owed. It may have an unbalanced capital structure in which an inconsistent cash flow puts the business at risk. If it has a cogent financial plan, it is no longer being following, or management has failed to make changes when business assumptions changed.

The problems of the shrinking business is having too many bills and not enough funds now or in the future to settle its debts, unless it reorganizes and restructures before it is too late.

Coaching Services

I am been fortunate to have been a founding member of the Professional Business Coaches Alliance. In collaboration with other business coaches I have been able to develop a comprehensive (more than 450) library of business tools, instructions, and systems to meet the needs of my coaching clients.

Business owners have a tough job. Not only are they responsible for the financial health of their own family, but they are also responsible for the financial health of the families of their employees. Even if you have as few as 10 employees, there are probably at least 50 people who count on *you* to grow the business and provide them security. That's a large load to carry sometimes!

People become business owners in many different ways. Sometimes they inherit the job. Sometimes they strike out on their own. Either way, they probably had a vision of what owning their own business would be like, and they discovered that the reality of being a business owner is probably quite different from what they expected.

Serving the customers is only a part of the job, and sometimes the rest of the work is confusing, even burdensome. Perhaps serving the customers (which excited you at first) has become more of a chore than a joy. In fact, you may have already accepted that it's "just the way it is."

Good News! There's a Better Way

You probably use some advisers now. You probably have an accountant, a lawyer, a banker, and perhaps even a family member with whom you share your challenges.

These advisers help you in many areas—compliance with tax laws and financial statements, compliance with employee and health and safety laws, and all the other legal things that are a pain in the rear. But who helps you with all the other areas such as:

- Getting more customers.
- Serving them more effectively so they come back.
- Maximizing your profits.
- Hiring and training good employees.
- Systemizing your business so that you don't have to be everywhere.

If the answer is *no one* up to this point, maybe it's time for that to change.

Small businesses fail every day. Hiring a coach will help you make your business better and help you become the business owner that you know you can be. Coaches understand the relationship between marketing, sales, customer service, leadership, human resources, systemization, and controlling costs and finances, which are just some of the areas in which you will need to be more effective if you want to be able to overcome your business challenges and operate your business by remote control.

Every high-performing person in the world has a coach in one form or another. From athletes to business leaders to political leaders, the highest performers know that having someone they trust who provides awesome advice is necessary to maintain high performance. The rest of the world just "shows up" every day.

How My Coaching Relationships Work

First of all, you must understand that *real* lasting change takes time. There is no magic wand! You will meet with me a minimum of once a week, for at least an hour per meeting. Early on, I will learn about your business and about your leadership style. As you progress, we will work on time-tested, world-class business strategies to get your business humming.

Every week, we will discuss what you want to address, brainstorm, discuss solutions, and set homework for the week. Yes—homework! But it's not the boring kind; it's the kind of homework that is going to change your business and therefore change your life. The homework will require approximately two to three hours of your time every week, because action is the only thing that will move you in the right direction.

Because *lasting* change takes time, the coaching process lasts for one to three years. You will progress from meeting weekly, to bi-monthly, to monthly, to perhaps quarterly. Think of it this way: you can lose 50 pounds by starving yourself for a month, or you can lose it the healthy way and lose one to two pounds per week. That's very similar to what business coaching is. Every week, you will take actions to improve your business while not interfering with your day-to-day obligations.

The reason that this process always works is relatively simple. It combines the best learnings of both personal effectiveness and business effectiveness through the ages. Successful people have a lot in common. Successful businesses have a lot in common. I can help you implement a combination of these powerful lessons.

Up to this point, your business advisers simply told you all the stuff that you should be doing. While the information may have been good, often life gets in the way of implementation, and you continue doing what you have always done. That's where personal effectiveness comes in: time management, goal setting, and other personal effectiveness strategies ensure that you actually make things happen.

Along the same lines, personal effectiveness has its limitations. I am sure you recognize that a positive attitude and passion are great, but if you don't know the first steps to take (as well as making sure those steps are in the right direction), you will be positive—but broke.

That's where business effectiveness comes in. I have literally hundreds of programs and strategies to improve your profits, make you a better leader, help you to systemize your business, and help you maintain a better staff.

While working with me, you will be exposed to over 450 strategies to:

- Drive more potential customers to your business.
- Sell to a higher percentage of them.
- Service them better so they come back again and again.
- Hire, train, and motivate your staff better than you ever have.
- Systemize your business to free up your time.
- Create a better balance between home and work.
- Become a better leader.
- Understand and manage your finances better.

Going it alone is no longer an option in today's fast-paced business world. Your competitors may be considering working with a business coach right now. In order for you to compete now as well as have a business that survives for your children or gives you the maximum possible sale price, having a business coach is crucial.

The dreams that you have had *can* come true, but it will take some effective hard work on the small things that matter most to push you over the edge. If you are busy putting out fires every day, the days will turn into years, and you may regret it later. It has happened to millions of business owners before you. Don't let it happen to you.

Seven Reasons You Should Consider Coaching

1. We will strategize about how you can make your business perform better.

2. You will grow your business by learning more effective marketing and sales skills.

3. You will hire, train, and manage your staff better.

4. You will systemize your business so that it works—and you can work less and enjoy your life.

5. You will be part of a confidential environment to gain input and knowledge from other like-minded business owners who share the same challenges you have.

6. You will become a better leader.

7. You will stop procrastinating and start taking better actions that move your business to where you want it to be.

To see what impact business coaching can have on your business, visit www.sbishere.com.

Index

Postcard, 356
Power outage, 184
Press release, 95, 357
Pricing decisions, 95–98
Primary target market, 86
Print advertising, 356
Private investors, 300–301, 307–311
Problems facing business owners
   business complexity, 368–369
   financial problems, 370
   human resources, 369–370
   management, 369
   marketing, 370
   price, 369
   product mix, 369
Process and procedures, 114–115
Procrastination, 11
Product attributes, 91
Product mix table, 61
Product/service life cycle, 65–66
Product/services mix, 60, 61
Products and services, 59–73
   background information, 60
   breadth, 61
   changes in costs/profits, 64–65
   costs, 62–65
   customer analysis, 66–67
   customer needs and preferences
     profile, 68–70
   customer preferences, 67
   customer profile, 66
   depth, 61
   describe product/service
     characteristics, 60–61
   expansion costs, 63
   getting started, 59
   growth, expansion, redesign, 64
   NWEP profile, 68–70
   positioning strategies, 62
   product/service life cycle, 65–66
   product/services mix, 60, 61
   proprietary rights, 70
   revenue, costs, profits, 63

   sample services section, 71–73
   start-up costs, 62–63
Professional advisors, 221–226
   accountant, 225
   attorney, 225
   business coach, 223, 371–374
   business plan writer, 359–362
   "coaching" side of business coaching,
     222–223
   historical overview, 222
   informal advisors, 225–226
   operations and management, 121
Professional Business Coaches Alliance,
   371
Professionals. *See* Consultants/professional
   service firms
Profit and loss (P&L) statement. *See*
   Income statement
Profit vs. shortfall, 152
Profitability ratios, 156–159
Pro forma financial plan, 125–170
   balance sheet. *See* Balance sheet
   breakeven analysis, 152–153
   cash budget. *See* Cash budget
   cash flow statement, 145–149
   financial goals, 163–164
   financial planning software, 165
   flowchart (what to do), 131
   income statement. *See* Income
     statement
   past performance/current situation,
     162–163
   purpose, 127
   questions to be answered, 127–129
   ratio analysis. *See* Ratio analysis
   research/study sample statements, 130
   review work with accountant, 164–165
   revise/make final adjustments, 164–165
   sample, 166–170
   sensitivity analysis, 153–154
   spreadsheet, 130, 132
   summary, 161–162
Promoter, 15

About the Author

Greg Balanko-Dickson is a third-generation entrepreneur, a Licensed Professional Business Coach, a founding member of the Professional Business Coaches Alliance, an author, and an entrepreneur with clients throughout Canada, the United States, South Africa, and the United Kingdom.

Having worked with hundreds of business owners in more than 32 different industries, Greg brings a unique, practical perspective to every client.

He has been profiled in national magazines, newspapers, TV, and as a guest on radio shows and as a keynote speaker to public and private companies. As a seminar facilitator and consultant, his advice and experiences reflect an in-the-trenches, street-savvy flavor with a practical edge.

Greg maintains numerous blogs and podcasts. His main Web site can be found at http://www.sbishere.com/, where you can learn more about his 2007 World Tour and Greg's March to Impact a Million business owners.

He can be reached at 1-866-281-8281 or by e-mail gregbd@gmail.com.